Tom Jones

A Biography

A Biography

STAFFORD HILDRED & DAVID GRITTEN

SIDGWICK & JACKSON

LONDON

First published in Great Britain in 1990 by Sidgwick & Jackson Limited
Reprinted May 1990

ISBN 0-283-999276

Typeset by Matrix, 21 Russell Street, London WC2

Printed by Billing & Sons Ltd, Worcester
for Sidgwick & Jackson Limited
1 Tavistock Chambers, Bloomsbury Way
London WC1A 2SG

CONTENTS

Chapter One

FIRST LOVE

The curtains in the front window of 44 Laura Street, Treforest were drawn tightly that cold winter night in November 1956, as two families faced a major domestic crisis.

Outside the tin bath swung noisily against the door in the winter wind while inside, in the small, scrupulously clean front room of the tiny terraced home, burly miner Tom Woodward and his wife Freda faced their old friends Bill Trenchard and his chirpy waitress wife Vi in totally new circumstances.

In the corner, well apart from the embarrassed adults, sat tearful teenager Melinda Trenchard and her sixteen-year-old boyfriend, tearaway Tom Woodward Junior. As the grown-ups, local stalwarts of the close-knit Rhondda Valley village community, considered their 'problem' in lowered, anxious voices the youngsters waited silently for their fate to be decided.

Shy, blonde Melinda was just fifteen years old and deeply in love with her swarthy sweetheart, an emotion she had expressed as enthusiastically as her young body knew how in the long grass in their secret spot on the hillside overlooking their homes. Which was why she was now four months pregnant.

Half a lifetime later, Tom Woodward Junior, now better known as Tom Jones, the international singing star, multi-millionaire and heart-throb, can recall the agony of the occasion as though it were yesterday. 'I remember

1

sitting in our bloody house and they were all discussing what was going to happen to us, and to our unborn baby,' said Tom. 'There was my mother and my father and Linda's people and we were sitting in the corner holding hands not saying anything.'

An abortion was out of the question, but although the teenagers were fond of each other, certainly, surely they were years too young to consider a life together with a baby. Other arrangements were considered, while Tom sat silently and Melinda sobbed. Maybe she could take a 'holiday', bear the child, and have it adopted. Perhaps Vi could even bring up the baby as her own. Then came the intervention which would so deeply affect the young lives. Tom recalls: 'Suddenly my father turned to me and said, "Hey, we're talking about them as if they're not here but we're trying to decide their life. Let's hear from them. What do you want to do?"

'I said, "I want to get married to Linda and she wants to get married to me." He just looked at me, it all went dead quiet for a moment and then he said, "Go ahead". I always loved him for it. He stood up against the rest of them who were busy making all sorts of plans for the baby which did not include me.

'Later my uncles, his brothers, argued against the marriage. So did some of Linda's relations. They said we were too young, had our whole lives ahead of us, would not cope with a baby. And my mother's mother came out with all this "Oh, he's sixteen years old, you've got to stop it" stuff, but my father always stood firm against them.'

The marriage had to wait until after Linda was sixteen on 14 January and took place six weeks later at the registry office in nearby Pontypridd on 2 March 1957. The young couple moved into the basement of Linda's parents' home in Cliff Terrace, Treforest and started married life. Their son Mark was born on 11 April in Cardiff Maternity Hospital.

Tom was hard-up, weighed down by new responsibilities and yet blissfully happy. Linda was quiet, sensible and adoring. The childhood sweethearts wanted only each other.

'It was love at first sight for me,' explains Tom. 'Linda and I were kids together, she only lived round the corner. She went to a Catholic junior school and I went to a Protestant one when we were very little so I didn't see much of her but when we reached secondary modern we went to the same school.

'I can still remember seeing her when I must have been eleven. I walked down her street and she was bending down and playing marbles. I saw these great legs and all of a sudden I thought of her in a new light.

'She wore earrings, lots of the Catholic girls did and we Protestant kids used to think there was something really mysterious about Catholic girls. So when we used to lark about playing games like kiss chase I would always be after her. It's a game where all the boys would chase the girls and if you caught one you had to give her a kiss. My first proper kiss was during one of those games and it was with Linda. It was her first kiss, too. Afterwards I had to run my wrists under cold water. I was an early starter.

'Gradually I really took notice of her and by the time we were twelve we were pretty well inseparable.'

In fact the couple were so inseparable that they first became lovers at a very early age. Tom says: 'I was fifteen and she was fourteen, I think. That was very special, too. I was never obsessed about losing my virginity because I was fairly sexually advanced beforehand. It happened up a mountain – it was very hilly where we lived, and in the summertime that was the place to be.'

Tom insists he did not boast about his youthful relationship with Linda to his contemporaries. 'I never said anything about her to my mates – she was always special you see. The boys used to ask "Have you given her one yet?" and I always used to say "No!". I was very protective about her. I used to chat about sex with the lads, but I could never have chatted about my sweetheart.'

But years before the legendary Tom Jones libido sprang into action his extraordinary singing talent had marked him out as something special. Second to rugby, singing is close to being a national sport in Wales. And in the tiny village of Treforest, Tom's father Tom Woodward and his two brothers

George and Edwin were well known for their fine voices.

Tom Woodward had met local beauty Freda Jones at a dance in 1933. They were soon married and lived with Freda's family at 57 Kingsland Terrace, Treforest. Their daughter Sheila was born in 1934, but the son the couple so desperately wanted did not arrive until 7 June 1940. The baby boy who was to transform all their lives with his remarkable voice was born at home, and when the birth was registered at Pontypridd Register Office on 1 July he was given the same name as his father, Thomas John Woodward.

The bed Tom was born in is now in the luxury mansion the adoring son bought for his parents in the exclusive Bel Air district of Los Angeles. His mother insisted on bringing it when they moved from Wales. The proud parents later said that when he was as young as six months old tiny Tom began to make noises 'like musical notes' and did not like to be interrupted in mid-performance. Freda says: 'From the earliest days I could see the talent there. When he was only two and a half he was like a little professional singer. In our living room there were drapes on the windows. Tom would pull the drapes over and get behind them and say, "Mum, call me out now." '

Tom agrees: 'I must have been born with it. My mother says that when I was a baby in the shawl and an up-tempo song would come on the radio I would start to move about in the shawl. When I was able to stand I was able to sing. When she took me to the corner shop I would stand on an orange box and people would come in and I would sing. At school I'd do the same thing. Any chance I'd get I would sing.

'One of my earliest memories is of being left in my pram outside a grocer's shop. I can even now see the grocer through the window, his eyes popping because I had grabbed a string of sausages and was eating one of them. He was one of my first fans, however. I remember one day being put on an orange crate in his shop and singing to a group of travellers.

' "Come on, give the boy a few coppers," the grocer said. My mother protested but the grocer said, "You can't have talent like that for nothing."

'A lot of my family were singers and at Christmas everyone would have to do something individually. I was always raring to go.

'I can remember my mother taking me to Women's Guild meetings and being asked to sing. Next there was a wedding in the family. The reception was crowded with relatives. I tugged at my mother's skirt. "Mum," I said in as loud a whisper as I could manage, "ask them if I can sing." An old gentlemen had heard and said, "Yes, yes, let the boy sing." "Yes," others echoed and I got up and did my best. I just loved to sing, I was never nervous, and there was an added incentive. When I had finished someone would say, "Right, let's dip into our pockets." That taught me an important lesson.'

Tom Woodward Senior was every bit as enthralled by the remarkable young voice as his wife. 'Tom was always singing as a kid, even when he was two or three. Then when he was older he went on to sing in working men's clubs and went in for talent contests. You could see summat was there.'

When Tom was four the family moved round the corner to the old Woodward family home at 44 Laura Street. Although it was still a terraced house it had three storeys instead of two and Tom soon graduated to a room of his own. The Treforest schoolteachers soon found that Tom was anything but a star pupil; the youngster always preferred to listen to Radio Luxembourg under his bedclothes than to do his homework. As his reputation as a young singer grew so his shortcomings in academic areas became more apparent.

Mary Layton, who was in Tom's class at Treforest Primary School, claims Tom was her boyfriend when she was ten. But she remembers: 'When it came to schooling Tom was always a waster. He was no good at any of the lessons, he just wasn't interested. But when they got him to stand up to sing even as a little boy it was wonderful. He once sang "Ghost Riders in the Sky" and you could have heard a pin drop.'

Tom Jones' sex appeal was in evidence as he became a teenager. Kay Davies, now deputy editor of the local paper, *The Pontypridd Observer*, says: 'He got a reputation as a bit of a tearaway but I can remember him at the swimming baths swaggering around wearing white trunks with his comb always stuck inside them. He was always posing and preening himself but it worked. The girls loved him.'

Treforest and Pontypridd in those post-war years were tough, working-class communities. Tom grew up in a society where teenage disputes were invariably settled with a fight.

His best friend as he began courting Linda in earnest was a burly youngster called Dai Perry, later to become his bodyguard in a brief spell which would transport him from the valleys to the world's most glittering nightspots. But in those days Dai and Tom were equals. Tom could sing like an angel but Dai produced his miracles on the rugby field. Now Dai is back in Treforest and still has fond memories. 'We were like brothers, me and Tom,' recalls Dai. 'We used to play together, fight together, and drink together. We got served in pubs from about thirteen or fourteen and after that we were young men.

'It was a hard area, still is, but in those days the fights were fair. There were no knives or any of that nonsense. There would just be gangs of lads come up from Cardiff, or over from other valleys, who would tangle with the Ponty lads. We had to look after ourselves. Tom was pretty tough, he could look after himself.'

The nose which was later to be remodelled in two operations by plastic surgeons came in for particularly heavy punishment. Tom said: 'I hate my horrible nose. It's been worked over, bent sideways and patched up more than any part of me. My nose has been broken so many times in punch ups that I can't remember which particular one made it this shape. Drinking was part of my trouble. I started to drink at fourteen. When I got into a rage it wasn't just fists. The boot and the butting were all part of the fight.'

The most savage attack Tom ever suffered happened when he was least expecting it. A brutal head butt sent him careering through a chip shop door and led to a confrontation with the perpetrator up on the 'Graig', the open land overlooking the village not so far from his favourite courting spot.

Tom says: 'This guy really let me have it and butted me

right through the door. It was a glass door but fortunately it opened when I hit it and I went right through. The funny thing was it wasn't over a girl. It was over a fight I'd had a few nights before.

'I'd had a problem after a few of us had been to an Indian restaurant after a few drinks in the pub. We were just coming out and this taxi pulled up and these hooligans jumped out and starting mouthing off at us. I had some words with one fellow and he said something back to me so I hit him. Hard. He went down and then jumped up and jumped back in the cab. I lost my rag and I was half into the cab after him. These other fellows with him must have thought I was mad or something but they didn't stop and the cab driver drove off with them all in it. Then a few nights later the word went round that one of the mates of this guy I'd hit was a real hard man and he was coming after me. They said he was looking for me, I said "Fine, whenever he shows, I'll be around."

'I was with Dai and he kept saying, "He's looking for you so be careful." I knew who this guy was and thought, he's got no chance, who gives a shit? Dai and I came out of the pub one night and went and had fish and chips and we were standing in this doorway and up the guy came. He said, "You remember the time you hit that friend of mine?" I said, "Yeah." He said, "I couldn't get out of the cab. If I'd got out it would have been different." I said, "Why don't you run along, you've got no chance," and I was so confident I kept on eating my chips and Dai whispered, "Keep an eye on him." I didn't care. I said, "Where do you want to fight? Let's go up on the Graig," and while I was talking he suddenly let me have it – wham – and I was smashed right through the door into the fish and chip shop.

'I jumped up and was just about to let him have it when two policemen arrived and told us to stop it. So then we went up on the Graig and I was tamping by this time because he caught me one. I was with Dai and the guy had his father with him. I was saying "I'm going to kick this bastard all over the Graig," and Dai was saying "Why don't you take off your overcoat?" I was so confident I said, "This

is going to be over very quick, I don't need to take it off." I
remember I had a collar with a pin behind the tie and Dai
kept telling me to take it off and get ready to fight properly
but I was so mad I thought I didn't need to.

'Then, when we got up there, like a bloody fool I just
launched myself on top of this guy and his father, getting an
arm round either one. I must have thought I was bloody King
Kong. I shouted, "I'm going to get both of you." But you start
off very strong and pretty soon, as you struggle, the strength
seems to go. Still, I banged this guy and knocked him down
and I jumped on top of him to spreadeagle him and knock the
shit out of him.

'But his father jumped on my back and he had his
arms round my throat and I screamed at Dai to get him off.
Then this guy's mother came flying into the action and his
brother ran out of the house and together they beat the shit
out of me.

'Dai didn't get involved because this guy's father was
an older fellow and Dai didn't feel he could hit him or
the woman so I got a hell of a pasting. I've still got the
scar where the guy bit my finger.'

Dai Perry recalls that the man whose teeth left a mark
was Dai Hunt, one of a large family of bruising rivals for
local supremacy. He still feels a tinge of guilt for not leaping
in to the rescue but says: 'I couldn't hit a woman. I just had
to stand by and watch the fight take its course. But we weren't
always fighting, most of the time we were just young lads
enjoying ourselves. But Tom's singing is something I'll always
remember. One night we stopped in a pub in Taff's Well where
I played rugby and Tom started singing and accompanying
himself on four dustbin lids. It went down so well we didn't
buy a drink for ourselves all night.'

Today Tom reflects thoughtfully: 'They were tough times
but they were very happy times. I have a lot of friends there
still, I wasn't a bully but I wasn't a weakling either. You had
to prove that you could look after yourself without resorting
to dirty ways of fighting with knives. I was always in trouble
with the cops for fighting. Most parents in Ponty wouldn't let

their lads talk to me. That's the kind of name I had. When I got drunk I'd fight anybody, even my best mates.'

Tom now prefers to play down the times he got into skirmishes with the law. But other people in Treforest have long memories. Billy Russell is Tom's second cousin and he remembers a darker side of Tom's adolescence.

Billy has long been reluctant to break ranks with the traditional family support for Tom Jones which holds sway across his home valley. But in his first-ever interview he said: 'The truth is that Tom Woodward was a young thug. He was a lout. People round here like to forget it nowadays but Tom and a cousin broke into a lock-up tobacconist's shop just near the end of his street. The poor old woman who ran the shop was absolutely devastated by the break-in. I don't think she ever recovered. Tom tried to lie his way out of it, of course, but they found the cigarettes under the sofa in his mother's house. His parents thought the world of him but he made their lives a misery tear-arsing around. He broke his mother's heart.'

With little or no scholastic success to save him and without ever considering his voice could be his fortune, as he approached his mid-teens it looked as though Tom's future was to follow his father down the pit. Then the youngster was struck down with tuberculosis.

In those days this disease killed scores and left many others wheezing cripples, so TB was a shattering blow to the Woodward family. Tom was very ill and spent a year confined to bed while his anguished parents did their best to nurse him through the disease. He spent most of his time listening to music and drawing.

It was during this period that the seeds of Billy Russell's seething resentment were sown. Billy says: 'My wife Elaine is the same age as Tom. She is his cousin and while he was ill she was round at their house helping to look after them. That is when he made some sort of a pass at her – his own cousin. He tried to interfere with her. That's the sort of person he is, a dirty bastard. What we call in Wales a "shagarse". Women were all he was interested in. His wife Linda knew even before the baby was born what he was like but she loved him. She was a lovely girl.

'That's not the story you'll get from the rest of the family or from all of the people in Treforest who suck up to Tom Jones as though he is God. But it's the truth.'

Tom was obviously on the mend. Gradually the cruel disease receded and as he returned to school his romance with young Linda resumed in earnest. Once the baby was on the way and the family conference had decided they were to marry, young Tom realized he had to buckle down and earn a living to support a family.

'When Mark was born I didn't have two halfpennies to rub together,' recalls Tom. 'I was excited but the first thing I thought was, "God, how can I support him?" I was working night shifts at the paper mill and I couldn't even afford to take the night off when Linda went into hospital. I set off for work on a pushbike as the ambulance was taking her to hospital.

'My first job was in a glove factory. I got £2 a week as an apprentice glove-cutter and I hated every moment of it. By the time I got married I had moved on to work in the local paper mill.

'I did all the overtime I could but because I was so young my rate was very low. We were living with Linda's parents, in the basement, and times were certainly hard with three mouths to feed. After about a year I went to the manager and said, "I think I can run this machine," and he said, "If you can do a man's job then you will get a man's pay, have a go," so I did and it made a lot of difference to our income. Then the bloody union fellow who was related to me went bloody nuts. He said, "You can't be on there. You're not old enough." I said, "Talk to the manager."

'Even now I wouldn't like to name this union fellow because he is a member of my family but it really riled me that he was trying to stop me getting the full rate for the job I was doing just because I was under-age. I was doing the bloody job, for God's sake.

'Fortunately the manager stood up to him. He said, "If I pay him less than the union rate you can speak up but if

I pay him more it's none of your business." So then it was fine – once I got a man's wage life was fine. The only thing that got in the way was that I was working shift work and I really wanted to become a professional singer so my job was in the way.

'It wasn't until I was twenty-one that I got out of that job, when I finally didn't have to worry so much about trying to hold that job down because I knew I could get the full rate anywhere I worked.

'Those first five years of marriage were very hard, living with my in-laws, and coming to terms with being a husband and father at that age. It was hard for Linda too; she was even younger.

'There were men at work who were jealous of me because I was under age and getting a man's wage so they used to try to mess me up at work. It was a paper coating factory and I was on a winding machine as the paper, hanging on rods, came into this big bay to dry and then I would have to hang it to dry in reels. When I used to come in to start my shift this guy that was on the machine in the shift in front of me used to try to screw me up all the time. He would put too much heat on in the bay so the paper would all start to crack up or too much humidity so it would be soaking wet. So as soon as I got in to work I would race for the valves to sort it out as I knew he would try to cock it up for me, to get me the sack.

'They didn't like me. I was seventeen at the time and they were in their thirties and there were a couple of hard cases there. There was one guy who used to try to get me mad enough to try to make me have a pop at him. But I couldn't because I knew I had to hold my job down.

'I was big when I was young and I can remember when I was on night shift I would wake up in the day and I would be wanting to strangle this bloody fellow. But it was hard. I just had to swallow my anger and get on with the job.'

There were happier moments during this youthful toil and Tom remembers one former workmate who had a more positive and inspirational effect upon him. 'He was called Bill Larcombe and I'll always remember I was eighteen when he took me to one side for a chat one day. It turned out to be the best piece of advice anyone has ever given me.

'He was an old fellow and one day when I was working these long hours he asked me, "What are you doing here?" I said, "Trying to make a bloody living like you are."

'But he said, "Yeah, but I'm an old man, I've been in the British Army, been to India and all over the world, I've done the best I could with my life, but you: I've heard you sing, people are talking about what a great voice you've got."

'I said, "Thanks." He said, "If you see your chance, go for it. Don't let it slip by you because there's fellows walking around in this factory who could have been great soccer players or great this or great that, but they didn't really go for it. You give it your best shot you can. You can always come back here."

'When I got home I thought about that a lot. I used to sing all the time I could in the pubs and clubs, in concert parties and that, and people always said nice things about how my voice sounded but there was something about what he said, something about the way he said it that made me think just talent is not enough. I've often wished I'd gone back years later and told him how right he was.'

Like many Welsh families in the Rhondda, the Woodward family was large and very close. Tom's cousin Margaret Sugar, two years younger, recalls: 'We were brought up in a singing family and Tom as a child always loved the singing. At family celebrations, weddings or Christmas or whatever, we all had to get up and sing a song. It was no good being shy, everyone had to do it. But Tom never needed persuading. Even when we were little he always knew that he wanted to be a singer.

'The two things Tom loved as a lad were singing and Linda. Together they are Darby and Joan. Linda knew that if she married Tom he wouldn't be around like normal husbands. She has always been happier to stay in the background.'

And Tom himself recalls: 'When I was a kid, all my mother's brothers and sisters and their children and all my father's brothers and sisters and their children lived in Pontypridd. It was only later, in talking to other people, that

I realized how rare it was to have all your aunties and uncles around you like that. But it was great because you never felt alone. There was always a member of the family close at hand.'

The relationship between Tom and his namesake father was particularly close. He grew to emulate his father's smartness. Tom said: 'My father was a sharp dresser and I grew up watching him. He always had suede shoes and used to polish the soles and the edges of the soles and I thought that was wonderful. He wore coloured shirts and different coloured ties to go with them. He had a narrow moustache he always trimmed immaculately and he wore a pork pie hat.'

Today Tom shrugs off the emotional effect of marrying early. 'Sure we were sixteen and married with a baby but we were happy. We had loving families around us and we loved each other. You grow up quick in the valleys, I didn't feel so young.'

He learned that he was a father by ringing the hospital from the telephone box which used to stand in Laura Street. He nervously phoned to find out if the baby had arrived. In those days it was not so fashionable for fathers to be present at the birth but in any case, in Tom's relentlessly male chauvinist view, this was definitely women's business.

Chapter Two

THE SENATORS

Tommy Redman and the Senators were never a great group. Even their greatest fans and closest relations knew that their main function was as background music to a night of serious drinking. Yet as the 1960s began, very slowly, to swing into the lower reaches of the Rhondda Valley, the group graduated to regular Friday night bookings at Pontypridd YMCA. There the inmates simply had to listen to the sound of Tommy and the Senators as there was no booze at the YMCA.

But the group were something less than totally dedicated. Lead singer Tommy Redman, whose real name was the only marginally less glamorous Tommy Pittman, frequently found a game of cards to be a more stimulating way of spending the evening. Without vocals to help disguise their limitations, the Senators were a distinctly underwhelming musical experience.

But they were not without ambition. So, tiring of three consecutive weeks vainly attempting to cover up for the absent Mr Redman, acknowledged group leader and bass guitarist Vernon Hopkins made a decision.

He recalls: 'I knew Tom Woodward quite well, he used to sing around the clubs a bit as a solo act with a guitar and I always admired his voice. I thought he was a great singer.

'I knew he would be drinking in the White Hart down at the other end of the High Street. So when Tommy Redman didn't turn up for the third Friday in a row, I raced out of the YMCA and ran down the length of the High Street to ask him to stand in. When I got there he was sitting at the bar with his powder blue Teddy Boy outfit on, clutching a pint of bitter as usual.'

Even for an enthusiastic young singer the prospect of stepping in front of the sound of the Senators was not something which instantly appealed to Tom Woodward. In that familiar laid-back manner he told the breathless Vernon: 'Friday night is my drinking night, my night out with the lads. They don't have any booze at the YMCA.'

The guitarist was desperate. 'Well, I'll smuggle a crate of beer in if that will get you to sing for us,' said Vernon. 'Fair enough,' replied the casual young conscript, and, as Tom remembered later, 'It wasn't a bad night. In between songs my friend Roy Nicholls would hand me a bottle of beer from behind the curtain.'

Keith Davies was then the group's rhythm guitarist. He recalls: 'Tom just bounced onto the stage and I remember saying, "Do you know 'Great Balls of Fire' in C?" He said, "Yes" and that was it. He was fantastic.'

The performance produced a mixed response. Vernon Hopkins was ecstatic but the audience was largely unimpressed. Vernon said: 'When he got on stage he started belting out all the Little Richard, Jerry Lee Lewis stuff. He was a bit heavy for the audience. With Tommy Redman we had been more into songs from Elvis Presley or Cliff Richard. The audience was taken aback and didn't quite know what to make of him. At the end we said, "Thanks, Tom," split our £6 fee for the night with him and said, "See you around." '

But for Tom Woodward it was a stimulating experience. Until that night singing to him had meant solo efforts accompanying himself without distinction on guitar at concert parties, or in pubs and clubs. He knew he had a strong voice. Everyone told him so. And he knew enough about work to realize that it was a lot less attractive than singing for a living. Suddenly, as groups began to take over from individual acts on the national musical scene, Tom saw that standing up there in front of a group, his group, was the way to go.

'Once I had that taste of singing with a group I realized that was what I was looking for. I actually started as a drummer for a group of other guys but that was strictly amateur stuff. I had bought a guitar when I was fifteen and I used to sing in concert parties but I was very limited on my own,' said Tom.

Separately, Vernon Hopkins had come to the same decision. He recalls: 'From that moment on I wanted Tom to sing in the group. A couple of the other lads were not keen. So we decided to have a showdown in our front room to decide. My mother died when I was nineteen, a year before all this happened. My father was a musician, a pianist, so he loved the group and let us use his front room. My sister used to bring in sandwiches, biscuits and tea. Both Tom Woodward and Tommy Pittman were there, we all said our piece and eventually had a vote. I said to Tommy Pittman, "Well, Tommy, three consecutive Friday nights missed. Tom Woodward stands in and does great. Personally I prefer him because we can't rely on you." '

The meeting backed Vernon's view and Tommy Pittman was exchanged for Tom Woodward, although the move appears to have exhausted the group's imagination when it came to providing the new singer with a snappy stage name. Tom Woodward was soon to be renamed Tommy Scott.

Vernon Hopkins recalls: 'We were thinking of a name when he joined the Senators and I thought I'd nip out to a telephone box and pick up the directory. I thought something with S maybe and saw the name Scott. I went back in and said "Tommy Scott and the Senators" and they said "Great".'

The two rival singers left the emotional meeting together and began the long walk back from Vernon's home in the nearby village of Rhydyfelin. The group members watched their old singer and his replacement set off to walk the couple of miles back to their homes in Treforest and wondered if there would be a punch-up.

But Tommy Pittman took the sacking very well. He still lives in Treforest where he works as a welder and still occasionally sings in public. Tommy Pittman's son Stephen screams: 'We think Tom Jones is a load of shit' at visitors who bring up the past but Tommy himself takes a more relaxed view of past events.

He remembers today: 'Tom and I did have a long, lonely walk home together and I was very down, but we were friends before this happened and I believe we remained friends.

'I was more ballads and Tom was more rock 'n' roll, if that's what they wanted that was up to them. I did get involved in a game of cards with some other lads so I cannot blame Vernon for asking Tom to stand in. For a time at the meeting it looked as though we might have two singers in the group but Tom wouldn't have any of that and the band members had a vote and picked Tom. I did tell him not to make the same mistake as me, that is put his money into the band and not be able to get it out. I'd invested in the equipment but I never got paid back.

'I was very envious later when I saw Tom really making it big, and I always thought he would find time to help out his old mates but no call ever came.'

Tom recalls: 'I started to take the group round the clubs. The working men's clubs had not seen electric guitars before and they got a bit scared when they saw me coming in there. But when we got on stage they wouldn't let us off. In the ballrooms we were doing rock and roll but when I went into the working men's clubs I had to give them big strong ballads that they would enjoy. It was a great training ground.

'My first television spot was for BBC Wales on *Donald Peers Presents* and I sang "That Lucky Old Sun". They wouldn't let me do my heavy stuff but I thought if that's the only way I'm going to get my foot in the door, then OK.'

The popular and carefully cultivated image from those early musical years of Tom Jones is of a hard-working young man busy providing for his young family with a series of tough labouring jobs while singing in the clubs at night. Contemporaries remember him slightly differently.

Gerry Greenberg, from nearby Caerphilly, was manager of one of Pontypridd's rival groups, the Sapphires, as well as being the writer of the 'Teen Beat' column on the local paper, *The Pontypridd Observer*.

'I first met Tom late in 1961. He was already well established as the leader of the Senators and as Tommy Scott the rock singer he was well known around Pontypridd,' said Greenberg.

'He was a layabout. He didn't like working and didn't hide the fact. You would often see him idling the day away on street corners, always clad in the obligatory T-shirt, leather jacket, turned up jeans and winklepickers. He looked like a Welsh model for the Fonz. Rumour has it that Tom was employed variously as a miner, a hod-carrier and a bricklayer but the only non-vocal work I ever knew him to do was a lone half-day at a local glove factory.'

Tom's regular chore was his Tuesday morning stroll along Taff Street to the dole office. With those payments and his share of the income from the Senators Tom never seemed to be short of money, or beer. Ten or twelve pints each was normal in a session, before they went on stage.

Tom certainly never liked to waste valuable drinking time, as the other Senators learned to their cost. One night at Pontypridd's New Inn, clad in his prized all-leather stage suit, Tom was sitting in the main bar while his group got the Wednesday night dance under way in the ballroom upstairs.

The other Senators were not blessed with vocal talents, and their entire repertoire without Tom was limited. Normally they would get the show under way with a few instrumentals and then Tommy Scott would appear, gyrating wildly, to roar through a string of numbers made famous by his idol, Jerry Lee Lewis.

This particular night, however, Tom was sidetracked. He got chatting to an attractive young girl in the bar and, as the drinks went down, an hour and a half later the Senators were going through their routine for a third time. Eventually Tom made his customary big entrance, without so much as a murmur from the band. Nobody wanted to question his behaviour, not if they wanted to stay in one piece. Tom's reputation as a hard man kept him clear of trouble most of the time. He exuded an air of menace which put off all but the most inebriated of the local roughnecks.

But sometimes a chilling glare was not such a very effective defence. Gerry Greenberg recalls the time Tom Jones arrived in the newspaper office with a face looking like an out-of-shape football. He was covered in cuts and bruises and his mouth seemed twice the normal size.

'What happened?' asked Greenberg.

'Some bastards jumped us at the Green Fly last night,' mumbled Tom. 'They came up from behind us as we were loading our equipment.'

The Green Fly, a working men's club in Caerphilly, was one of the Senators' regular gigs. But Tom's condition was anything but regular that day as he put his forefingers to his mouth, one either side, and gestured to pull it outwards.

'One of them jumped on my back, put his fingers in my mouth and pulled . . . like this,' said Tom, although he managed to add with a grin: 'Mind you, you should see the other bloke.'

Tommy Scott and the Senators gradually built up quite a reputation locally but the national music scene still seemed a million miles away. At this stage in the Senators' career, British pop music was going through turbulent changes. There had never been a better time for an unknown group to make it into the big time. The Beatles had turned London's music business upside down, after years in which the biggest rock and roll stars – Elvis, Jerry Lee Lewis and Gene Vincent – were American, and the biggest British names – Cliff Richard, Adam Faith, Billy Fury – tended to be bland.

But the Beatles' raw, youthful and enthusiastic approach changed all that. Teenage fans thought they were cute; they loved their mop-top hairstyles, their sharp, stylish clothes and their urgent, pounding records. And the Beatles gave an opportunity for other Liverpool groups – the Searchers, Gerry and the Pacemakers, Billy J. Kramer and the Dakotas and the Fourmost. In nearby Manchester, the Hollies and Freddie and the Dreamers were just starting to emerge. And in London, a quintet of mean-looking, long-haired kids called the Rolling

Stones were beginning to make a name for themselves.

But while Tom, even at this early stage in his career, had a terrific stage presence, it's fair to say the Senators had little chance to appeal to a national audience. They weren't pretty boys, like the Beatles or Billy J. Kramer's Dakotas. They didn't perform chirpy pop songs that young children and parents could enjoy along with teenagers like Gerry Marsden or Freddie Garrity did. And they didn't have the semi-intellectual pretensions of rebellious art school graduates like the Rolling Stones or the Pretty Things.

Instead the Senators were like throwbacks. They looked working class, which they were, but it was a 1950s version of working-class kids. They didn't comb their hair forward into a modish Merseybeat fringe; they swept it back and applied Brylcreem to it. They were rockers in an age when mods were storming the charts.

They got an insight into the real quality of the so-called big time when they were booked to support Billy J. Kramer and the Dakotas at the Winter Gardens in Porthcawl. Tommy Scott was unheard of in that part of South Wales but his first half performance sent the audience wild with delight.

Kramer, or Billy J. Quagmire as Tom dubbed him, was at the time top of the hit parade and a major figure in the Mersey revolution. The crowd listened to a couple of numbers from him, didn't rate them, and began to bay for Tom's return. Kramer, despite his chart-topping status, had to bring his act to an early close to keep the peace. And Tommy Scott and the Senators took over again to roars of approval. His sexually suggestive style of hip-swivelling and thrusting his pelvis drove the women into a frenzy.

This was a difficult time for Tom. He recalls: 'I knew I was different because I sang differently. There was no one in Wales who could give me a helping hand. There was no TV company and no local radio stations and no agents. London felt a long way away because there were no motorways and no fast trains.

'People around me in Wales would say, "For God's sake get to London and show the English what it is all about." I remember I was in a pub one Saturday afternoon betting on horses. There was a television in the bar and the Rolling Stones were on. This big rugby player, Glannoch Evans, stood there looking and it was a bit alien to him – Mick Jagger shaking his head and twitching his leg.

'I could see him looking and I was sitting in the corner with the lads playing cards and he said, "Hey, when are you going to get up off your fucking arse and go up to London to show these English bastards how to sing?" I said, "Christ, Glannoch, give us a chance," but I knew that in a way he was right.'

The reputation of the hip-swivelling young singer, who threatened to wear out his trousers from the inside as he sang, gradually began to grow. Eventually two young songwriters – Raymond Godfrey and John Glastonbury – came across this raw talent and recognized real potential.

Raymond Godfrey recalls: 'Back in 1962 John Glastonbury and I were partners struggling to try to sell our songs. We were living in Wales and we used to travel up to London regularly with manuscripts and go round the publishers. We were advised one day that the best thing to do was to make a demo disc.

'So the following day we went out to look for groups and we saw that there were three groups playing in a dance hall in Caerphilly. We watched them and one of them was Tommy Scott and the Senators. When we saw Tom we were very impressed. We waited until they came off stage and introduced ourselves.

'We explained we were trying to get our songs recorded and wanted to make a demo. They said they were interested.

'Over the course of the next three months I gave them some songs and used to drive over to see the group. But it was Tom I was interested in. He was the obvious talent. We drove over to see them after work. We used to try to rehearse with them because we became aware that we needed a bit more authority. The group was very lax and sometimes they were late and other times they didn't show up at all. Or we'd get there and they hadn't even bothered to set up their equipment.

'After a couple of months of this slack behaviour we said
we couldn't go on like this. So we became their managers
and started getting them bookings around Wales and then
did a tape in a Cardiff studio. Then we came up to London
and started hawking it around the companies. Not one of the
major companies was interested. My partner and I must have
spent a whole week getting appointments and getting in to see
people.

'There were so many groups going then it was very difficult to get in. Eventually we went to a guy called Joe Meek,
an independent producer who had been with Decca (Meek
had had a number one record in 1962 with an instrumental
called "Telstar" for the Tornadoes: he had partly produced
the record in his bathroom using the echo of the room). He
was a bit of a lad. He was very short-tempered, very full of
anxieties, very hyper and homosexual. He was very difficult
to deal with, he wouldn't talk logically. And London was
anything from a five- to a seven-hour drive away from Wales
then before the motorways. After a lot of disappointments and
hassles we finally got Tom and the boys in the studio and cut
seven tracks with Joe.

'But it was hard. We were still living in Wales and
keeping the band working. We didn't take any commission
as we already had jobs. It was extra to us, so we let them
keep their money thinking it was more important to them
than to us.

'We bought them a van and a PA system, spent quite
a bit of money. But it was only because we thought so
much of Tom. God, we had seen nobody like Tom. This guy
could really sing. We were probably very silly but we were so
enthusiastic. Every time we were turned down somewhere we
would go somewhere else. We were dogged in our pursuit.'

The two managers, nicknamed Myron and Byron by the
group, found that the relationship with Joe Meek developed
slowly. Godfrey said: 'Tom was signed through us to Joe as a
record producer, a record company, and then Joe would do
a tape-lease deal with one of the majors. We kept pestering
him about when there would be a release as he had seven

tracks – some of which he supplied, some were ours.

'He said he had done this deal with Decca and we would have a record out in three months. So we said great, what we plan to do now is move up to London to follow it through and find a good agency. So we were making plans like that and kept asking for a release date but we were just given a lot of excuses. This happened, that happened, Decca had put it off because there was a similar record out. This went on for the best part of nine months and we had several new release dates.

'Very often we would ring Joe and he would never come to the telephone. He seemed to have an army of people around him. Eventually we thought it had to be now or never. So we saw Tom and said, "Look, Tom, we are not happy with the way things are going and we are going to lay the law down because this could go on indefinitely."

'So we went to see Joe Meek and knocked at his door at 10 a.m. after driving up from Wales through the night. At first he wouldn't see us but we insisted and at last he came and we confronted him. He put his hands on his head and shouted and screamed. We said we didn't want to hear that. What we wanted to hear was what was happening and why we didn't have a release. Then he said he had had enough anyway and wanted to break the contract. We said that was fine by us because nothing was happening. So we agreed to break the contract with him and went back to Wales and told Tom and the boys we had broken with Joe.

'Next week we went back up to London with Tom and went into a studio in town called Regent Sound because unfortunately we couldn't get our tapes back from Joe. We cut a couple of tracks and Tom went back to Wales with the group while we stayed up there to see Decca. We were helped by Jimmy Savile. We had found out where Jimmy stayed so we popped in to see him and played him the tape and he was really excited about it. He said if he could take the tape into Decca we were to phone him the following day. I phoned him the next day and he asked me to meet Peter Sullivan, who later became Tom's recording manager.

'So we landed a new contract with Decca which we

were very pleased about. I remember the day we went up to their recording studio for the first time. I was on the floor when Tom started singing and was watching them in the box, Peter Sullivan and others, and they were all very excited about Tom.

'Tom asked, "Shall I just sing ordinary?" and they said, "Sing as if you were on stage" and he started to go through those amazing motions. Then they knew there was something there.

'We had such faith in Tom. The first time we saw him we realized he got such a great reaction from the girls because he was so visual as well as having the voice. He used to wear suits but if it was a venue for young kids he would wear black leather. If it was a club he would wear a black tuxedo and a dickie bow-tie. A normal gig was worth fifteen guineas but if it was a Sunday it would be sixteen guineas.

'He was a real raver in those days. Tom was certainly interested in girls. He was a raver but he was married so he had to be very careful. He wanted to be a singer, but like a lot of artists, he wasn't doing anything about it. He was just going round the same pubs and clubs over and over again. Without trying to be boastful the best thing Tom ever did was to meet us. We were so enthusiastic about him. We used to work night and day doing two jobs trying to get something going for him. I used to work shifts and to get up to London we would get up at 4 a.m. and drive. We used to stop off at the toilets at Shepherd's Bush Green and change into suits. We had to wear suits to look like managers.'

Tom remembers those difficult early days rather differently and without much affection for his former managers. 'Myron and Byron?' he snorted. 'They might as well have been called Pinky and Perky for all the good they did me. One of them – it could have been Myron and it could have been Byron – had been up in London for a week on expenses and we hadn't heard a word from him.

'I went up to London and tracked him down to his hotel room to find out what was going on. I was banging on the door and Jimmy Savile came out of the room next door. I couldn't believe it. We had a chat and he gave me some really helpful advice. Then Myron, or it could have been Byron, came out.

'I said, "What's going on?"'

'He said, "I haven't met anybody yet."'

'I said, "Bloody hell, Jimmy Savile is staring you right in the face. Haven't you tried to talk to him?"'

'He mumbled that he hadn't had a chance yet. And I realized that these two jokers were never going to organize our big break.'

Savile himself recalls his early contact with the group in his colourful autobiography *As It Happens*. 'One group presented itself at my door. Earnest and solemn of face, they were down from Wales but things were not going right. Several discussions we had at all odd hours. They would tell me their progress and I would suggest a course of action. It started things going the right way and the caterpillar of Tommy Scott and the Senators turned into the world-beater winged wonder of our own Tom Jones. I would never make claim to be responsible for anyone's success but when a top man has time to talk or eat with new arrivals it gives a tremendous boost to the morale of the beginners.'

Tom remains grateful to Savile. 'I was a bit drunk and I banged hard on the bedroom door. Jimmy popped his head out and I explained these two idiots had let me down badly. He told me to come and see him next day. I recorded four songs, he gave the demo tape to Decca and that was it. It's partly thanks to Jimmy I am where I am but when I say how grateful I am he just says, "If it hadn't been me it would have been someone else." '

Whatever the truth of the relationship between Tommy Scott and the Senators and their managers, it was becoming blindingly obvious to all concerned that, as new groups were discovered almost daily and launched to instant stardom, the band from Pontypridd were looking increasingly likely to go precisely nowhere.

One man was going to change all that and become the catalyst the boys needed to speed them to success. His name was Gordon Mills, a lad like the Senators from the Welsh valleys who had chucked in his job as a bus conductor in Tonypandy and made a name in the music world. Unlike the Senators, Gordon Mills was a fine musician who had built up a reputation on the harmonica. He finished runner-up in the grandly styled British Harmonica Championships at London's Royal Albert Hall.

That success was followed by an audition with the popular Morton Frazer Harmonica Gang, which provided a swift education into the working of the music business. Ruthless agents, clever publicity campaigns, enthusiastic and generous audiences and above all the considerable potential income which fame could produce were all quickly assimilated by the shrewd young Welshman. He was much keener on making money for himself than in the squeals of the fans. Gordon quickly move on to join a group called the Viscounts who enjoyed two or three minor hits.

To Tommy Scott and the Senators, in the faraway, small-town obscurity of Pontypridd and Treforest, Gordon Mills was someone remarkable, an ordinary bloke from their part of the world who had made it as a musician and songwriter in the music business, in London.

The credit for arranging that crucial first meeting between Gordon Mills and Tommy Scott is still argued over today. Club singer Johnny Bennett makes a strong claim. Johnny is a member of a well-known Tonypandy musical family who were very friendly with the young Gordon Mills.

Johnny was also a friend and admirer of the singing style of Tommy Scott. He recalls the young singer had ambition to match his talent. 'He was desperate to get on, to make it, he always knew he had it in him and he wanted success so much,' said Johnny. 'I remember once coming out of the Lewis Merthyr Club in Porth with Tom after a lunchtime session. There was a white E-type Jaguar outside owned by Eddie Brown, the bookmaker whose father had plenty of money. Tom said, "I'll have a dozen of those bastards one day." '

The meeting which was to lead to the sort of income

which could buy any number of Jaguars actually took place on 10 May 1964. Johnny remembers that Mills had come home to see his family and that his initial impression of the would-be superstar was not too favourable.

Johnny Bennett said: 'I took Gordon into the Lewis Merthyr Club in Porth on Sunday morning and I introduced Gordon and his wife Jo to Tommy Scott and the Senators. Gordon was not that impressed, when I pointed out Tommy Scott he said, "Not that scruffy bastard."

'My answer was, "Well, you don't think he's going to go on stage like that?" Tom was in leather jacket and jeans. I said to Gordon, "Come down to earth. You're a valley boy. Have a look round, all there is are workmen on a Sunday morning." '

Gordon Mills listened to the enthusiastic reports of this raunchy young singer and agreed to take a look at him in another local club that night.

Johnny Bennett said: 'Me and my wife Sonia took Gordon and Jo to the Top Hat Club in Cwmtellery. But when we got there we couldn't get in to the concert room so we had to go into the bar.'

The big-shot from London had reckoned without the club rules as rigidly applied by the all-powerful committee. Seats were for members only.

Johnny was embarrassed as he had persuaded the influential Gordon Mills to come and listen to the local boy but fortunately for all concerned Tom pleaded with the men from the committee: 'That's Gordon Mills the songwriter from London. He's come to listen to me,' and eventually a compromise was reached.

'You can stand by the door but don't get in the way or our members will play hell,' said the committee man.

And one of the most successful showbusiness partnerships in modern times was forged as the latent managerial genius of Gordon Mills peered over the flat caps of rows of distinctly uninterested Top Hat members and saw the man he was to mould into an international superstar sing for the very first time.

As a note of respect to Mills the Senators opened with their version of his hit 'I'll Never Get Over You' before Tommy Scott launched into his customary soulful rendition of 'Spanish Harlem'. Mills stood listening while struggling to protect his heavily pregnant wife from an endless stream of serious drinkers who filed steadily back and forth throughout the act. As Tom was followed by comedian Bryn Phillips, Johnny Bennett could not wait to hear what Gordon thought of Tom's performance.

He asked: 'Well, what's the verdict?'

Mills replied: 'There are plenty of singers around. In fact the comedian has got a better voice than him.'

'You must be bloody joking,' retorted Bennett. He added glumly, 'We'll have a little drink and forget the whole thing.' But Jo Mills knew what her husband really thought and she decided to put Bennett out of his misery.

'Do you want to know the truth?' she asked. 'I don't know what he's doing in a place like this, he's so good.'

'Well, Gordon doesn't seem to think so,' said Bennett.

'Look, if Gordon hadn't liked him he would have been through that door after the first number,' said Jo.

Jo Mills recalls today: 'I was pregnant with our first child, our daughter Tracey, and we had gone down to Wales to visit Gordon's parents as we often did in those days. I was quite a successful model then but Gordon had given up the Viscounts. He was skint. It was a tough time for us as I was giving up work because of the baby although I still had quite of bit of modelling money to come in. Gordon was concentrating on his new career as a songwriter and he had had one success with the Johnny Kidd and the Pirates hit "I'll Never Get Over You", but we were still waiting for some money to come in from that. For us it was a time when Gordon was at a crossroads, he really didn't know what he was going to do with his life.

'It was Gordon's best schoolfriend Gordon Jones who kept on at us to go and see this Tommy Scott. Gordon Jones said, "You have got to come and hear this guy sing and see his act.

Maybe you know people in London who could do something
for him, he's brilliant."

'We went to the Top Hat Club and it was standing-room
only but nobody minded. I was absolutely stunned by Tom's
performance, I'll never forget it, it was an amazing experience.
I came away just overcome, it was as strong as that, he was
fantastic. He wiggles nowadays but then, wow! He was just a
remarkable raw talent. Gordon felt the same. Tom must have
been on stage, on and off, for about three hours. There were
lots of five- or ten-minute breaks and in one of those breaks
Gordon went backstage and talked to Tom.'

Bennett said: 'Gordon wanted to have a chat with Tom
but Tom's two managers – Myron and Byron – didn't take
too kindly to that. They came over to me and said, "That's
Gordon Mills." I said, "Yes." "Well tell him to piss off," said
Myron. I said, "Don't be silly. This boy is in with Decca now,
he is writing some nice songs for Cliff Richard and Johnny
Kidd and the Pirates. So it would be far better if you got your
heads together." '

All concerned have slightly differing recollections of that
first meeting. Rhythm guitarist Keith Davies had by then left
the group and been replaced by Dave Cooper but he still
spent every Saturday and Sunday night with them as they
performed. Davies said: 'I stood at the bar with Gordon Mills
all night drinking pint for pint as we watched the show and
just before the interval he turned to me and said, "I wish I
had that guy under my belt." '

Jo Mills says today: 'I don't think at first that Gordon
even thought of managing Tom. He didn't know what
management was at that time. But on the long drive back
to London we were both shattered by what we had seen.
At one point Gordon suddenly pulled the car over to
the side of the road and said to me, "I've just got to
do something with that guy, I've just got to something."

'Tom was also very excited about meeting Gordon. At
that time people in Wales were impressed by people coming
down from London and Gordon had had a big hit with the

Viscounts with a song called "Who Put The Bomp?", a cover of an American song.'

Gordon Mills said: 'As soon as I saw Tom I knew he had what it takes to go all the way to the top. He was sensational. That night at the Top Hat he had the audience in a frenzy. All he needed was to get out of that pitiful mining country to where his talents would be more highly appreciated. The first few bars were all I needed to hear. They convinced me that here was a voice which could make him the greatest singer in the world.'

Tom recalls today: 'It happened like I thought it would happen. I knew that one day somebody would see my talent and say, "I'm going to take you to London and I'll get a hit for you," and that is exactly what happened. Gordon Mills saw me singing. I knew who Gordon Mills was, I knew him because of the Viscounts. He was a real entertainer, a professional, and I knew this could be it, and it was it. I talked to him afterwards and he said: "By God, you should be in London."

' "But I don't know anybody there," I replied.

' "You do now," said Gordon.'

And one of the most lucrative partnerships in show-business began in that meeting. Tom explained: 'Gordon was so important for me. I needed someone to recognize my talent and handle all the agents and producers and all the rest of it. In those days before the motorways and the Severn Bridge, South Wales was a long, long way away. It took a long time to get to London and I didn't know anybody. If I went to London on my own, what was I going to do? Walk around the streets singing? Gordon was in showbusiness. I knew he knew what he was talking about because he had done something and I liked the way he talked. He was telling me what I felt about myself. That I could sing all these songs. That I was versatile. That I had a powerful voice. That I had a great range. He said, "If I can't write you a hit record I'll do my damnedest to get you one."

'I knew when I met Gordon that the chance of success was staring me in the face. And I simply had to grab hold of it. My mind went back to Bill Larcombe telling me to "Go for it." '

Co-manager Raymond Godfrey recalls the crucial meeting rather differently again: 'After we had done the original recording for Decca we wanted some more material for Tom. We said we would try to write some more songs. We went round the music companies again and then we remembered there was a guy called Gordon Mills who was a harmonica player who had written a couple of songs including the big hit for Johnny Kidd and the Pirates.

'We thought, well he's from the valleys, he'll keep the Welsh flag flying, we'll give him a ring. I went to see him and introduced Tom. At the time Gordon was doing something with Les Reed. They played some songs for us, one of which was "It's Not Unusual". We really liked that song. Peter Sullivan was eager to get a record out with Tom and put out one called "Chills and Fever" which was one of the songs we had recorded with Joe Meek.

'When we heard it we thought it was horrible. It had a million instruments. It didn't sound like a group with a singer but the Halle Orchestra – there were millions of pianos and trumpets and brass. We thought it was grossly overproduced. It didn't do anything.'

Not surprisingly, the meeting between Tom Jones and Gordon Mills was bad news for Myron and Byron.

Raymond Godfrey recalls: 'Then we learned that Tom had been propositioned by Gordon. Gordon told Tom that if he moved up to town with him he could stay in his flat. So one day Tom rang up and said he had had this offer from Gordon and asked what should he do. I said, "Do what you like. Although you have a contract with us we won't hold you to it if we can have some kind of deal." I had a chat with my partner and what we decided on was that we would relinquish management but have five per cent of Tom's earnings. Tom agreed on that.'

Tom himself remembers: 'All that was going on in my mind. So I said to Myron and Byron that I wanted to talk to them and we met in this pub run by the parents of my rhythm guitar player Dai Cooper.

'I said, "Look, fellas, I've met Gordon Mills and I feel he

is the man to really do something for me. I want to call it a day with you." I told them I believed in Gordon, that what he said was true and that he could back it up. There was this contract that I had with Myron and Byron and it had a month or two to go on it, but Gordon wanted to get the ball rolling right away.

'So instead of waiting the couple of months before this contract ran out, which with hindsight would have been a lot easier, Gordon said, "Look, fellas, I'm not trying to steal him from you. I'll have a separate contract with Tom and you can have five per cent." But we couldn't put any dates in because I hadn't then got anywhere so we left the dates open. It just said Myron and Byron will be paid five per cent from blank to blank.'

The introduction of Tom Jones, with all his raw talent and naked sex appeal, to Gordon Mills, the potentially ruthless businessman determined always to close the toughest deals, was crucial to the careers of both men. 'I wouldn't have made it without Gordon,' said Tom. 'Lots of people said I should go to London and make records but Gordon was the one who made it happen.'

Chapter Three

SWINGING LONDON

They say the best thing about Wales is the road out, and that was the route taken by Tommy Scott and the Senators in June 1964. They were off to the bright lights and excitement of swinging London to join in the musical group explosion sparked by exciting new bands like the Beatles and the Rolling Stones.

Their slick new manager Gordon Mills had lined up the accommodation. Big bookings and fame would surely follow. At least that was the mood of the naïve young Welshmen who set off on that brave adventure.

Vernon Hopkins, the dark, good-looking, bass guitarist, was twenty-four, the same age as Tom. He gave up his steady job as a printer with *The Pontypridd Observer* in the hope of musical success. Dave Cooper, the rhythm guitarist, was twenty-one. His parents ran the Thorn Hotel in nearby Abercynon where the group rehearsed and planned their assault on the capital. Chris Rees, who changed his name to Slade, was the baby of the group at seventeen. His parents were upset when he left Pontypridd Grammar School to join the Senators. Mickey Gee, twenty-one, from Cardiff was the lead guitarist. He quit his job as a delivery man with Brain's Brewery to join.

By the time they hit the capital their name had changed. There was already a Tommy Scott on the scene so Gordon switched names for Tom to become Jones, inspired by the film hit of the time. And the Senators became the Playboys to fit in with the new cosmopolitan image.

It all sounded fine but the real picture was slightly different. 'We were just a bunch of Welsh yobs,' recalls Mickey Gee, the talented guitarist recruited to replace original member Mike Roberts who preferred to stick to his steady job as a TV cameraman. 'It wasn't very hip to be Welsh in those days,' he said. If you were Irish or Scottish, or best of all from Liverpool, you had a bit of credibility, but a Welsh group was so unfashionable. All the other groups we met used to sneer and put us down, 'Oh no, anything but bloody Welsh.' We were definitely not the in thing. Welsh kids then were so naïve, and we were more naïve than most. We used to support bands like the Rolling Stones and all those other hairy groups and Tom would come out with his hair slicked back in a DA and wearing tight trousers and a frilly shirt. And we would all be there in our little Marks and Spencers shirts that Gordon had got us. We hardly looked as though we came from the same planet. They all had weird and wild looks and we all had to have our hair dyed black to match Tom's.'

Tom himself was very aware of the difficulty. Today he says: 'I was a very unfashionable talent for the time. This was the problem we had when we came to London. Gordon thought when we got to London it would happen for me but we did a lot of auditions for agents and they would say "too adult", "too old-fashioned", "too fifties rock 'n' roll".'

They might have added that he was too old. Tom looked much more than his twenty-four years by then, thanks to his rugged, swarthy looks and his dated hairstyle. This was an era of baby-faced, almost girlish-looking pop stars – Paul McCartney, George Harrison, long-haired Mick Jagger, Billy J. Kramer and Peter Noone of Herman's Hermits. Many of the kids in groups from the Merseybeat era looked innocent; Tom Jones didn't even look like a kid. He might have passed for a worker on a building site, or a long-distance lorry driver. He was definitely no one's idea of a fresh-faced star in this new age of British pop.

Tom says: 'I had a Tony Curtis haircut instead of a Mick Jagger haircut. It was strange. They said I was too masculine.

It was the time of the Beatles, the Rolling Stones and Herman's Hermits. All groups.'

Mickey Gee remembers the poverty of those early days very clearly: 'It didn't help that we were living on the breadline. For years I always had to go on stage from the left to hide a big iron mark I'd made in my pants. At first Tom was all right, just like one of us. We were all in the same boat really. Gordon had got us this flat in Ladbroke Grove and we had £1 each a day to live on. We were just young Welsh yobs away from home up in London. All we wanted to do was to get drunk and pick up girls and that was what we did. Tom was a real yob. He and I had one or two fights. I remember once he pushed me up against the wall and said he was going to hammer me. Next day we were both too hungover to remember why. It happened at lot at that age. He was your typical macho Welsh man. He liked to get drunk and he liked to pull a bird. He wasn't choosey, he'd pull anything. His favourite trick was to run out of restaurants without paying the bill. He was always the first to make a break. At first it was because we were so hard up but later, even when we could afford to pay, he would rush out and we would all panic and follow.

'We'd say, "Look, we've put our money aside so we're just going to eat our biryianis and pay the bill like normal people." But then at the end of the meal Tom would be making jerking movements as if to jump up and we'd all shout "Don't you dare", then suddenly he'd be gone and then we'd all be gone after him. That used to frighten me a bit.

'We all lived in this hovel and we hadn't got a tin of baked beans between us, but on Saturday night we would put on our best tab collars, and go marching out towards Hammersmith – the yobs on a big night out. We must have had happy times otherwise we wouldn't have stayed, but more important than that was that, happy or sad, for all of us this was the first time of really being away from home. We were constantly bemused. We were thinking, "We're in showbusiness, man", "We're going to make it".'

The flat itself was decidedly basic. Acknowledged group leader, bass guitarist Vernon Hopkins said: 'It was just four of us in the same room, one big room, a miserable flat. We were given £1 a day each to live on. Either it was a few beers and nothing to eat or something to eat and no beers. That was £1 for everything: transport, food, clothes, toiletries. Most of the time we were starving.

'But they were still great days, it was so exciting, even down-market Ladbroke Grove. We would stay up all night and the local prostitutes would come in, just for a chat mind; we couldn't afford them. In fact we felt sorry for them, used to try to persuade them to go home and get back on the straight and narrow. It was a basement flat.

'The girls would knock on the door in the middle of the night and come in and we would give them a cup of tea and chat and they'd give us a few cigarettes. We didn't have a lot to do as we were waiting for things to happen.

'The early days were an adventure, just pure, total adventure. We all had the same ambitions to make it driving us on so we put up with the hardships. I thought once we got Tom on board we would really be able to crack it. We were all close friends from Wales, I thought nothing would ever split us up – Mickey the lead guitarist, Dave the rhythm guitarist, me on bass and Chris the drummer, and Tom. We lived together, drank together and dreamed together. We were so intensely ambitious we just didn't care that we were so hard up that we had had to borrow shoes, clothes, everything. We shared everything, we were totally skint.

'We were much harder up than we had ever been before. Back in Wales I had a good job as a printer and with working with the group at nights as well I was making a nice living. Tommy Scott and the Senators used to get paid around £11 a night before we left and we would always split it equally. Everything we did and everything we had went into building up the group. We used to eat, sleep and breathe the Senators.

'We played our final gig in Pontypridd upstairs at the White Hart the night before we left. Then we went round all our friends and relations saying goodbye. Tom was driving us in our old Thames van which frightened us all as he was wild behind the wheel.

'In London we first went to Gordon Mills in Notting Hill Gate. His wife Jo made us tea and Gordon said: "I've found a place for you."

' "Where?" we asked.

' "Ladbroke Grove," he said.

' "That sounds nice," we said. We were so green we'd never even heard of it.

'But first we stayed in a grotty hotel, a real dosser's place, with no fire precautions or anything. Then we moved into the flat in Ladbroke Grove. Nice was not a word that came to mind. It was a dismal little two-room basement in a very rough area. There were four beds in one room and two in another. And with just £1 a day from Gordon to live on we were desperately hard up from the beginning.

'We lived on egg and chips from greasy spoon cafés and on sandwiches and hampers friends and relatives used to send us up from Wales.

'Gordon had £3,000 from writing "I'll Never Get Over You" for Johnny Kidd and the Pirates so he had a bit of cash. And almost as soon as we got up to London we played at The 100 Club in Oxford Street supporting the Rolling Stones. I thought we went down well but we didn't seem to get many gigs, and gradually our enthusiasm began to run out.

'Tom and I were like brothers. I was closer to Tom than I was to my own brother. I remember one day Tom was raving on about how he hated policemen for some reason. "All policemen are bastards," he kept shouting.

' "Hang on a minute," I said. "My brother Norman is a copper, Tom. He's all right. He's not a bastard."

' "I'm more of a brother to you than him," said Tom. And I knew what he meant. We became very close. Some nights we slept in the same bed, not that either of us were homosexual you understand. We shared sausage sandwiches when we couldn't afford decent food.

'There was never any animosity or quarrels between us. Never a cross word. And we always said if any one of us makes it we'll always stick together, it will be one for all and all for one.

'And of course we did have some laughs as well. Gerry Dorsey was a friend of Gordon's and we got to know him as well, long before Gerry changed his name to Engelbert Humperdinck. One night he asked us to back him at a club in Barnes, West London, and we all went over there with Tom. When we arrived Gerry went to his dressing room and we were shown to another room. We found we were sharing it with one of the other acts on the bill – a belly dancer and her performing python.

'Fortunately the snake was asleep in its basket but the other disturbing thing about our dressing room was that it was just outside the kitchens. So there we were, all starving hungry, and the tantalizing smells of delicious foods kept wafting our way. It was agony.

'Then we realized the waiters kept leaving trolleys loaded with meals just outside our door. Eventually we just cracked. Someone opened the door, lifted the cover off a meal and snaffled a beautiful T-bone steak dinner. Within a few seconds we had pulled it to pieces and eaten it, taking care to replace the cover.

'The next thing we heard was the commotion when the waiter got to the table and grandly lifted the lid to find nothing underneath. He came racing back and shouted at us but he was Portuguese so that didn't make too much sense to any of us. He was followed by the manager who gave us a real ear-bashing until Tom had a brainwave.

'He pointed at the basket and said darkly, "It was the snake." Then we all picked up that line and tried to convince him the snake had eaten the steak. I'm not sure that he ever believed us but we got away with it.'

The alcohol-assisted excitement at being in the big city on the ladder to showbusiness success gradually wore off as the bottom rung proved to be increasingly uncomfortable. The Playboys found themselves swiftly renamed the Squires as London already had some other musical Playboys but their fortunes stayed the same. All of the group members suffered bouts of depression but Tom felt the disappointments more deeply than the others. Apart from the occasional demo disc or live gig way down the bill the young Welshmen all found themselves kicking their heels. But Tom was the only one who was married with a young son to support. His wife had to go to work in the glove factory to provide for herself and Mark as Tom was perpetually short of money.

He felt the weight of gloom so strongly that one day Vernon Hopkins found him in the flat sobbing his heart out. Vernon recalls: 'Tom was terribly down. After about six months we didn't seem to be getting anywhere and we were getting the odd food parcel from home. We were desperate to get on but we were proud too. It was hard to admit we needed charity. I came into the flat and Tom was there on his own, and he was crying. I went up to him and put my hand on his shoulder and said: "What's wrong?"

' "Nothing's going. Nothing's happening. I can't stick it here any longer. My wife is nagging me to go back, and she's got a kid, and she's having to go out to work," said Tom.

'I said, "Look, we've come this far we've got to stick it out, we'll get a break, we're all in this together, we all feel the same way."

'And then he told me he was going to kill himself, he was going to commit suicide, he was so low that he had been standing on the platform at Notting Hill underground station determined to throw himself under the next train. That black day it just seemed like the only way out.

'I talked and talked to him and even then he was going to chuck it all in and go back to Wales. Eventually I managed to convince him to stay.'

Tom recalled the incident himself later: 'A Tube train was coming into Notting Hill Station and I stood on the platform thinking, "Shall I jump off and end it all?" You see, I was terribly depressed. This was at the end of six of the worst months of my life. I didn't know what to do with myself. Gordon was very good.

'He gave me £1 a day but there was never anything left over while we were looking for work. Then I asked him if he could send Linda £5. She was working in the factory to keep herself and Mark while I was in London. We needed the extra money badly. When I asked Gordon he said, "I can't really afford that £5. I've spent nearly all my own money trying to keep you together. Now I'm existing on a loan from the bank." That's why I felt so depressed. I didn't want to go home again to Wales without being a success, so I waited at Notting Hill, wondering what to do with myself. Just like that.'

The moral support from Vernon Hopkins helped to pull Tom through this black period. Vernon explained over and over again how they must stick together and pull through and gradually Tom came out of his depression.

Jo Mills recalls: 'We just didn't have the money. My modelling money was drying up and I even did a few jobs after Tracey was born but it broke my heart to be away from her. Gordon's money soon went and our overdraft just kept growing and growing. Sometimes Tom and the Squires did get a gig and they would get paid about £30 or sometimes it was up to £50, which we thought was fantastic.'

Their first record, 'Chills and Fever', was released in August 1964 and swiftly climbed the Pontypridd charts, largely, as reporter Greenberg recalls, 'Because it was the first pop record anyone could remember anyone from the town being involved with.' Sadly this local enthusiasm was not repeated nationally and the record disappeared without trace.

Manager Mills was the saviour. He and Les Reed wrote a clever little song called 'It's Not Unusual' which was the perfect showcase for Tom's remarkable voice. Unfortunately, it had been written for Sandie Shaw, the popular young singer whose gimmick was performing in her bare feet. Jo Mills explains: 'She was very hot at the time and her management had asked Gordon to write a song for her.'

But Tom and the Squires were needed to provide a demo disc so the new creation could be more easily assessed. Mills arrived at the dank basement flat just before noon one day, not a time of day which figured prominently in the Squires' calendar.

'Get up,' he exhorted. 'I've got this song called "It's Not Unusual", and I've booked the studio in Denmark Street for 3 p.m.'

Mickey Gee recalls: 'We used to cut a record in twenty minutes in those days and I said to Gordon, "How does it go?" Gordon played it for me, he was a good musician, and straight away I smelled some interesting chords.

'I thought, "Yeah, that's for us. That's nice, that's different. But Dave Cooper and Vernon couldn't get it at all. They couldn't learn it. They were great blokes but not great musicians, so we went in and recorded it without Dai and without Vernon, with no bass and no rhythm guitar. Tom sang, Chris Slade the drummer played tambourine, I played lead and we dubbed some rhythm on.

'The trouble was Gordon and Les Reed had written the song specially for Sandie Shaw, who just had a hit with "There's Always Something There To Remind Me", and Gordon was trying to get the follow-up song. We finished it and we all went over to the pub, The George, in Tin Pan Alley.

'I always felt I was sharper than the other guys; to me they were valley yobs while I was a city boy from Cardiff. They never smelt a rat and I could smell a rat then – call it paranoia if you like.

'I always felt they were a bit too gullible, that's why I was the first to leave. In the pub I really let rip. I said, "Look, we're up here living in a pigsty. What's it all for? So we can be famous. And here you are, Gordon, you're our manager, you've written a hit. Of course Sandie Shaw is a guaranteed hit and Tom isn't, but bloody hell, give us a break. That's a great song."

'Tom sat quiet and said nothing. He never liked to go against anything Gordon said, but eventually even he piped up, "It is a nice number. I'd like to do it." That was his contribution.'

But Jo Mills remembers: 'Tom really did bug Gordon about "It's Not Unusual". All one weekend he went on and on about it, pleading with Gordon to let him have the song straight away but Gordon had agreed to write it for Sandie Shaw and he stuck by his word.'

Eventually Gordon conceded they had a point. 'I'll tell you what,' he said, 'if Sandie Shaw turns it down I'll let you have it.' As it turned out the singer more famous for her feet than her voice did reject the offering and so the song was handed back to Tom.

But Mills had not failed to register the Squires' musical limitations. As Mickey Gee recalls: 'Gordon made Tom go into the Decca studios and record it again without any of the Squires playing. What was great about that was that the recording was a disaster. But these were determined people. They cut it again and that was the one that came out.'

The squalid flat and seedy living conditions forced Tom and the boys in the band to make frequent trips back home to Wales. Often they would hitch a lift with a Pontypridd lorry driver who took pity on their poverty. Tom hated hitching and would do anything to avoid the indignity. He once sold his leather jacket to Mickey Gee for £2 so he could travel by train.

Although never short of female companionship in London, Tom missed Linda and Mark very badly. And when he had a real black shiny new record with his name on the side to show off he raced back to Treforest to let his family hear the new sound.

Gerry Greenberg was called in as the Rhondda Valley's sole pop columnist and gravely asked for his verdict. Greenberg colourfully recalls the scene: 'I picked my way up the cobbled streets, strode up to 3 Cliff Terrace and stamped my feet on the grill outside the front door.

'It was late 1964 in dank, gloomy Pontypridd. The green, green grass of home was nowhere to be seen. Just the grey, grey walls of rows and rows of miners' cottages. A shadowy figure appeared beneath me and glanced briefly upwards.

' "Hang on, Gerry. I'll be there now." Seconds later the door opened and I was face to face with Tom Jones. The foot-on-the grill routine was normal procedure for Tom's friends. He and Linda lived with young Mark in the basement of his mother-in-law's little house, and the local code of conduct was clearly laid down. A knock on the door meant a call for Linda's mum Vi, a chirpy woman who worked as a waitress in a local café; a rap on the grill signified a visitor for Tom and his family.

'I was in Cliff Terrace at Tom's request. He wanted me to hear his record. With no critical competition on the Rhondda he actually valued my opinion. And it was in that tiny basement flat that I heard "It's Not Unusual" for the first time, on a demo disc.

' "What do you reckon?" asked Tom intently.

' "Great," I lied, privately convinced that his second effort on wax would go the way of the first.

'The over-produced "Chills and Fever" had made the top ten in Pontypridd, mainly because it was the first record ever cut by a pop performer from the town. But it had made absolutely no impact elsewhere. And I couldn't see "It's Not Unusual" faring any better. It simply didn't have enough melody and was too repetitive.'

Gerry Greenberg's false praise must have convinced the would-be singing star for he was rewarded with a boiled egg from Linda as Tom enthused about his prospects. Greenberg liked Linda.

But although the record had been made, a definite release date remained elusive. Jo Mills said: 'We suggested the boys stayed at home for Christmas because we simply had no more money to pay the £1 a day to each of them.

'They had virtually nothing to go home with, they stopped down there because it was cheaper that way but secretly Gordon and I wondered whether they would ever come back. Christmas 1964 was our worst time ever. Decca kept putting back the release date; we were £1,000 in debt at the bank; and I was having problems with my second pregnancy and was laid up in hospital.'

The record was at last released towards the end of January 1965 and from her hospital bed, having sadly lost her unborn baby, Jo Mills watched its first national exposure on a television programme called *Newly Pressed*. 'I had always rated the song but when I heard it on the show I just knew it would be a hit,' says Jo.

His brief respite at home over, Tom returned to London and set out to launch himself into the big-time. 'He's Tom Jones, he's twenty-two, single and a miner,' said one of

Gordon Mills' early press releases, managing to avoid the truth on every detail. But Gordon did manage to get Tom Jones and the Squires on a nationwide tour with Cilla Black, Tommy Roe and assorted others. Tom was the replacement for top-of-the-bill P. J. Proby who was sacked in the famous 'pants-splitting' row.

Proby was then a big star and the press helped to build up a ridiculous rivalry between the two singers. They were solo singers in a pop world dominated by groups and both relied heavily on a raunchy stage act to inflame their growing followings of female fans. Both men looked vaguely similar; on stage they wore tight trousers and loose, smock-like shirts. Like Proby, Tom had started to wear his hair swept back in a pony tail secured by a bow.

But Proby's habit of 'spontaneously' bursting his trousers at the straining crutch helped to tip the battle in Tom's favour. Proby played up the press interest by sneering that he had: 'spent more money than Tom Jones would ever see, he's nothing', perhaps one of the least accurate of all pop predictions. Tom, who had nicknamed his rival P. J. Probably, retorted by challenging Proby to make his comments face to face. Proby wisely shut up and faded quietly into obscurity. Yet as 'It's Not Unusual' was released in January 1965 it was certainly Proby who was the established star while Tom was unknown.

But as the tour began to roll Proby's pants-splitting brought the wrath of authority down on him. Powerful showbusiness figure Joe Collins, the father of Jackie and Joan Collins, was in charge of the tour and he became the man who provided Tom Jones with what proved to be his crucial break. He said: 'I challenged Proby myself about what was happening. He was most upset. "The same thing happens to Elvis Presley. His pants split too and everyone knows it's an accident." '

But problems with Proby persisted and eventually he had to go. Collins recalled: 'Before I had even begun to search for a replacement, the agent Colin Berlin came on the telephone to me, "I've heard what's happened to Proby, I've got just the right chap to step in. A boy with a great voice from South

Wales, name of Tom Jones ... if you listen to his new disc 'It's Not Unusual' you'll get the idea that he's just right for the Proby audience. And the women go wild over him." I accepted Collins' offer of Tom Jones and agreed to engage him for £600 for the week.'

Proby was dropped from the tour in a blaze of publicity and on 4 February 1964 Tom Jones and the Squires joined the line-up in Plymouth.

As Mickey Gee remembers: 'When the management chucked Proby off the tour, Cilla Black became top of the bill and everyone moved up a peg. That was the best thing that could have happened to Tom because we had no promotion organized for the record but one or two radio shows played it and we started to get a great reception for the song on tour. We crept into the charts and that got us moved up another notch on tour.'

Tom said: 'Proby never liked it when I took over from him on the tour. But he was busting his pants all the time and although he said it was an accident I know for a fact he did it on purpose. No matter what he says I know the story because he was getting his shirts made by the same fellow that was making my shirts.

'Proby asked him to use the material to make a pair of pants and the tailor said,"No. This is velvet, it's made for shirts. It won't stand up to the wear." Proby said, "I don't want them to." So he used to drop to his knees and they would split.

'But now he says there was some great plan and he was bought out of the way so I could move in. At the time he was doing very well. After I joined the tour I used to go on to sing and all the front row would be holding up posters of him and I'd have to do my act looking at his bloody face. But the bigger "It's Not Unusual" became the more those posters got rolled up.'

Gradually the earthy sexual appeal of the singer and the catchy melody of the song started to catch on. TV producers took notice and Tom was sent an air ticket to Glasgow and invited to appear on *Scottish Round Up*. Manager Mills hated flying so, as Tom said at the time, 'I've never been on a plane before and as Gordon won't travel by air I've got to go on my own.'

But Gordon went and many more TV appearances followed. The live audience of *Ready Steady Go* applauded wildly when they realized that, unlike so many of his contemporaries, Tom could actually reproduce the sound of his record. By 8 February 'It's Not Unusual' had sold out in Pontypridd and topped the local charts, by 15 February the record had risen to number ten in the *New Musical Express* and Tom was the first Welsh pop singer since Maureen Evans to reach the national hit parade. His mother Freda proudly told *The Pontypridd Observer*: 'We always knew Tom would make it. He has always had singing ability and bags of confidence. He was singing in public when he was only five or six years of age. I remember taking him to Women's Guild meetings and he used to make his own beat on a table and sing to the members.'

By 22 February 'It's Not Unusual' had maintained its meteoric progress and stood at number two in the *New Musical Express* and number three in the *Melody Maker* charts. 'It's all happened so quickly I can't believe it,' said Tom when reporters tracked him down to Gordon's apartment in London's Campden Hill Towers. 'It's Not Unusual' reached the top of both national charts on 1 March 1965, appropriately enough St David's Day, and the celebrating in the valleys was even more riotous than usual.

In London they went pretty wild as well. Tom led a liquid celebration which lasted until dawn. Mickey Gee reflects today: 'We began that tour unknowns with a record that wasn't so much released as escaped and we finished it top of the bill, above Cilla, and at number one. It was fantastic.'

Jo Mills, out of hospital by then, says today: 'Our lives were turned upside down within a few days. If "It's Not Unusual" hadn't happened I can't imagine we could have gone on long like that. The £1 a day the boys got was little enough but it was money we simply didn't have. But Gordon always believed in Tom, he knew that Tom was something really special, so I suppose we would have found a way. But when it happened it was a wonderful, magical time. And somehow it was a great boost for us. We all believed "It's Not Unusual" was a hit record. It was fantastic to be proved right. Our tiny flat was totally overwhelmed by it all. We got loads of fan mail which I struggled to answer. I had never typed before but I thought it was important that people got a proper letter back. Almost straight away I couldn't cope.'

P. J. Proby was not the only established star not too keen to share the limelight. As his name was becoming known Tom met Scottish singer Lulu in a record shop. Tom was not backward in coming forward but Lulu turned her back on him and stormed off without a word. It wasn't behaviour Tom was accustomed to, even from a celebrity.

'Stuck up bitch,' he snorted over a pint the next time he recalled the incident in Pontypridd.

Tom's triumph was tarnished a little by a rash of newspaper revelations that he was neither twenty-two nor single nor a miner. The revelation that, far from being footloose and fancy-free, Tom was married with a son made the biggest headlines. Friends in Treforest had thoughtfully written to national papers pointing out that Tom's wife Linda lived with his son Mark at 3 Cliff Terrace, Treforest. At the time Tom was embarrassed to be caught out by such a transparent lie. He said: 'I never really wanted people to believe I was single. It wasn't fair to my wife Linda and son Mark. In fact I was going to let people know the truth but then the papers came out with the story.'

Jo Mills recalls: 'It was very different in the sixties. Then it was unheard of for a male star whose image was so blatantly sexual to own up to being married. Gordon felt he simply had to try to pretend Tom was single at the start because all the people in the business said the female fans wouldn't go for him if he was married. That made it a very difficult early time for Linda. It was only a few months before she was discovered but during that time they tried to hide her away completely.

'She is a lovely person. She did do interviews but it certainly never came easy. I think it shaded the way she viewed Tom's whole career. She never looked confident after that. In a way I think those early days have coloured her whole life.'

Chapter Four

LIFE AT THE TOP

'When I saw my name on top of the charts in the Sunday papers, I thought, "Oh thank God. This is it, this is the start." I've never really had a feeling like that since,' said Tom Jones, reflecting on his sudden arrival at number one.

After struggling for years around the pubs and clubs of South Wales, and starving for months in a squalid London flat, the big-time arrived not a moment too soon. Tom was twenty-four years old and celebrated his eighth wedding anniversary the week 'It's Not Unusual' reached number one, so he was not some impressionable teenager unable to cope with his sudden fame and wealth.

Not that there weren't some long liquid celebrations. Tom and the Squires normally needed no excuse for a booze-up, but they went wild when they learned 'It's Not Unusual' had hit the top, even though the group weren't actually used on the record. Back in Pontypridd Tom's health was drunk in his absence. Tom Senior said in an interview later: 'It was a Sunday and when I got to the surface after my shift some of my mates gave me the big news. "Your Tom's got to number one," they said. And there in the chart published in the Sunday paper was the proof. No. 1 – "It's Not Unusual". The song that became his signature tune. We went home and celebrated. Champagne and whisky and all the neighbours knocking on the door. It was quite a party.'

Tom had been waiting so long for success that, when his big day arrived, he was determined to enjoy it. He said: 'My rise to "stardom" was overnight really when it came, everything happened so quickly. I remember being mobbed by fans for the first time – it terrified me. We were having a drink in a pub near the theatre when a load of screaming women came racing over. I just assumed they were fans of Cilla Black but they swarmed round me, grabbing my clothes and demanding autographs. I was totally shocked. In that moment I realized that things were never going to be quite the same again.' Tom was forced to sprint for safety as the excited ladies struggled to claim a souvenir. He sacrificed a perfectly good raincoat as he bolted back to the stage door.

Life on the road was suddenly quite different. After years of battling for attention Tom was now the target for that most dangerous species of the pop world, the frenzied female fan. His most embarrassing encounter with this peculiar animal which normally travels in excited packs came in the least glamorous of surroundings, the Watford Gap motorway service station on the M1 during a trip back to London from Birmingham. Tom was followed into the gents' toilets. He said: 'I was literally caught with my pants down when these girls jumped over the top of the toilet door. I told them if this was their way of calling on me I didn't care if they didn't buy my records any more, just as long as I could go to the toilet in peace. That was the most embarrassing experience I ever had but there were lots of benefits to making it. Suddenly I realized that after years of being desperately hard up I had money at last. I could buy things,' he said.

'I could never afford a car before I made it so when "It's Not Unusual" happened I bought my first motor, a gleaming new S-type Jaguar. I could never afford a house before I made it so the first place I owned was a mansion in Shepperton. I'd never had my own house in Wales. I lived with my mother and father and then I got married and I lived with my wife's mother and father.'

The change in fortunes was as swift and dramatic as any rags-to-riches showbiz story. Tom splashed out £7,000 on a stylish detached house in Shepperton, London. The first house he ever owned was almost as large as the whole terrace in Laura Street, Treforest, where he grew up.

'I coped pretty well with fame,' observed Tom modestly in an American radio interview some years later. 'I suppose at first I went a bit mad. The house and the car came. I had always wanted to own my own place and I had always fancied a Jag. I started going to discotheques at places like The Cromwellian. For a time I thought I was Jack the lad but I learned very quickly.'

Manager Mills was learning to cope pretty quickly as well. His ex-wife Jo firmly believes Gordon and Tom needed each other.

She says today: 'Tom was a very vibrant, sexual young man, totally dedicated to making it. He knew he had the talent, not in a big-headed way. He just knew he could sing and he knew women reacted to him. I think he would have made it in some way no matter who had managed him, but without Gordon's brilliance I don't think he would have become a world star.'

Gordon Mills might not have had much managerial experience to speak of but he had plenty of ambition. While many showbusiness executives might have still been congratulating themselves on reaching the top of the British charts, Mills was busy plotting how to conquer the world's biggest market for his protégé – America. Fortunately the trail blazed by the Beatles was still warm and British music was still very much in demand in the United States. Mills managed to sell his unknown singer very well; he swiftly lined up five appearances on the influential *Ed Sullivan Show* which had provided a platform for Stateside success for the Beatles.

Mills was so determined to make his boy do well in America that he overcame his lifelong fear of flying to travel out with Tom on 29 April 1965 for the first appearance, which was carefully timed to coincide with the US release of 'It's Not Unusual'.

The Welsh wiggle was unchanged on the other side of the Atlantic but Sullivan's producers were appalled at what they saw. The thrusting pelvis which had powered Tom Jones up the British charts was too blatant for American television.

'Shoot him from the waist up only,' came the order from up on high, and even after that prim directive Tom recalls he was warned: 'Now listen, son, keep it cool, move sideways only. Otherwise we'll black you out.'

But the main surprise for the American viewers was not concerned with any absence of animal antics. Many millions of them were much more shocked to discover that Tom Jones was white. That throaty soul voice conjured up images of a black singer in the US.

Tom says: 'They all thought I was black. Lloyd Greenfield, who was bringing me over to New York, started getting phone calls from radio stations asking him to bring Tom Jones over. But those stations were black radio.

'He told them, "Tom's not black." But they said, "You can't tell me 'It's Not Unusual' is not a black record." I had got to know Dionne Warwick in London and we met up again on my first trip to New York. She wanted to show me round and asked me where I wanted to go. I said The Apollo in Harlem to see the 'R and B' singers. Chuck Jackson was topping the bill. I looked out front and then went backstage into the dressing room and I swear I was the only white person in the building.

'Chuck Jackson said to me, "Will you come on stage when I do my finale? Once they know who you are you won't have a problem." At the end of his amazing act he introduced Dionne to wild applause, then the Shirelles to wild applause, then he introduced, "Soul brother from England, Tom Jones".

'You could have cut the atmosphere with a knife. It was as if someone had just pressed off the applause button as I started to walk on stage. Chuck threw me the mike and I belted into "What I'd Say" and brought the bloody place down. I did fifteen minutes and got a fantastic reception. I'll never forget it.'

Back home after their whirlwind introduction to the sunnier side of showbusiness, manager Mills insisted Tom and their respective wives take a quick holiday break in the south of France.

Jo Mills recalls: 'The pressure had been absolutely unbearable. Every day something happened that exceeded everything else, more deals, more reporters, more offers, more fans. So we decided to go to France. Gordon refused to fly this time so we drove in our first car, a Ford Consul. We had a lovely time, it was a great break, but the only thing that sticks in my mind is Gordon's crazy driving. I was screaming on the floor of the car, terrified of Gordon on the French roads. I think it was such a relief for him to get away he went a bit mad behind the wheel.'

Life with the Squires was never quite as glamorous. But as Tom swiftly came to terms with his new-found wealth and fame so did his faithful backing band, his closest friends who had struggled together for years for their big break. Only they were quickly discovering that the 'equal-shares-for-all' days had been left far behind in Wales.

'At first it was great,' recalls Mickey Gee. 'Most of the times we would just get pissed and knock off birds whenever we could. Even when Tom was number one and we were touring circuits like the Top Rank, before we went on you would find us up in the bar pouring beer down and holding court in our mohair suits.

'We would have eight, nine or ten pints and then go on. We were real pissheads. It was a bad habit to get into and I had a real problem for a time. It got out of hand. We were living in swinging London at its height and we had more booze and girls than we could handle.

'I was twenty-one and I went to the doctor and he said, "If you keep drinking at this rate by the time you're thirty you'll be twenty stone." I was around thirteen stone. Then we went to Australia on tour and it got worse, you would buy a round and get a great jug full.

'We were just yobs trying to play at "Look at us, we've made it." We used to buy little fake rabbit's feet from Woolworths in Portobello Road and the girls would battle to tug them off. The minute you dangled them from your belt the girls would grab them. Tom was just one of us, a normal red-blooded Welsh guy but he was the only one of us who was actually married.

'I remember at the start Linda used to arrive at the flat and it would be, "Oh fuck, it's your wife," and we would have to quickly clear other birds out.

'At the point "It's Not Unusual" got to number one we were still getting paid our £1 a day as Gordon said it took a long time for the money to come in. I now know that is true but it was no argument for us starving. There could have been an advance.'

The 'all for one, one for all' ethos was certainly an idea of the past as Tom bought his mansion in Shepperton and the Squires were rehoused in a modest, rented semi-detached house in Hounslow. While Tom's earnings were never disclosed to the other group members, the musicians who had lived with him through the darkest days of the Ladbroke Grove hovel found themselves on musicians' wages of £20 a week.

Early group leader Vernon Hopkins recalls: 'As soon as the money arrived it was Tom and us. We were still in the van and Tom had a Jag. It was wrong. It shouldn't have been like that but we had all worked so hard for the success we couldn't leave. We never saw the books.

'From the very beginning we were partners, we had shared everything. We used to split our earnings equally, there was never any suggestion of anything else. Tom used to say that when we made it we'd all have flash cars and gold rings and the rest of it.

'Of course it didn't turn out like that. We had no idea how much Tom and Gordon were making but we knew it was a whole lot more than us.

'But at the time we didn't worry too much. Soon we had gone up to £30 a week while the average wage then was only £20, and we were having such a great time. We did tours and gigs all over the country. Although the wages were low it was all happening for us. And at least after starving in that flat at last we were staying in hotels and getting plenty to eat. It was great on the road, everybody wanted to jump on the bandwagon. It was parties and girls all the way, they just couldn't seem to get enough of us.

'We were still steadier than a lot of the groups. We worked with the Who once and we were amazed when they started throwing all these Vox amplifiers down the stairs. We didn't smash anything up. We just used to drink as much as we could and score with as many birds as we could and have a good time. It was great fun. Tom was always the leader at pulling the birds – he would jump on anything.

'We were a very tight band. We weren't just one of those manufactured groups. We had been together for years and we worked together really well. We could tell just from a movement of Tom's head how to interpret a song. All those years together counted. He was a powerful singer and we were a good band. We used to drive each other on.'

But Mickey Gee, who had by then been promoted to 'musical director' as he was the only member at that time able to read music, was not so easy-going about the new financial arrangements.

He says today: 'It was the classic rock and roll story. Tom Jones was just a typical yob who used to get typically pissed and had a typical accident of a hit record and reacted typically.

'I didn't join a band to be famous. I joined a bunch of blokes to get pissed with and have a laugh together. We were Welsh lads all on the dole together. The joke was that back in Wales, apart from Vernon, they were all on the dole while I had a job on the beer lorries. And it was me constantly moaning at them, "Come on, we've got to do something better than this." When we got to London it took me a year to get used to lying in bed all day. I soon found out there was no point in getting up as I had nothing to spend. I missed work. Whenever I went home I would go round with my mates on the beer lorries without getting paid.

'I don't think Tom meant to cut us up badly. I've been with lots of people before they were famous and seen what sudden fame and fortune does to them. I know I might go crazy if I had a hit record – meanness, thoughtlessness and not giving a damn for anybody else is a common quality. Tom is no exception.

'But it was fun while it lasted. Of all the things I feel about Tom I would never take away his singing. He had a remarkable voice. He used to like Jerry Lee Lewis, Chuck Berry and Solomon Burke and even in the van when we were going to a gig he would be singing away with that amazing voice.

'I used to think he could become a great singer singing great songs but too often he would churn out rubbish like "The Young New Mexican Puppeteer" which used to depress me no end. But it was a living so I went along.

'Once Tom was famous I was made musical director and Tom used to fly me out to places like Bermuda to work on routines with him. But I only got the job because none of the others could read music. Tom found his best-known song, "Green, Green Grass of Home" on a Jerry Lee Lewis album, *Country Songs for City Folks*, and he gave it to me to write out the chords for the boys. Tom said, "That's a great song, I want to do that," so I just sat in a hotel in Wigan and wrote out the chords and said, "There you are, lads, we're doing that tomorrow night."

'Dave Cooper, the rhythm guitarist, got the sack. He wasn't a good musician but none of us were good musicians compared to the London musicians. The drummer, Chris Slade, was dreadful and I used to get some stick for criticizing. Not that I was any good but they were crap. But when we got to London Chris used to go across town and take lessons from Billy Cotton's drummer from the *Billy Cotton Band Show* and he did become a great drummer.

'Vernon was not a good musician but it was his band. He chose Tom to be in the band and he was always Tom's mate. Vernon was a great guy. He should have had something out of it. Then Tom went on a long tour of America without us, and we all had to go home to Wales. We had to get together with a keyboard player called Vic Cooper who had been working with Johnny Kidd and the Pirates. Vic was brought in to replace Dave Cooper. After that Tom went to Bermuda and sent for me. That is when Gordon got me the visa and, when I looked on my passport, it said "musical director". I thought, "I'm not a musical director, I'm a 22-year-old yob, and here it is I'm going to Bermuda in the big-time all legit." I couldn't believe it. I flew out with Linda, who was missing Tom badly.

'When we got to Bermuda, Tom and I were supposed to be going on to Los Angeles where Tom had some more concerts booked. More than anything in the world it was my ambition to meet Elvis Presley and I kept saying to Tom, "Let's meet Elvis" but Tom scoffed. He didn't think it would be possible. He didn't think we could get to see Elvis, but I did and I kept on at him, telling him that he had had a big hit in the United States. I remember telling him, "How can you think about just lying on the beach when Elvis is only a few miles away?" I knew we could fix it.

'But then Linda said to me quietly one night that she was supposed to be flying back to Heathrow but she wanted to go with Tom to LA. Did I mind swapping tickets with her and going home? *Mind?* I minded like hell. I was devastated but I couldn't refuse her. She hadn't seen much of Tom for months, but he didn't seem bothered either way. Anyway, I flew back to Britain and then I remember a week later I was in the house in Hounslow when Tom came in and proudly showed me a picture of him with Elvis. I was green with envy.

'Gordon was always ruthless as the boss. I remember he used to come into the flat in Ladbroke Grove and be appalled. It was like *The Young Ones*. The dregs of society would be in there. We didn't realize people saw it as a place to hang out. We just thought everyone wanted to be our friends.

'Gordon would come down and kick them all out and shout at us and tell us they were "bad people". We had starved in that hovel from July of 1964 until the spring of 1965. After the number one I would often complain about our treatment but Gordon would always tell me, "There are plenty more guitarists in Wales, Mickey."

'If I went on he would say, "Wanna go back to the hills?" to us, which I always particularly resented as they were from the hills but I was from Cardiff, the flat lands. We were touring regularly, promoting the records and by the time I left in 1967 the wages had gone up to £40 a week.

'But we had to pay our own hotels and other expenses and

he never even paid our stamps. That was the start of all the
shit and the bitter feelings. When I came home I couldn't get
any dole because my stamps hadn't been paid. The backlog
opted me out of the system. Because I'd been up in London
for that long and I'd earned money and I hadn't paid tax or
stamps, when I came home I couldn't get dole. I was out of
the system so I continued to be a sort of self-employed person
for about twenty years. They caught up with me in 1982 and
really threw the book at me but it all came from that. If only
Gordon had paid our stamps it would have saved me a great
upset and not messed up my life and caused me a lot of trouble.
I remember at the end Gordon told us, "You're self-employed,
but you've got to pay your own tax." Great. Big deal, I thought.
Now you tell us. But we were naive.

'Tom, Vernon and Dave got most of the women. Tom's big
fears then were getting a girl pregnant and catching VD. He
must have had thousands of women. He was a hell of a boy
with the girls. He was a true yob. Watching him chat up a
girl was like watching a caveman dragging a woman home
by the hair. I could never be like that. Tom used to try to
sexually educate me and gave me long talks that I had to
break the barrier and go for it. But he did not really have
more women when he became famous, he always had loads
of women.

'I remember Tom decided that because he had black hair
all the rest of us had to have black hair. I'm sure that's why
I've gone bald, all that dyeing your hair is not good. There
were two girls from Pontypridd who used to be hairdressers
and come up to London to dye our hair. And provide a few
other services as well.

'I got involved in the groupie scene for a while but the
appeal soon wore off. I just grew to hate the whole lifestyle
of Tom taking the band for a ride. I used to despise the other
guys in the band who were Welsh guys who had come up with
Tom and starved together. I used to despise them for allowing
that to happen. The only concession Tom ever made to our
feelings about the new set-up was to let one of us go with him
to America on his promotional trips. People from the office

used to go with him at first and then I grumbled, "Why can't we come, Tom?"

'Tom allowed it once and we were all supposed to get a turn on a rota basis but somehow that petered out. Underneath all my resentment at the situation I always thought Tom would look after us. We were mates for goodness sake.

'Ironically, when I left it was over not enough pay, but it wasn't me, it was the band.

'I'll never forget it, we were playing in Southampton in the autumn of 1967 and getting £40 a week, and they all grumbled to me. I was sent to see Tom and Gordon in the dressing room to say we either wanted £50 a week with our tax paid or £60 a week and we'd pay our own tax. They said if we don't get it we'll all leave. I agreed, I said OK. I had been moaning for some time so I went and put the case to Tom and Gordon in the dressing room. Tom was in dark glasses and Gordon was all stern and businesslike. I told them what we wanted. It was like a scene from a Humphrey Bogart film.

'Gordon said, "Call the band in."

'They all filed in and Gordon produced one of his big statements. He was great at big statements.

' "I was in a band once," he said. "It was called the Viscounts. And when I didn't like being in the band any more, I left. You can forget this money you're asking for, you're not getting any more money and if you don't like it you can leave."

'Well, as all the band had agreed that we would leave if we didn't get the rise, as spokesman I said: "Right, we're leaving."

'Unfortunately, when it came to it they all backed down and I was the only one to leave. And that in a nutshell is why, although in many ways they were great blokes and we had a lot of laughs together, I don't keep in touch. Because on the big one, when I really thought we were all standing together, they let me down. Because they asked me to go to Tom and Gordon. I don't think they maliciously set me up, I think they thought, right, we're going to stand our ground, but once Tom and Gordon got them lined up like that they crumbled.

They went through us, me first, and said, "Mickey, you're not getting any more money, what are you doing, staying or going?" I said, "I'm going."

'Then the others were asked and one by one they said they would stay. I was surprised, to say the least, but really I didn't care. I thought it showed them up for what they were.

'The only reason we went up to £40 a week was because we had started to work with proper session musicians and had found out what the proper rates were. Even then the other guys in the band were easy-going about these session men getting more than us. I kept saying, "For God's sake, they never starved with you or went on the road to all those awful places. He's paying them session rates, let him pay us session rates." Of course, he got rid of them in the end as I knew he would, but the thing that really pissed me off was that after I left they did all get to America and they met Elvis which was always my dream. So I missed out in that way.'

Vernon Hopkins also recalls the cash showdown with bitterness. 'When it came to the wages it was just accept it or go. That was Gordon's management style but Tom went along with it. He could have said something and he should have said something to veto it. He should have looked after us. But now if he's asked about his old days with the Squires he tries to keep it quiet.

'Mickey Gee was disgusted and he left. I admired him for it. But I decided to accept it. I wanted to see the world and also I had put in a lot of energy for six years to the band building us up in Wales and spending a lot of money on equipment. I wanted to get something out of it.

'Tom and I had been like brothers but we got further and further apart. When he made it he just changed. He became very, very hard. I never saw it in him before but the fame and the money changed him.'

Tom recorded the song which became his unofficial theme tune, and the second of his two number one hits in the British charts, 'The Green, Green Grass of Home', in 1966, and that also heralded the arrival of a new member of the Squires, Londoner Vic Cooper who replaced his dismissed namesake

Dave Cooper. The two were not related. Vic Cooper had been playing keyboard for Johnny Kidd and the Pirates when he was approached by Gordon Mills to join Tom Jones and the Squires. 'I wasn't sure if it was a good move at first. I thought Tom might just be a flash in the pan,' says Vic Cooper. 'But I joined and the first time I played with them was live on television on *Ready, Steady, Go*. At first I was the outsider as they were all Welsh and I was from London. They were a little bit clique-like but gradually we became friends.

'Gordon asked me if I would drive Tom as well as playing, so I would do that, first in a red Jaguar, later in a Volvo sports car like the TV Saint used to drive, and then in a Rolls Royce. The rest of the band would travel in the van, driven by Chris Ellis, another Welsh guy who had been with Tom since the beginning.

'It was an amazing life. We toured all over Britain and went to America, Australia and various European countries. Wherever we went there would always be loads of girls. We were all young then so we just took advantage and rode on his back in that way. It was Tom they were all after. Yet even Tom couldn't cope with them all so we did well out of it. Sometimes I think we had more girls than he did.

'I remember once when we were up in Stockton on Tees and we had played a club and we were driving to another club because we did two shows a night sometimes. I was driving the Volvo and the boys were behind in the van.

'It was a really foggy night, I was in the front and Tom was in the back grappling with a sixteen-year-old girl who certainly wasn't complaining. It was pretty obvious what they were up to. They certainly weren't playing backgammon.

'Being a nosey sod I was concentrating more on the sexy action that was going on in the back than on the road in front. Tom saw I was looking in the mirror and kept barking at me to stop looking. Suddenly we came to a roundabout and I didn't have time to turn. We just went straight over, followed by the boys in the van. Bang, bang, bang, bang the car went up and down over the roundabout. Tom went spare.

' "Stop the car," he screamed. I pulled over to the side

of the road. "Now get out and walk away from the car, and don't come back until I tell you."

'The van had pulled up behind us and we all had to stand around in the fog waiting for Tom to finish with the girl. Bloody marvellous, I thought.

'That's how I remember him, a great professional singer but not too bright, not too quick on the uptake for a joke or anything, very keen on the women and very, very mean. The original guys in the band always used to say that he wouldn't even buy a microphone in the early days, although they'd all spent money on equipment. Certainly when I was with them he would pay the absolute minimum and the way he ditched the boys without a bean was disgraceful. He could be very foul-mouthed and sometimes in quite the wrong circumstances he would let fly with the strongest language. We were backstage in the Copacabana in New York with Dionne Warwick one night and she was so appalled by his swearing she stormed out almost in tears at the verbal abuse Tom was using.

'And he was a tough guy, too. One night in Cork in Ireland we were doing a concert and there was this guy at the front who kept flicking cigarette butts at Tom. He stood it for a while and then eventually he just went up to this guy and head butted him. He laid him out cold. I thought we were all going to get lynched but the crowd loved it and cheered Tom.

'He wasn't a good conversationalist and if there was someone bright in the company he would shut up altogether and let Gordon speak. He trusted Gordon implicitly. Tom didn't ever seem to understand the financial side of the business. I remember his saying to me in 1967: "How much money do you think I'm worth, Vic? I've got £9,000 in the bank and a £20,000 house."

'Of course that was a lot of money in those days but I don't think at that time he grasped the millions and millions he was going to earn. He could comprehend his bank account and the price of his house.

'We used to take the mickey out of Tom a lot but he didn't

appreciate it. If you saw him in a new suit and said, "What a great suit, Tom. Do you think they'll come back into fashion?" he would just grunt and say, "What do you mean?"

'And he was pretty ropey when it came to reading and writing. Often if someone wanted an autograph and said, "Could you sign it to Margaret?" he would say to me, "Now, Vic, is that M . . . A . . .R . . . ?"

'Yet technically as a singer he was brilliant. Once I went with him to Brussels in Belgium to record a TV show and when we got into the studio they hit him with a load of complicated instructions about "first you look at this camera and then you walk over here and sing into that one" and it didn't faze him at all. He just did everything they said without a sign of nerves.

'Tom was always dead against drugs. I used to smoke a little marijuana back in the sixties, which wasn't that unusual in the pop business, but I never let Tom know. Then once I'd been smoking with Vernon Hopkins before a show at the Talk of the Town. And when we went on Vernon was still a little bit out of it. We played one song and he started to put his guitar down and walk off. He said later he thought for some reason he was on a boat. Tom went bananas and of course I got the blame. He really yelled at me for letting Vernon try the stuff. But we were never into anything serious.

'The funniest thing I remember about Tom was just before I left in 1967 when we were playing the London Palladium with Jack Benny. Tom was delighted because he had been given a huge box of one hundred cigars by Bernard Delfont.

'Tom had a taste for the finer things in life like champagne and cigars so he was as pleased as punch with the gift. But while we were on stage Jack Benny removed every cigar but one and left a £1 note in the box which said: "Thanks for the cigars, Tom. I'll collect the change later."

'Tom most certainly did not get the joke. By the time we came off stage Jack Benny and the cigars were long gone. I'll never forget Tom's expression when he found the note. He was like a kid who's had a bag of sweets pinched at school. "What does he mean change? I'll give him bloody change," he shouted. "It's not right, he can't take my cigars like that. It's not right."

'We tried to tell him it was a joke. That Jack Benny was supposed to be the meanest man in the world, but he didn't want to know. He just kept on raving. It wasn't even as if he'd bought the cigars in the first place, the mean sod.

'Tom was a very insecure man in many ways. He was always brooding and worrying about something. Every time we filled the Rolls Royce up with petrol he would moan about the price per gallon.

'His biggest scare seemed to be his dreams about his grandmother. He often used to say he'd had a nightmare about his dead grandmother coming to get him and he would look really scared when he told us about it.

'But he was very jealous of his status. When we played in Melbourne, Australia, for some reason a few girls in the crowd were shouting at me. A few of them began chanting, "We want Vic, we want Vic." I suppose I must have reminded them of someone or other. I didn't think anything of it but afterwards Tom came up to me all hot and bothered and snarled, "What's all this shouting about? I'm the star." And he certainly wasn't joking.

'Tom is basically a rock 'n' roller. That was why I got the job in the first place, because I could rattle off all those Jerry Lee Lewis numbers that he loved on the piano. He would really rather be down the pub with his mates than in some plush cabaret room.

'But essentially he was just a very selfish guy. That came home to me most strongly when I left. That was the strangest experience of all. I was in the Copacabana in New York when I was approached by Harry Saltzman, the producer of the James Bond films, and Don Kirshner, who helped to create the Monkees.

'I couldn't believe what they were saying because they said they wanted to make me a film star. They saw me as a Tommy Steele character in a new film they were planning with Olivia Newton John. This was pretty hard to swallow for a humble piano player, I can tell you.

'But amazingly they were for real. It wasn't the most elaborate wind-up on earth; it was the chance of a lifetime. I left Tom Jones and the Squires to star alongside Olivia Newton John in the most hyped film of the sixties – *Toomorrow*. Sadly it was probably also the least successful film of the sixties as well, the flop of the decade. But it was a remarkable experience and I earned a lot of money. I wouldn't have missed it for the world.

'But it didn't please Tom. When I had left Johnny Kidd three years before, Johnny said, "Good luck and thanks for all your help, I hope you do well." When I left Tom Jones for what looked like a real chance to become a movie star Tom Jones said, "I'll make sure you never work again in the music business" and the other band members told me later that he went storming round for weeks saying, "How dare he leave me!" '

The boy from Pontypridd who hardly travelled at all until he was twenty-five was certainly making up for lost time. And although he was no stranger to women he suddenly found himself involved with one of the world's most beautiful and successful women. Mary Wilson was a member of the all-conquering female group the Supremes, rich, elegant and sophisticated. And this alluring lady, who in her time admits to affairs with film producer David Puttnam and film star Steve McQueen, among many others, fell head over heels in love with Tom Jones. In her autobiography *Dreamgirl* she records how agent Norman Wise played matchmaker for the two amorous singing stars.

She describes their first meeting in 1967 in Munich: 'I opened the door and there he was, dressed in a ruffled white shirt, black tuxedo, and – of course – skin-tight pants. Sparks flew; he was gorgeous. Why had I waited so long?'

The couple were kept apart until later that night because Tom had to travel to an official function in a limousine with Richard Burton and Elizabeth Taylor. Tom later remarked he was appalled by Miss Taylor's bad language. His Welsh background has instilled a lifelong dislike of women swearing. But, just like in the movies, Mary Wilson believed that by the end of the evening she was in love.

Apart from the physical attraction, evidently she and Tom spent hours and hours talking, a novelty for Tom who did not normally approach females for their conversational capacity. 'Tom made a great friend in addition to being a fine lover and our relationship was wonderful,' she gushed. But Mary Wilson must have been one of the few people in the music business unaware that Tom Jones was not as fancy-free as he appeared. He had a wife and son and when she found out about them she said: ' . . . Tom was married. I couldn't believe it. Maybe Tom figured that since every other woman in the Western world knew that he was "unavailable", I should have, too. . . . I resolved to break it off the next time I saw Tom, but when that time came, I realized I couldn't. It was too late.'

To the guys in the band it became obvious that for Tom, too, this was much more than the usual casual fling. Keyboard player Vic Cooper recalls: 'I was in the group when he was going out with Mary Wilson. Tom always liked black girls and would often choose one of our coloured fans as his partner for the night but his thing for Mary was different. I think that was a real love job, he was really stuck on her. I remember we played a concert in Germany with the Supremes and it was common knowledge among us that Tom was knocking her off.

'For some reason Clint Eastwood of all people was at the concert and he came backstage. Another musician dared me to ask for Mary's autograph for some reason when we were in the dressing rooms afterwards. Tom and Mary were talking to Clint Eastwood and I went up and said, "Excuse me, Mary, could I have your autograph?" She gave me it but then afterwards Tom came storming up and demanded to know why I wanted it. He was always a bit paranoid.'

Mary remembers: 'I treasured every moment with him. We would laugh and talk, and just be so happy to be together. . . . I didn't care what anyone thought. I was young and in love. If one of us missed the other's call, we would leave a coded message saying that "Jimi Hendrix" called, which must have kept people in our entourages buzzing.'

This was one relationship that did get back to Linda and when Tom and Mary were cosily sharing Tom's rented house in Bournemouth in August 1968 they were interrupted by an angry phone call. Mary said: 'She told Tom she suspected that he had a woman there and she was coming to see for herself. Tom and I decided that I should leave. He put me in his limousine and kissed me goodbye. I cried all the way to London.'

When Linda arrived she did a swift search of the house but Tom and Mary had cleared away all female traces. The only thing they had forgotten was the gourmet meal simmering in the oven. Linda knew Tom did not cook but Tom quickly improvised an answer, suggesting that his road manager Chris Ellis was preparing the meal: 'He's taking cookery lessons,' he added hopefully. But Linda knew about the affair and several times since then Tom has admitted that 'Linda gave me hell about it.'

The writing was on the wall after that. Mary observed afterwards: 'Ironically, Tom's devotion to his wife and child was one of the things about him I admired most. Never once did he even hint that he would leave her, but I couldn't let go. Sometimes I'd been so foolish, going so far as to telephone his home in England, only to hang up when his wife would answer.'

Eventually it was Tom who ended the affair at Mary's Hollywood home: 'Mary,' he said, 'I don't think this is fair to you. There is no future for us, and I think we should break away from this affair now.' Mary thought: 'I had to agree. He wasn't going to leave his wife, and I had always known that. I was crying, but when we said goodbye at my door, I knew we were doing the right thing. After that, we kept in touch, and deep inside I still nurtured the faintest hope that things might change.

'I finally accepted that they never would when he brought his wife backstage after one of our shows and introduced her to me. She was very nice. After I was married and got to experience first-hand what she had gone through, I understood the pain and humiliation she must have suffered. Still, Tom remains one of the very special people in my life.'

Comedian Jimmy Tarbuck became a firm friend of Tom's, which caused the singer to be on the wrong end of some practical jokes. Tarbuck recalls: 'One man whose voice I have enjoyed imitating on more than one occasion is Tom Jones, who recently left his body to medical science, except for one part which is going to the Hall of Fame. Many years ago we had a memorable night out together in the Midlands. I was in pantomime in Coventry and he was in a show in Birmingham. After the panto he sent his car over for me and I went to Birmingham to watch him. He finished his show and we had a few drinks together. The night went on, turned into tomorrow, and at about six in the morning we drove back towards Coventry. There was snow on the ground and we passed a group of fellas waiting for a bus to take them to work. We pulled in at the bus stop and lowered the dark-tinted windows of Jonesy's car, a big black Rolls. I called out: "Where the hell have you lot been till this time in the morning?"

'We got a great response. Snowballs everywhere thudding into the car. We made our escape and got back to the hotel in Coventry. At this point our schedules proved to be very different from each other. We were both knackered, but whereas Jonesy could sleep all day – I called him Count Dracula and he seemed to like it – I had to get up and do a matinee.

' "Have a good show," laughed Jonesy, "I'm gonna have a good sleep now." And he shut the door of his room.

' "Rotten bastard," I thought and rang reception. "Mr Jones 'ere," I said in my best Valleys accent. "Will you send me up a nice grilled trout?"

'The trout was cooked and taken up to Jonesy's room while he slept on. For about five hours he and the trout rested in the same room but while Jonesy was growing steadily fresher as the minutes passed the trout was doing the opposite. In the centrally-heated stillness the smell given off went from a mild fishiness to a foul and dreadful stench, finally pushing up the nostrils of Mr Jones with sufficient force to wake him. "Bloody hell, what's this?" shouted Tom and raced from the room. I only wish I'd been there to see it.'

And Tarbuck recruited his friend Kenny Lynch for a more public prank. Tarbuck says: 'When Tom came back to England for the first time since conquering Las Vegas a big spectacular TV show was planned and the dress rehearsal was set up at a packed Elstree studio with a forty-piece orchestra, the lot. Jonesy was due to knock 'em dead with "Letter to Lucille". I gave him the big build up: "Ladies and gentlemen, now for the young man who has just taken all America by storm – our very own Tom Jones."

'The curtains pulled back and the spotlight hit the centre of the stage. There was Lynchie with his trousers round his ankles, bent over with his backside pointing at the audience. "Oh gawd," I thought, "not at a dress rehearsal. That's really done it."

'Then from high in the control room came an instant instruction from the unflappable producer Albert Locke: "Make-up!" '

To those who had known him in Wales, success had changed Tom Jones quickly and profoundly. Old friend Gerry Greenberg remembers meeting up with his pal turned superstar in Manchester in the late sixties. Greenberg says: 'I phoned his hotel and arranged to see Tommy at 4 p.m., but when I arrived he was still in bed. It was Tom Jones all right but not quite the same Tom I had known in Ponty. The nose was now as straight as a rod and considerably less prominent and those gleaming front teeth looked as though they had more caps than Bobby Moore.

'I went in to the hotel room and he got up and went into the bathroom for a shower. When I looked round there was money everywhere, fivers and tenners all over the place. We arranged to meet later that night. I wanted to introduce him to the girl who was going to become my wife. We met in the foyer of another hotel and Tom emerged from the lift with two girls, one on each arm. I am sure they were local prostitutes; they were certainly very tarty-looking women. And they looked absolutely exhausted and he looked raring to go. One of them thrust a card into his hand and said, "You can get me on that number any time" and she and her friend walked off.

'My wife-to-be couldn't resist a wisecrack as I introduced her to Tom. "Couldn't you do better than that?" she laughed, nodding in the direction of the two departing women. Tom shrugged his shoulders as if to say, "I'll take anything that's going."

'An elderly man stood nearby, holding an oil painting of Tom. "Excuse me, Mr Jones, do you like this?" he asked, holding up the indifferent picture.

'Tom frowned, "Is that supposed to be me?" he asked. "How much do you want for it?"

' "£25" was the answer. Tom turned to a member of his entourage and said, "Pay the man," not bothering to take the picture. Two teenage groupies were showing obvious interest in Tom and his group. Vernon Hopkins kept them entertained for a while and my last sight of Tom Jones was getting with Vernon and the young girls into the back of Tom's chauffeur-driven Rolls outside the hotel. It was never like that in Pontypridd.'

Chapter Five

AMERICA

It's now taken for granted that Las Vegas did a lot for the career of Tom Jones – but it's easy to overlook that, around 1968 and 1969, Tom Jones did a whole lot for Las Vegas.

His presence as a dynamic showroom act helped bring at least one gambling casino back from the brink of extinction. And in later years, other casinos would bid furiously for Tom Jones' services, knowing that his presence in their showrooms would bring huge audiences into their hotels. Those audiences, of course, would gamble, which was how the gambling casinos made their real money.

Along the way, Tom Jones' early Las Vegas appearances indirectly helped to rekindle the then dormant career of Elvis Presley, who was preparing a comeback in the Nevada gambling resort. And Jones' arrival contributed to a spell of astonishing prosperity for Las Vegas; by the late 1960s, the city was playing host to 15 million tourists a year, who were spending about $400 million.

In 1968, Tom Jones played some dates on the east coast of America and drew raves from critics and audiences alike. His big triumph was at New York's Copacabana, where the first signs of mass hysteria among otherwise rational adult women were beginning to break out. And word quickly spread west to Las Vegas, almost 3,000 miles away.

Nick Naff, who now publishes entertainment guides for Vegas tourists, was working at the time at the Flamingo. Gambling had been legalized in the state of Nevada in 1931, and the Flamingo, with its huge, gaudy pink sign at its entrance was one of the first gambling casinos to be built after the Second World War. Back then, it was a glamorous place. Vegas was controlled largely by mobsters, and they catered to 'high rollers' – gamblers who would breeze into town with thousands of dollars to spend at the gaming tables. Such people dressed in tuxedos in the evening to play blackjack or poker or craps. Because they were such big gamblers, they rarely paid for hotel rooms; the casino managements provided them for free. It was an elegant era.

But as Las Vegas became more of a mass tourist attraction, some of the old gambling casinos started to fall by the wayside, unable to adjust to the changing needs of the market. The Flamingo, once the pre-eminent place in town, was suffering badly.

'I was part of a small group that went to the Flamingo from the Sahara in 1967,' Naff remembers. 'There were about thirteen of us in this management group.' A financier called Kirk Kerkorian had bought the Flamingo, and had also announced plans for a huge new lavish hotel and casino for Vegas, to be called the International. 'So we set up house at the Flamingo,' says Naff, 'and we were only going to use our stay there long enough to build the International, and then the management staff would move over there, and the Flamingo was to be sold off.

'Kirk Kerkorian bought the Flamingo as a bargain. By the time it was taken over, it was out of business. When we arrived, there were only two vacuum cleaners in the place. It was a terribly run-down hotel, but it was OK for us to spend two years there to staff up the International.'

However, Kerkorian also wanted the Flamingo to stay in business and open to guests. 'So we had to do a lot of promotional work to keep people coming,' says Naff.

Charles Mather, a British-born entertainment agent working in Las Vegas, advised the Flamingo that they should consider Tom Jones, who was creating such a buzz back in New York. His recommendation, and his description of Jones' torrid stage act, convinced Alex Shoufy, general manager and president of the Flamingo, to send a reconnaissance party to New York to check out this new Welsh singer. Bill Miller, the Flamingo's entertainment director, flew east, and with him went Alex Shoufy's then wife, Joan. The pair returned from New York with glowing reports of Tom Jones.

But Gordon was interested in Tom playing Las Vegas even before the Flamingo party came to visit. He had considered offers from smaller hotels – offers which his then wife Jo persuaded him to turn down. 'I advised Gordon not to let Tom become a lounge act in Vegas,' she remembers, 'and people were begging him to come. I had worked Vegas as a Bluebell Girl, and I said to him – whatever you do, say no to him becoming a lounge act, because it's very difficult to cross over from being a lounge act to a major showroom star.

'The lounges were offering wonderful money, but I was able to help Gordon out there, because I'd been to Vegas and he hadn't. We held out, and eventually signed him at the Flamingo as a headliner. Tom never looked back in Vegas after that because he began as a star, not as a lounge act. He would have been a great lounge act, he would have been a great draw. But he may never have become a superstar draw in one of the main hotels.'

Tom Jones and the Flamingo at that time were made for each other. 'We had such a good management staff in there that we turned the Flamingo around in no time,' recalls Nick Naff. 'But we had to get out there and promote the hell out of the place to get people to come. It was in this fervor of promotion that we booked Tom Jones, and we were determined to utilize that occasion, to present it as a fresh new booking policy.'

Naff devised an entire publicity campaign to herald Tom's arrival in Vegas, some elements of which sound hopelessly corny now, but which were clearly quite effective. 'I coined the phrase "Tom Jones fever", and used it on a lot of promotional material,' he recalls. (Later Tom would release a US album called 'The Tom Jones Fever Zone'.) 'We had a bottle of "Tom Jones fever pills" on each table in the showroom, guaranteed not to cure you, but to make the

fever more tolerable. We had gimmicky radio commercials
in town, stating what the Tom Jones fever temperature was
that day. We put an ambulance at the back of the showroom,
just in case anyone succumbed to Tom Jones fever. That kind
of thing. By the time he arrived, you could say he was heavily
pre-sold.'

Even so, Tom was an unknown quantity, and he shared
billing at the Flamingo with Kaye Ballard, an American singer
and comedienne who would be more familiar to the Vegas
audiences. Out of deference to her reputation, she was to
close the twice-nightly shows. 'Tom had never played in
Vegas before,' she remembers, 'and he came up to me after
one show, and said: "I have eight amplifiers on stage. Would
you mind if I closed the show?" '

Kaye Ballard was smart enough to agree to Tom's proposal.
'In every ringside seat for every show, there was a single
woman. And they certainly didn't want to see a comedienne.
Anyway, I'm a softie, so I said OK.

'Think about it. I could never in a million years have
followed Tom Jones. The fans were throwing bras, panties,
room keys on stage. Not my crowd. But Tom Jones was a
very nice chap.' She adds wryly: 'I'd never want to work
with him again.'

The Flamingo's showroom was small – it only held 500
people. That meant only 1,000 people could get to see the
newest star in Vegas each night. 'The lines started to get
bigger and bigger,' Nick Naff remembers. 'At the start of the
engagement, there was a show further down the strip called
"Tom Jones", which was a sensual show with production
numbers. It was based on the successful movie *Tom Jones*,
which was a hit at the time. And at the beginning, there was
some confusion between that show and our Tom Jones. But
not for long.'

Still, the early days before the mass hysteria in Vegas
started happening at least gave Tom some personal freedom.
'He could walk through the lobby of the Flamingo at first,' says
Naff. 'I remember we had this photo request from a London
newspaper who wanted pictures of him being besieged by

ladies and signing autographs. That really wasn't happening, so we had to go out and find six or seven ladies who would have to act like they were devotees. We took that picture in the casino. But that situation only lasted for our first and second engagements – after that he couldn't walk through the casino without being mobbed. He would be just deluged with people.'

Tom Jones had arrived in America, in every sense of the word. He had wowed them at the Copa; he had met with similar success at the Deauville Hotel in Miami, and now he had found, in Las Vegas, a place that would become a kind of spiritual home. From these auspicious beginnings in 1968, he would build a career in the USA, the country he feels has been kindest to him, and the one which has treated him most like a superstar.

Yet it was by no means his first visit to the States. That had come in 1965, hot on the heels of 'It's Not Unusual'. His experiences in America that year were far from happy. On his first trip, he had been shot strictly from the waist up on *The Ed Sullivan Show*. And even though that invaluable national TV exposure had given him two immediate top ten Stateside hits with 'It's Not Unusual' and 'What's New Pussycat?', he was not treated like a star when he returned in July for his first US tour.

The tour was one of those package tours with a lot of artists making brief appearances – the kind that was common in the US in those days. It was promoted by Dick Clark, host of the long-running TV show, *American Bandstand*, and it was called 'The Dick Clark Caravan Tour'. Tom was on a bill with the Shirelles, Sonny and Cher, the Turtles and a couple of lesser-known acts.

The Caravan visited thirty-six cities in two months, which meant travelling on a chartered Greyhound bus the length and breadth of America. It was a gruelling experience – hot, sticky and fatiguing. Because of the constant pressure to drive on to the next city after one show ended, the performers often walked right off stage into the bus, in which they slept until the next show. This tour may have done more than any other event in Tom Jones' life to give him a genuine distaste for discomfort. He promised himself that he would never again travel anywhere except under first-class conditions – and that when he was the sole attraction on a tour he would fly between cities. As if to prove the point to himself about travelling in style, he returned to Britain and bought himself first a grey Rolls-Royce, then a Mercedes sports car.

The tour also gave Gordon Mills plenty of food for thought. It brought home to him the fact that in America, having a top twenty record does not necessarily mean you will be treated – or paid – like a star. Gordon had seen his protégé Tom treated like a piece of baggage, being shuttled in squalid conditions from one end of the USA to the other, with the other performing artists who accompanied him. It was not what Gordon had had in mind.

Around this time, Gordon began to realize that there were limits in continuing to promote Tom as a pop idol whose appeal was primarily to teenagers. He determined that he would gradually broaden Tom's appeal and re-direct his talents towards older fans – fans in their twenties and thirties, who had more disposable income to spend, and whose loyalty could provide Tom and Gordon with a more affluent lifestyle.

Still, that 1965 American tour had provided Tom with one indelible memory – he had met Elvis Presley. When the Caravan stopped off in Los Angeles, it was arranged for Tom to drive over to Paramount Studios, where Elvis was shooting one of his forgettable movies.

This was a big moment for Tom Jones. Elvis was the King, a superstar with no real competition, and he seemed so remote and unreal as to be virtually godlike. Presley had an added mystique for British pop fans; he had never set foot in Britain, although the music papers at the time ran stories on an almost weekly basis, stating (hopefully rather than accurately) that Elvis was considering a British tour.

The meeting between the two men was brief indeed. Tom hovered on the side of the movie set during shooting, and then in between scenes, Elvis' manager, Colonel Tom Parker, walked Tom over to meet him.

'When I met him,' Tom recalled, 'he was walking towards me, singing "With These Hands". I couldn't believe it! And he knew every track on my album. It was amazing! Here I was, ready to tell him how much he had influenced me, and he was telling me how much he liked my records!'

By 1968, Tom Jones felt less of a new kid in town when he visited America. His live appearances were by now massively successful, and Gordon's strategy of re-tuning Tom's stage act to appeal to adult women rather than teenagers appeared to be paying off handsomely.

But it was in Las Vegas that he really blossomed. Maybe something about the fantasy quality of the desert resort, with its 24-hour activity, its garish architecture, its crowded casinos offering the faint chance of unimagined wealth, enhanced the kind of sensual fantasy that Tom Jones was offering his female fans on stage. You don't see many clocks in Vegas, and inside a casino or a showroom, it's easy to forget whether it's the cool night-time outside – or the blistering, scorching dry heat of noon.

Whatever it was, the Flamingo management was now doing standing-room only business with Tom Jones, and the word had spread around town so fast that other major celebrities were coming by to watch his act. Among them, as it turned out, was Elvis Presley. As Nick Naff, who arranged their meeting, tells it, the reunion between Elvis and Tom was vastly different from their 1965 meeting at Paramount, when Tom was noticeably starstruck. This time, Elvis was coming to learn a thing or two.

'We had booked Barbra Streisand to open the new International,' he says, 'and Elvis was contracted to follow her. Elvis was booked in a whole year ahead, and in 1968, he really didn't have a stage show. He began visiting Vegas, and giving some thought as to what kind of show he would do, because he hadn't been in Vegas for years. It was aimed at reviving his career somewhat. One of the things he specifically wanted was to be introduced to Tom Jones. But before Elvis met Tom

Jones, he wanted to see his show without anyone knowing. So we had to escort Elvis into the showroom quietly. He sat there in the shadows, and he watched Tom intently. Not even the waiters knew he was there. He saw two shows that night, and then we took him into the dressing room, and they became acquainted.'

Photographer Peter Borsari would capture the historic reunion between the two entertainers. He had driven back home to Los Angeles from Las Vegas earlier that day, having shot pictures of Tom Jones on stage at the Flamingo, and outside beneath the famous Flamingo sign. 'I hadn't been home long when I got a call from the maitre d' at the Flamingo,' recalls Borsari. 'He told me that Elvis's road manager, Joe Esposito, had made reservations for five or six people to watch Tom Jones' show that same night.'

Knowing he had the potential for a great picture, Borsari consulted the airline timetables, found there was no convenient plane to fly him into Vegas – then jumped into his Pontiac Firebird, and broke the speed limit in getting to the desert resort. 'I covered 285 miles in three hours and twenty-five minutes,' he remembers.

Unfortunately for Peter, by the time he had raced into the Flamingo, Elvis had already visited Tom in the backstage area, and had gone. 'I missed him by ten minutes,' he recalls ruefully. But Elvis had now gone across the Strip to Caesar's Palace for dinner with his party. Peter called in on the Jones' camp backstage, told them he was trying for pictures of Tom and Elvis together, then bumped into Joe Esposito, and put the proposal to him. 'Could Tom and Elvis meet at 2.30 a.m. beneath the Flamingo sign?' he asked.

It was quite a question. Would the King of rock 'n' roll make a trip across the Strip just to be photographed with a singer who some thought might be a pretender to his throne? As it turned out, he would – though he was a little late. 'At 3 a.m. they met beneath the sign,' says Peter. 'And then we all drove over to a bungalow behind the Flamingo, where Elvis was rehearsing, and I just shot pictures of the two of them together.'

Peter snapped away and sold his pictures of Tom and Elvis around the world. They were so popular that they even appeared in a special souvenir magazine, filled with nothing but snapshots of that night. 'Most of the shots were very similar,' admits Peter Borsari. 'They were standing together, sitting on a couch together. I know they were talking, and I think it was about music. I don't remember, because I was trying so hard to concentrate on taking as many pictures as I could in the time I was allowed.'

During those two shows, Presley got a first-hand insight of exactly what it was that was working for Tom Jones on a Vegas stage. Says Nick Naff: 'Elvis never emulated anyone, and he was quite a different person from Tom, anyway. But I know that Elvis picked up quite a lot from Tom Jones' performance, that showed up in Elvis's own style when he opened at the International next year. Tom Jones played to screaming ladies in a very sensual way – he practically thrust his pelvic area in their faces, and of course he had a lot to show them. Elvis wore his clothes more loosely, but his fans were fanatic about him in a different way. Most of the ladies who loved Elvis, I think, weren't envisaging being in bed with him – the women who loved Tom Jones were, quite definitely.

'When Elvis made his comeback in Vegas, he had his charismatic moves, those karate chops he did. He'd always been known for his wiggling and his movement. I'm not saying that Elvis was a Tom Jones copier – he wasn't. I'm saying that Elvis did what they all do – he took those bits of Tom's performance that worked for Tom, and could work for him.'

The meeting between Tom and Elvis formed the beginning of what was to become a cordial friendship. Backstage, Elvis's wife Priscilla had accompanied the King to meet Tom – and had requested an autographed picture of Tom for her daughter, Lisa Marie, who was less than a year old at the time. During this meeting, Elvis invited Tom to join him at his home in Hawaii.

When Tom arrived, Priscilla greeted him. 'Elvis has just gone out to buy two guitars for the two of you to goof around with,' she said. And later that evening, Tom and Elvis each strapped on a guitar, and sang songs together – including Elvis's early hits, 'Hound Dog', 'Heartbreak Hotel' and 'Blue Suede Shoes'.

Even at this stage, almost ten years before his death, Elvis was having weight problems, and confided in Tom that he used 'medical methods' to keep his weight down. Tom reportedly gave Elvis a lecture on the dangers of drug use. In later years at Caesar's Palace, Elvis came backstage to meet Tom, who was showering after a show. Elvis talked to Tom through the shower partition while he was using the adjoining toilet, and then called for an aide called Red to come and lace up his tight leather trousers for him. The problems that would lead to Elvis's death were already in evidence.

Still, the relationship between Tom and Elvis blossomed, and Tom found Elvis to be a genuinely caring friend. 'Once he gave me a prayer book in which he had written a very sincere message,' said Tom. 'He's a very deep-feeling man.'

Vernon Hopkins, Tom's bass player from the earliest days, recalls that Elvis would occasionally drop by to see Tom in action – a gesture which was both friendly and a means of checking on the opposition.

'I'll never forget one time we were playing Caesar's Palace in Las Vegas,' he says. 'In between shows I was in the casino, playing a fruit machine, and I looked back and did a double take. There was Elvis Presley coming down this carpeted aisle with his wife. He went into the main room where we were working. I went and told Tom, and he said: "God, we'd better put on a good show tonight."

'The curtains opened and there was this vast auditorium, and we could make out Presley and his wife three tables back. So halfway through the spot, Tom said: "I'd like to introduce you to a gentleman I have admired for many years, who has been a big influence on my career." A spotlight came from nowhere, zooming round, the lights went up, the audience screamed and Elvis stood up and clapped towards the stage. And Tom said: "Enough of that – I'm the star."

'Afterwards, Tom said: "Come and meet Elvis." He was in

a corner chatting with Elvis, and he beckoned me over. We chatted and he joked that he thought we would be decked out in Carnaby Street gear, which was supposed to be the height of fashion then. But we had all changed from our stage gear into American sweat shirts and jeans.'

Another time, Tom was having difficulties in Las Vegas with his black back-up singers. Onstage in Vegas, he had made an off-colour joke about the Ku Klux Klan which offended them, and they refused to perform with him. So, unknown to Tom, Elvis dispatched two planes, one to Nashville and one to Los Angeles, each to bring him three girl singers. 'By the time I got up the next day, he'd assembled a choir for me,' said Tom. But Tom apologized for his tactless quip, and order was restored. Still, the six singers Elvis had imported stayed around for the entire week, and entertained him and Tom after showtimes.

In his relationship with Elvis, Tom admitted he became 'closer to him than any other entertainer'. This made him privy to some of the King's more colourful eccentricities. 'He used to blow up televisions by shooting at them with shotguns,' Tom admitted. 'If there was something on that he didn't like or understand, that was it.'

Professionally, the two men carried on a good-natured rivalry in Las Vegas. When Elvis made his big comeback at the International, the hotel put up big billboards announcing his presence. 'Elvis Presley is at the International,' they fairly screamed. For Tom, the management at the much smaller Flamingo did exactly the same. 'Tom Jones is in town,' they proclaimed, tongue in cheek. But after their respective shows, the two men would get together socially. The following year, Tom graduated to the International himself, and easily outstripped other attractions in town.

But for Nick Naff, who himself went to work at the International, it was Tom Jones' shows at the Flamingo that stood out in the memory. 'He was at the Flamingo for eighteen months, and by the time he played the International, he was more of a known quantity,' he explains. 'But the room at the International is three times as big, and to me his magnetism was not as powerful. I have never seen in a

showroom the essential excitement like in those early Tom
Jones appearances. It was uncanny. We'd unearthed a gem;
he was an absolutely incredible find as far as Las Vegas was
concerned.'

There was, of course, more to America than Las Vegas,
and Tom Jones slipped into an American lifestyle with relative
ease. By the time he made the decision in 1974 to live in the
US permanently, he had comfortably assimilated it. He liked
the size of the place, the feeling of wide-open space – and
the unsurpassed luxury that those in his high income bracket
could enjoy.

There were big differences between Britain and America,
of course, and some took more getting used to than others.
Tom found America a very violent country, in which guns
were commonplace. Elvis, who had received death threats
from an unbalanced fan, took to wearing a gun, and sent Tom
one to his dressing room as a gift. 'Elvis gave me a Walther
9 mm,' Tom recalls. 'He always carried one on stage himself
hidden in the small of his back, after President Nixon made
him an (honorary) narcotics agent.' Tom paused briefly, with
an ironic smile. 'Elvis should have arrested himself.'

Despite his misgivings, Tom himself packs a gun. 'I
carry a .38 in the States,' he admitted, 'and I take it with
me wherever I can. They made me an honorary sheriff of
Tennessee, a deputy sheriff, that is. The biggest threat that I
feel is if someone tried to kidnap my grandson. I think about
that a lot. I had a wall built around our house, and we have
our own security force in Bel-Air. I've got "panic buttons" in
every room of the house.

'One night I looked out and saw a guy outside my pool.
Like a fool, I walked out and asked him what he wanted. He
said he thought there was a party going on. I told him to piss
off – but of course, he could have had a gun.'

Tom was also alarmed to find himself on the hit list of Charles
Manson, the crazed murderer whose followers had killed
actress Sharon Tate, her unborn baby and some friends at
their house, in a bloody carnage which for many people
signalled the end of the hippy era.

'A girl [in Manson's "family"] was assigned to come to one of my concerts, make it her business to get close to me, and kill me while giving me one,' he remembered. To be specific, Manson's plan was for the girl to slit Tom's throat with a razor during sex. 'That rather put a block on any thoughts in that area,' he recalls.

'I used to have high security in the States, but like John Lennon, if anyone really wanted to do something, I couldn't stop them. When it happened to John, it all struck home – and I stepped up my awareness after that.' Overall, though, Tom Jones has adapted well to America. His TV show *This Is Tom Jones*, made for Sir Lew Grade, was extraordinarily popular among his fans. And when he went to Los Angeles to tape six shows there, the ABC network received a staggering 30,000 requests for tickets over and above the number it could accommodate. 'I can't even get a ticket to get a friend in myself,' Tom reflected at the time.

Strangely, the show, which started in February 1969, lasted less than two years, and had its final broadcast in January 1971. It never became a top twenty show, and in its first season, it used to lose the ratings battle to the popular *Ironside* starring Raymond Burr. It was cancelled before the end of its second full season. The only explanation was that those viewers who liked Tom Jones liked him a lot, and were very vocal in their support. But the majority of American viewers preferred to watch something else. Of course, to say that fans of Tom's show were in a minority must be qualified – they were a minority comprising several million people.

America loves people with regular looks, and Tom Jones was prepared to go under the surgeon's scalpel to correct his facial irregularities. When it became clear that he would stake his reputation on an American career, he had a nose job, though the press was told he was undergoing an operation to correct sinus trouble. At this point, he also had his teeth capped to give him a more even smile. But that was not the last time he would undergo plastic surgery. In 1975, Los Angeles gossip columnist Dorothy Manners reported that Tom had 'a handsome new nose and correction in his crooked smile. Now thirty-five, Tom's new face has taken years off his appearance.' In his late forties, he went under the knife again, to have some tucks placed underneath his eyes.

Los Angeles is a place where looking good, looking young and feeling secure are of paramount importance. Those who can afford to stave off the visible signs of old age do so without compunction. To look fit and slim and tanned and young, despite one's age, background or metabolism – that's the secret. And having a personal bodyguard tailing your every public move has become a kind of status symbol. In recent years, Chris Montgomery, a tall, well-built blond Briton who was formerly attached to the elite SAS commando corps, has been retained to act as Tom's personal security. With his bodyguard, his workout routines, his truly deep dark chestnut tan and his willingness to re-invent his face through a surgeon's skill, Tom Jones has become far more American than maybe even he realizes.

Chapter Six

OLD SCORES

The Squires were by no means the only people left disenchanted by the relentless rise and rise of Tom Jones. Hits like 'What's New Pussycat?', 'Green, Green Grass of Home', 'I'll Never Fall In Love Again' and 'Delilah' kept the career bubbling along and Tom soon became a key part of the 1960s scene. His audiences were a shade older and more mature than those for the Beatles or the Rolling Stones, but they certainly screamed just as hard.

But as the rude, crude valley boy turned into a sophisticated international star, two men grew increasingly bitter about their failure to share in the untold riches being generated. Raymond Godfrey believed that he and his partner John Glastonbury had been cheated out of a fortune and they meant to fight back.

Raymond Godfrey recalls that the agreement under which he and his partner got a 5 per cent cut of Tom's earnings kept them in close touch with Tom and Gordon. But when 'It's Not Unusual' showed that Tom was destined for long-term stardom, the relationship soured.

'They already had our van in London and they had left it parked in a street in Notting Hill Gate with flat tyres, a burned-out clutch, and a totally knackered engine. It was completely unusable. They also had our PA system. But we said, "That's all right, we've got this 5 per cent anyway so we will swallow that."

'When Tom's record reached the charts and he started earning we called round to see Gordon about when he was

87

going to start paying us. But he was out. Then he broke the news to us – on the telephone, I might add – that he wasn't going to pay us anything. Gordon was determined to bluff his way out of the deal. I remember he said: "Your contract's not worth a light."

'We were annoyed and bitter and we decided to sue him. But it took us five years to get him to court. Our contract had said, "5 per cent in perpetuity". We were so convinced he was going to make it that we said we would forget about the van, the PA and our back commission. If we had 5 per cent we were happy because we had that much faith in him.

'It's not the sort of thing I would have done. I've got certain morals. Through my time in the business I have tried to be fair with people and I don't like it when people are not fair with me. I was not impressed by the way Tom dealt with the situation. At least he did ring me first but what was embarrassing was that he did not insist that his manager held that agreement. My own opinion was that Gordon Mills was such a strong character that Tom went along with what he said.

'We were always totally convinced Tom was going to make it, there was never a doubt in our minds. It's absurd looking back and it's easy to talk in hindsight but it wasn't "if" he was going to make it but "when".'

The case eventually came to the High Court in London in January 1969 at a time when Tom Jones' annual earnings were estimated to be approaching £1 million. The ex-managers were represented by Mr Brian Neill QC who described his clients with considerable understatement as: 'Very bitter'.

Mr Michael Eastham QC, for Tom Jones, argued that the singer had agreed on the 5 per cent payment only until he had paid off what might be due under an earlier agreement.

Eventually an out-of-court settlement was agreed to pay off the two disgruntled ex-managers. Outside the court John Glastonbury told reporters: 'We are very happy about the settlement. It is substantial. What we have done for Tom Jones cannot be measured in terms of money.'

Today Raymond Godfrey still finds it difficult to talk

about how one of the world's biggest stars slipped through his fingers. He says: 'Because we had spent all our money we were reduced to getting Legal Aid. One of the problems with Legal Aid is that they let you go so far with a case and then they put the screws on you to settle. They say, "You have had an offer now. Either you accept that or we will withdraw Legal Aid and from here you are on your own." And that's what we did. We had a settlement; otherwise we could have lost our Legal Aid and ended up in the red after all that, after all the money that was owing to us. We were very bitter about it. We certainly didn't make any money on it.'

Not surprisingly Tom's recollections of this crucial court case are slightly different. He remembers the judge, Mr Justice Megarry, being astonished at the demands of Messrs Godfrey and Glastonbury.

Tom says: 'When we went into court the judge said, "What kind of money are you talking about?" They said, "We want 5 per cent." He said, "Yes, but what date do you think it should have started and what date should it end?" They said it should have started in 1965 when "It's Not Unusual" came out and gone on until the end of time.

'The judge said, "What? You want 5 per cent of this man for ever?" and they said, "Yes" and he said, "Come on".'

Whatever the accuracy of the memories of the case, neither side is prepared to recall the size of the pay off. But the by now jettisoned lead guitarist Mickey Gee, who was subpoenaed to appear for the plaintiffs, remembers it well.

He says: 'Our old managers wanted me to come and speak up for them because of some conversation I was supposed to have heard. I didn't want to go but they subpoenaed me. But it was all settled outside court. They got £50,000 each so I don't see why they should feel so bitter. They did nothing. They never got him a hit record. They just booked him round the pubs and clubs in the valleys. I wish every one of the Squires had got £50,000.'

Tom is still dismissive of his former managers. Just before his European tour of 1989 he was interviewed on BBC Radio One by Simon Bates and referred to Messrs Godfrey and

Glastonbury as 'Pinky and Perky', which brought an angry reaction.

In an interview with one of the authors afterwards Tom said: 'I can't remember now how much they were paid but that was the end of it. And they knew that I thought they hadn't done much for me, but now when I call them Pinky and Perky they don't like it. I told the story on the BBC and all of a sudden they want to sue the BBC. It was a bloody joke.'

But the court case was also a crucial time for the Squires. And it was certainly no joke for them. Four years of touring the world as Tom's backing band was a glamorous way of life but the musicians still felt aggrieved at their low pay. What they did not know was that as Gordon and Tom cut their ties with the original management they were also planning to free themselves from the band as well.

Vernon Hopkins recalls: 'When the old managers decided to raise their contract I got a call from Chris Ellis, Tom's road manager, saying: "Can you come to court tomorrow? They want you as a witness. You were there when the contract was signed in the pub. Just say what happened."

'Chris picked me up with Tom at 7 a.m. and I hung around waiting for a couple of hours and then they decided to settle out of court. So we all went across to the pub and had a drink. As we were leaving Tom said, "I can't run you back because I'm going on the town. Gordon will drop you home. He wants a word with you."

'So I went with Gordon and on the way back he said, "I've got a song I'd like you to hear. It's for the Squires to record because Tom is laying back a bit now, he's taking a long rest. I've got this song for the Squires, we'll see if it can put them on their feet." '

' "What does this mean?" I said, instantly concerned.

' "Probably it means you're going to split," said Gordon Mills, making no effort to lighten the blow of the news he was breaking to the bewildered guitarist. "Tom has done a lot of work in the States and he is going to be doing a lot of TV work there." '

When they arrived at Hopkins' home Gordon Mills played the song he had selected for the Squires, which was a Joe South number called 'Games People Play'. The irony of the title was not lost on Hopkins.

The guitarist recalls bitterly: 'The next day there was a big headline in *The Daily Mirror*, "Tom Jones and the Squires in amicable split". It was so amicable we knew nothing about it. That was another crafty move by Gordon.

'We went into the studios and recorded the song and brought it out. But it was just a half-hearted attempt by Gordon Mills to soften the blow of us being dumped. We rushed through the song and had just one advert in the *New Musical Express*, no promotion really and it died a death. That was the end of Tom Jones and the Squires.

'I never saw Tom again for years after that. He hadn't even told me personally which I thought was terrible. He was a millionaire by then living in St George's Hill, Weybridge, and I was totally skint. The most we ever earned was £80 a week and that stopped straight away.

'After all those years I was left floundering. All those years with no contact with other musicians and other bands. I only knew fifteen songs. We did fifteen songs a night year in year out for one person and then we were left like that.

'Today every time I see Tom Jones on television it brings it all back. It's not the money, I've gone past worrying about that really, it's just what happened that hurts. Of course there have been times when I have been desperate for that money. I was forced to do all sorts of jobs to survive. I drove a lorry for a time. We were in shock for a long time after it happened, especially the way it was done. One minute you are in court trying to defend someone . . . I was bitter for a long time after that.

'Tom wants to forget the Senators and the Squires, forget that any of it happened, but if we hadn't been there in the early days he might be still living in Wales and working in a factory and singing at weekends.

'If he hadn't been in a band Gordon would probably never have seen him because Gordon was looking at bands. And it was me who persuaded him to stay on in London when he was all for topping himself or going home.

'I understand that bands come and bands go and people come and go, people leave and join. Nothing lasts for ever but it's not as if we were manufactured by a manager or an agent. So much had happened to us together, we had starved together, slept together, drunk together, dreamed together for years and years. We had shared so much, sleeping in stinking awful holes, sinking into unbelievable despair, but we had come through all that and I really thought we knew each other very well. Then for it all to end like that was just devastating.

'If I had just joined him I could understand but it was like a birth, a seed, growing up in the same village, and there was no animosity between us. It was like a brother relationship. I was more of a brother to him than I was to my own brother – living together all of those years, doing exactly the same things, trying to get on, with this determination, this fire we had which we shared. That was the heartbreaking thing.

'I think it was Gordon who made the decisions but Tom has a strong character. He could have vetoed anything Gordon had suggested. To go through all that with Tom, right back to me persuading him to stand in with us at Pontypridd YMCA, and then to be thrown aside like an old sock was heartbreaking.

'After the split our last gig together was playing at the investiture of Prince Charles at Carmarthen Castle so we weren't exactly nobodies who deserved to be brushed aside.

'And then I got a bill from my accountant for three or four thousand pounds. He said it was for the tax on all my TV appearances. There had been a fee each time but it had never reached us. We just got a flat wage. I just said, "You send that bill to Tom Jones" and I never heard any more about it.

'To this day I do not understand why we were dropped. Except that maybe it was because it was around the time the employment protection legislation came in so that people couldn't be sacked so easily. They were to be protected under law. I think perhaps Gordon fixed up for us to make a record on our own so he couldn't be accused of unfair dismissal.

'We were so loyal, we never let him down. The money

stopped just like that of course. We had never been able to bank anything, we had never made enough. But we helped make that huge fortune they had. We were all so disgusted and shocked that we didn't ring Tom and ask what was going on. Psychologically it was a huge blow. It took me years to get over it.

'I didn't see Tom for about five years after that. Then one night he came in a pub where I worked with my wife Maya, who is a singer. I saw this white Rolls Royce outside but I didn't twig at all it was him. Then I saw him standing at the bar. I carried on playing, finished my set and walking over said, "All right?"

' "How's it going?" said Tom.

' "It's a bit different from what it used to be," I said.

' "Well, it's a living, isn't it?" said Tom. And that was the end of our conversation.'

But if 1969 marked a sad end to his career with the Squires it also heralded a happy beginning to a new career as an international television star. Tom had guested on shows for years and was no stranger to cameras but ATV boss Sir Lew Grade offered him a £3 million contract to star in his own series which would be transmitted on both sides of the Atlantic. Lew recalls that Gordon Mills was a particularly tough negotiator and it took three meetings with him and Tom to thrash out the deal.

Eventually noting that cigar-loving Tom had smoked his way through a good number of his best cigars while they argued over the figures, Lew said: 'Gordon, that's my final offer, and I'll tell you what else I'll do. I'll give Tom a box of cigars for every programme he does.' Then, according to Lew, Tom, who always remained silent at the meetings, spoke for the first time: 'You've got a deal,' he said.

To this day there has never been a more elaborate musical extravaganza of a series as the one Lew and producer/director Jon Scoffield put together for Tom Jones. The list of guest stars reads like a musical *Who's Who*. Everyone from Tom's beloved Jerry Lee Lewis to Janis Joplin, from Johnny Cash to Raquel Welch, and from the Bee Gees to the Moody Blues came on the show. For three years the glossy, elegantly produced programmes delighted Tom's fans around the world and Tom made many friends at the ATV studios in Elstree just north of London where they were made. Tom quickly earned a reputation as an untemperamental professional among the TV crew. Production manager Billy Glaze said: 'He was always very pleasant but he was never one of the lads. In a way, although he had his small entourage – with Gordon Mills and Chris Ellis the driver always around – he was a bit of a loner. He was very easy to work with, he didn't get irritated if he was kept waiting and he was always prepared to learn.

'Tom was an established star when he came to us. The first time I saw him was in concert in Los Angeles and when I first saw him squirming around in those tight trousers making all the women scream I was absolutely knocked out. He was terrific. When he arrived in the studios I was surprised to see how much he relied upon Gordon. If Gordon said stand there he would stand there, if Gordon had said, "We're going to do a tour of China, Tom," he would have said, "When does the plane leave?" He listened to Gordon all the time. We never had to wait for Tom and although soon after the start he had his own caravan he never played the big star.

'He always drank champagne, Moët and Chandon, and always the best Moët and Chandon, with orange juice. Gordon had told him this was a good drink and he stuck with it. But he would come and eat in the canteen, he would sit at any table and have typical working-class food. His favourite was lamb's tongues, he loved them and he would sit and eat six lamb's tongues at a meal, no trouble. He knew what he liked and it was what I call peasant food.'

Tom Jones was certainly not one of those pop singers who shirked comparisons with 'real' singers. His duets with the most exalted names in the recording world became one of the highlights of the show.

Billy Glaze recalls: 'We had the very biggest names but they never topped Tom. We always had a big duet. I remember when we were in the States we had Janis Joplin on the show. She came into the rehearsal as though she was going to sing Tom into the ground, she thought she was going to eat this man up and she sort of sneered at him.

' "What key do you sing in?" sneered Joplin.

' "I just sing," said Tom with a grin.

'He never said this is my show, don't come any shit. But when they came to sing together he matched her perfectly note for note and she changed her attitude completely.

'But in many ways he was very naïve when he came to us. For instance, Jon Scoffield had to teach him how to tie a bow-tie. He was wearing those fake bow-ties held round his neck with elastic and he would pull it off as he started to sweat and loosen his collar and finish up getting it taffled round his ears. Jon said, "You can't wear a false bow-tie on one of my shows" and stood behind him and showed him exactly how to tie a double-ended bow so that he could undo it and leave it casually dangling like Sinatra.

'Jon put together some fantastic production numbers with stars like Burt Bacharach, Cleo Laine and Perry Como. When he arrived he was a sex symbol, you know in those skin-tight trousers he would go out waggling his arse and showing his cock. Well, Jon kept all that but he made him do a few ballads as well as all that raunchy stuff.

'The artists would get $10,000 expenses and an agreement for Tom to guest on their show in the future. But just about nobody turned us down. Tom was the hottest act in town. When we went to Hollywood to record the second half of the series I found out just how big he was.

'We had just about got off the plane when a traffic cop pulled me over for driving on the wrong side of a six-lane freeway. He was going to throw the book at me until he found out I was working on *The Tom Jones Show*. He tore up my ticket, brought his wife to the show and we became firm friends.

'Tom was very aware that a good television series would be good for his career. He was very professional. He would be there on his marks every time when he was called and there were never any tantrums. If you kept him waiting he certainly wouldn't storm off to his dressing room or caravan like some stars. But then there was no real warmth about him.

'After three years of working closely with him on the show I never felt I knew Tom Jones. He kept himself to himself always. There were no big, lavish parties. After three years of TV we had a drink in the local pub when the series finished. I don't think I ever shook hands with Tom Jones. And years later when I was working on a special in Paris with him and Shirley MacLaine he just about managed to say "Hello, Bill". Underneath all that sweaty macho warmth I found him a very cold guy.

'But the most impressive thing about him was his effect on women. They really did throw themselves at him. He often had birds in his caravan and you'd have to be careful to knock a few times on the door and wait if you went to see him. He had all sorts of birds, some famous, some just fans, some beautiful, some very ordinary. Sometimes he would say to a minder, "Ask that blonde on the third row if she would like to join me for a drink afterwards." And I can't remember any of them ever saying no.

'We all knew that Tom screwed around. He was just a great puller of birds. Anything people say about Tom Jones and women is true. Sometimes girlfriends were in the caravan with him before the show but it never affected his performances as a singer.

'When we were in Los Angeles I saw him pulling birds off the street. He would just smile and give them that come-on look. He was legendary about his crumpet. He didn't care whether they were stars or not. He did pull several of his co-stars. He pulled Vicki Carr and Nancy Wilson but he certainly didn't pull Janis Joplin.

'The whole thing about him was sex, his image, his attitude to life, everything. He may have been dreadful at actually doing it, I don't know, but he always scored. He always wore very, very tight trousers showing his cock as big as he could show it. At the time there were lots of funny stories about young girls and their mothers: "Yes, deary, you can have me but I want your sixteen-year-old daughter as well". But I'm not sure if they were true. Probably today he is scared shitless by Aids but those were different times.

'I am not surprised that he is married to the same woman after all this time, he was never a guy who was going to fall in love. He was horny so he would screw. He was not a guy for involvements. He was very much a South Wales hod-carrier at heart and he always went home in the end. Probably if Linda had been different, if she had been the domineering kind and insisted on coming on tour with him it might not have lasted. She must have been aware of what he was like.'

Nina Blatt, who worked on the series and eventually became its associate producer, has similar memories – but she remembers Tom's warmth rather than his coolness.

'Tom Jones is a terrific guy. He has never changed from the beginning. I will always remember when we got delayed on the floor for hours with some technical hitch. The studio was hot and Tom was kept waiting for three or four hours. I went down to apologize to Tom and he just said, "It's better than hodding bricks. I've got a glass of champagne, I'm sitting here, don't worry." He was a very straight, uncomplicated man.'

So straight and uncomplicated in fact that his first amorous advance to attractive Nina was impossible to misunderstand. She recalls: 'We were sitting in the canteen one day and there was no salt on our table. I turned to reach for some. This was in the era of the mini skirt, remember, first time around, and I was wearing a tight leather mini. As I turned back he just looked at me and said: "Nina, I'd like to give you one."

'It all went quiet and then Jon said, "Thank you, Tom, as subtle as a freight train", and the moment passed. Jon said to me later, "We could be in trouble here," but we devised this wonderful understanding with Tom where I kept laughing off his advances because Tom was always propositioning me and I always said, "I'll be the reserve team, when you run out", knowing that there was no way he was ever going to run out of women.

'What I could never understand was that someone who could have, and did have, the most beautiful, wonderful women, very big stars among them, would also have funny little middle-aged women and girls who turned up to his concerts. I used to answer the phone to so many women who rang for him. We would pass messages on, of course, and I remember one woman who just said, "Ask him if he remembers Duncan Road." I asked Tom and he just laughed and said, "Oh yes." I could never understand it if you could have the tops.'

Tom's affair with Supremes singer Mary Wilson caused particular embarrassment when the couple were pictured together in an American magazine while the TV show was in production in Hollywood.

Nina Blatt recalls: 'We went all the way up Hollywood Boulevard buying up every copy so that Linda wouldn't see it and then Tom told me afterwards he bought it himself by mistake and took it home for Linda to see. I think he and Linda have an understanding about his behaviour nowadays. I know they have, and he is a little franker about his lifestyle now but in those days one did try to keep it quiet.

'I have never known anyone keener on the opposite sex. It was like heroin to him. There were so many stories about the famous caravan which had tyres that had to be replaced even though it never went anywhere. I don't think it's something he'll ever grow out of. Like most men he gets more attractive as he gets older. I wasn't in favour of his nose job, he was better before, now he has a slightly mongoloid look under his nose.

'I can't repeat some of the fruity language he used to use when he chatted to me but it was funny and it was just Tom. It is a great game with him, and the women, whether they were great stars or ordinary middle-aged ladies, accepted that it was not going to lead to any great romance.

'He was like a little boy in a sweet shop. He went after anybody. I couldn't understand it. We didn't call them groupies at the time; they were just these women who used to follow him around and I could understand it when he went with one of the young pretty ones but there were also these plain older ladies who waved their knickers and squealed and he loved them just as much. He adored it all. This was long before the Aids scare, of course, and he may be more careful now but I wouldn't bank on it.

'It was amazing to watch him whenever he spotted someone in the audience he fancied. It would really give an extra edge to a love song and it was terrific, although one didn't know in detail what happened overnight, but that magic had gone by the next day if the lady was in the audience again. He just wasn't interested any more.'

In those early television days Tom was still very naive and at first refused to have a dresser. He insisted on dressing himself. In one particularly explicit number, producer Jon Scoffield decreed that the sight of Tom's pulsating pelvis was just too much and the star was ordered to wear a jockstrap. Nina Blatt's recollection is: 'Tom had never worn a jockstrap before and he first put it on back to front.'

But Nina noticed much more about Tom than his extraordinary libido. Although no one could accuse the singer of being the world's most articulate entertainer he does have a real flair for coping with difficult situations. As his sound gradually crossed the Atlantic many listeners thought Tom Jones must be a black singer and when he made an early chat show appearance a slick host thought he could cash in on some of the growing black power publicity by asking the inexperienced singer: 'Do you think you are entitled to sing coloured songs?'

Nina Blatt recalls: 'Tom's reply was completely his own. It was a live show and I can't remember the name of the host but I remember what Tom said because I thought it was the most brilliant answer and it showed that he was perhaps a whole lot brighter than we had thought. Tom said: "Where I come from in Wales we white men dig for black coal and in America your black men pick white cotton. To me it's the same thing. You can be just as much put upon down a mine and singing those songs because you mean them as you can be if you're a negro picking cotton." '

For Tom the TV series was also an introduction to some of the world's biggest stars, some of whom turned out to be anything but what they seemed. Nina Blatt said: 'We booked

Bobby Darin on the strength of his great "Mack the Knife" songs but by the time we came to record he had gone all love and peace, changed his name to Bob Darin and he was anti-war, anti-everything. He refused to sing anything uptempo. He wouldn't sing "Mack the Knife" because of the implied violence. In the end he agreed to sing "Aquarius" but only much slower than it is normally sung; it was like a dirge. In the dress run the musical director Johnnie Spence, who was a great pal of Tom's, speeded up so Tom went with him and you could see this struggle on Bobby Darin's face as he decided whether or not to go with them.

'He decided reluctantly to speed up and we got the most sensational "Aquarius". Afterwards he snarled, "Don't you dare do that on the night." But that was the one that went out on television. Johnnie Spence became a great pal of Tom's before he died tragically young. Heaven knows what they used to get up to on their nights out together. I just remember answering the telephone one day from a young girl who rang up asking to speak to Johnnie about her audition. This was unusual to say the least so I asked her what she did. She said, absolutely deadpan, "I ice-skate in the nude on a bicycle."

'We had some great stars on the shows. Edward G. Robinson came on and was so sweet and kind we were all enchanted. Shirley Bassey was the opposite. I think she was the most highly strung. We had Anne Bancroft on, very nervous because she had to do a number in a bathtub with a revealing costume on. I had to hold a towel up for her to hide her modesty. Now, she was a little out of Tom's league.

'And Zero Mostel was a great character. Jon Scoffield was doing this long elaborate routine about the season and Zero was the part where the autumn leaves are blown away. By the time cameras came to him he had got a little bored and taken his trousers off for a gag. Jon's language was frightful but Tom fell about laughing.'

Nina recalls only one occasion when Tom Jones' libido made her uncomfortable. 'There was one time when he actually had nothing to do for twenty whole minutes and we were all going on from the studios to a party with the Fifth Dimension. I was in the hospitality room as it emptied and Bill Ward, who was then the controller of the studios, was watching as Tom came on to me really heavily.

'Bill asked me if I was OK and I just said Tom was being a little bit more fruity than usual but then it began to get awkward. Tom wanted me to come with him in his car to the party. I said, "No, I've got my own car, thank you," but he kept on and on trying to get me to go with him. Bill Ward tried to step in to save me and eventually he got Tom talking. He had to talk to Bill because he was the boss of the studio. I drove off on my own to the party but Bill was so worried about me he sent a rally driver friend who was at the studios to intercept me. Bill made me have dinner with him. He was really very shocked by Tom's behaviour. I think if Bill hadn't intervened there might have been a very ugly scene that night because I'm not a sleeper-arounder and I never have been. I have to say that I liked Tom enormously and I still do but I never found him physically attractive. He's magic as a performer, of course, but frankly I never felt the urge.

'When you went up to his caravan you had to knock four times and be very careful because you never knew who was in there. It's part of his legend now that people see him as the great sex symbol. Half the world doesn't believe it, the other half thinks it is really true. And of course if you've seen it in action you can hardly believe how it works.

'He never really chatted girls up. He just sort of looked at them and they all used to melt. I suppose that with women it became like with Kennedy, a sort of kudos thing. It became like a badge that they wore: "I've slept with Tom Jones." '

Chapter Seven

TOURING

The year was 1969, and Ben Segal remembers it as if it were yesterday. By this time the veteran Segal had been in showbusiness, mostly as a concert promoter in the eastern states of the USA, for twenty-eight years. But when Tom Jones came to perform at Oakdale, his theatre-in-the-round in Wallingford, Connecticut, even the hardened Segal was astonished.

'I actually saw adults in the audience doing things that until then only teenagers had done,' he recalls. 'For the first time, I saw panties and bras being thrown. It wasn't a set-up, it was not being shilled.

'There was one young lady in the audience, not a girl, but a woman of maybe twenty-seven or twenty-eight, and very slimly built, only ninety-eight pounds or so. She threw off her top and ran from the back of the theatre, and almost made it on stage. The security guards stopped her, and she seemed to cool down a bit, but then she tried it again, and as she neared the stage, she jumped – high. Thank God our security guards were bright enough not to let her fall – they held her up, and you could see her bare little boobies hanging down. She was in such hysteria, we took her outside to the parking lot. She didn't know what she was doing.'

Segal's daughter Rebecca, who then worked in her father's theatre, also witnessed those early shows: 'I remember being at the back of the theatre, and watching a quite respectable woman in front of me wriggling in her set, shifting first to one side and then another. I couldn't imagine what she was doing, and then finally I realized she had wriggled out of her girdle, and was preparing to throw it at Tom. And she didn't seem to have the slightest compunction about doing this.'

In neighbouring towns in New England, Ben Segal remembers Tom Jones being mobbed not only by fans, but even by reporters. 'I did a press conference with him in Hartford for all these TV, radio and newspaper people,' he says. 'And when Tom came in the room they just stormed him. I had to get him out of the building.'

Stories of mass hysteria like these would be repeated time and time again at Tom Jones concerts throughout America. 1969 was the year that set the pattern for the most successful phase of Tom Jones' career – concerts and touring. Because his spell of selling records by the million was relatively short lived, and would effectively end around 1971, playing concerts became central to his career.

This was true whether he was performing in a ritzy Vegas casino showroom like the Flamingo, Caesar's Palace, MGM Grand or the Hilton, or a convention centre in a small southern city like Pine Bluff, Arkansas. In all these settings Tom Jones was a superstar.

In terms of the lavishness of his show, he behaved like a superstar, too. From those early days of touring the States, the flamboyant, extravagant Gordon Mills decided that a Tom Jones live appearance would always be a major event. To this end he would book a full-sized band, a comedian and a support group, so that fans would feel they were getting their money's worth. Ben Segal saw a Tom Jones show in Columbia, Maryland, in which Tom had Gladys Knight and the Pips as his backing group, the full Count Basie Orchestra and comedian Norm Crosby all on the bill.

'Nobody else spent that kind of money to put a show together,' says Segal. 'He always had the best musicians, the finest conductors.' This extravagance flowered in his 1971 tour of America, which earned Tom Jones an estimated £2 million. Gordon leased a Boeing 707 jet to carry the huge entourage across country and the tour resembled a military operation.

Tom took a full-size orchestra on board the Boeing with him, while in first class were comedian Pat Henry, Tom's trio of black back-up singers the Blossoms, his management people and road crew. At every stop half a dozen limousines would be waiting on the tarmac to whisk away the artists to the poshest hotel in the city, while the other members of the party followed behind in specially arranged tour buses.

Singer Darlene Love, who was a member of the Blossoms on the remarkable 1971 tour, recalls: 'I had never seen luxury like it before or since. It was astounding.' The itinerary for the tour was meticulously planned: she remembers being given a thick dossier which detailed where all the members of the touring party had to be at any given time. 'If we missed the plane, there were always back-up flights listed,' she says. 'Nothing was left to chance.'

In fact, there was scant chance of missing the plane, since it never departed early in the morning: the tour schedule was devised around Tom's own sleeping habits on tour. And by 1971, these had become clearly established. 'He comes alive at four in the bloody morning,' says an exasperated Sylvia Harrison, who for fourteen years worked for Tom's American tour manager Lloyd Greenfield.

'On tour, his life is working and sleeping. He sleeps until noon, or even two in the afternoon, gets up, goes to the gym, has dinner, does his show, then parties from midnight until six or seven in the morning.' This meant that the Tom Jones jet would stay in its hangar until he crawled out of bed in the middle of the day, and was ready to travel on to the next town – a factor that made him popular with the late-rising musicians who accompanied him.

These tours were like an endless party, with all sorts of indulgences being rife. One former Jones associate reports that even an average dinner with Tom Jones' inner circle while on the road was no experience for the faint-hearted. 'He'll have a bottle of white to start with, maybe a Montrachet,' says the ex-colleague. 'And he reckons a bottle per person. Then it's red wine, maybe a mature Château Lafitte Rothschild, a bottle a head all round. At the end of the meal he likes to see a bottle of brandy on the table, Napoleon if he can get it. And he's not the kind of guy who likes to leave a bottle – even of brandy – until it's empty.' Then if there's a cheese board, vintage port will accompany it.

Not that dinners are all liquid by any means. He is a meat and potatoes man who likes red meat (fillet steak or rack of lamb), roast potatoes, chips and lots of gravy. For dessert he likes dark chocolate in a gâteau or pastry. Clearly this is not a diet that a heart specialist could love.

Typically the revelry continued in the marathon after-show parties, which would take place backstage if the group was in Vegas, or in his hotel suite otherwise. Everyone involved agrees that these nightly parties lasted from six to eight hours; outside the sun was usually high in the sky before everyone crawled off to bed.

The expensive champagne Dom Perignon is the drug of choice for Tom on these occasions, which he accompanies with a fine Cuban cigar, Monte Cristo No. 1. Every associate of Tom Jones interviewed for this book agrees that he drinks prodigious amounts of champagne: 'Gallons of it,' says one. Tom himself has admitted it. 'Weight could be a problem if I didn't watch it,' he once said. 'I would drink twelve to fifteen pints of beer a night if I could, but instead I just drink two pints of champagne. It's less fattening.'

At the same time the consensus is that he carries his drink well. 'He doesn't get mean or abusive or violent after a few drinks,' says a former tour member.

Still, this amount of drinking has its consequences, and Tom Jones frequently flushes out his system after a heavy bout with alcohol by drinking several pints of water the following day. This does the trick and later the next evening he is back to big meals and heavy drinking again. 'I've seen him do it again and again,' says Annie Toomaru, who was the long-standing girlfriend of Gordon Mills.

This is a routine that alarms many of those around him, who fear it is bad for his heart. 'He has an incredibly energetic stage show,' says one confidant, 'and he has a strenuous exercise routine too. He is nearly fifty years old, and it's a way of life that has got to put a strain on his system.'

This exercise routine depends on where he is. At his Bel-Air mansion he runs a couple of miles before breakfast, then plays squash and swims in the huge indoor sports centre he built on his own grounds.

In Vegas, for example, he may finish a show around 11 p.m., go for dinner, then party until the early hours, maybe 8 a.m., sometimes eating breakfast before retiring. He will sometimes sleep until 4 p.m., then take a sauna which helps protect his vocal chords from the dry desert air, and work out in the hotel's gym before a massage. Then it's time to get ready for the evening's show. The Jones workout has become quite an institution in Vegas, and when he was contracted to Caesar's Palace, the casino hotel built a workout area especially for him.

However, it does all add up to a gruelling lifestyle on the road, and those same people who worry about Tom's health also worry whether Mark Woodward, now his manager and controlling influence, is the man to curtail his father's excesses – Mark himself learned to drink and be merry with his father, they say, and he may lack authority to admonish Dad.

Still, Tom Jones apparently has some discipline of his own when it comes to alcohol.Roger Wall, who was his tour manager over a seven-year period, recalls that Jones regularly drank after shows, but often abstained from alcohol while he was in Vegas. 'The dry desert air and the air conditioning there used to dry out his voice, and the drink only made it worse,' says Wall. 'In Vegas, he would be at his parties drinking Mountain Valley water from a green bottle, and apparently quite happy. And still the parties would go on till 7 or 8 a.m.'

To Roger Wall, an American who joined Tom in 1973, sometimes it seemed that touring was one long party. 'Tom loved to see people having a good time,' he recalls. 'Many nights it was like a disco backstage. We'd see who could drink the most, which is a very Welsh thing to do. I had some really good times.'

Back in those heady days everyone connected with

the Jones touring party lived like kings. 'They were good employers,' says Roger Wall now, 'and even though the British are not the best when it comes to salaries, I still travelled all over the world with them. And I had the "magic pen" – which meant that wherever I stayed I just signed for what I wanted. I didn't pay for laundry or food or booze. Once I'd been on the road for so long with them that when I got back to Los Angeles I didn't have a place to stay and they put me up in a hotel for a month. I didn't have a car so I got to use Gordon's until he got back in town. In ways like that they came through.'

The same opulent lifestyle existed aboard the leased United Airlines jet, and continued when they touched down in a new city. 'We'd get into town and there'd be six limousines, a bus and two or three station wagons,' recalled Roger Wall. 'There'd be one limo for Tom, one for Gordon, maybe one for Lloyd Greenfield, all just sitting there twenty-four hours a day. This was when the music business was fun.'

Darlene Love agrees. 'On board that plane there would be fifty to sixty people. We had a full orchestra, with strings, leaders, a horn section, then Tom's rhythm section, a comedian, his back-up group and his management people. It was a great atmosphere, very free and fancy. Usually when you got on board a lot of people were tired, but before too long, people were lively and they would start singing.Not Tom though – he would be asleep from the time he got on the plane. I have pictures of Tom asleep on board, wearing a blindfold. We'd clown around and he slept.'

Then there were the gigs, astonishing for their intensity and the fan reaction they provoked. 'There was always hysteria,' remembers Darlene.

And it was on these early tours that the curious socio-logical phenomenon first occurred which entailed women fans throwing panties on stage at Tom Jones. Others threw their hotel roomkeys, and still others their bras, but panties were the favoured projectiles.'I performed with Elvis when he made his Vegas comeback,' says Darlene Love, 'and no one was throwing panties at him. Tom Jones was definitely the first. But his crowds were wilder than Elvis's – they were younger, for a start.'

Tom claims the pantie-throwing craze started in 1968 at the Copacabana in New York. 'A lady offered me what I thought was a napkin because I was perspiring so much, and it turned out the napkin was her knickers.' Syndicated columnist Earl Wilson wrote a column about the arrival of the underwear and it caught on fast. By the time Tom Jones reached Vegas he would be surrounded on stage by piles of knickers and roomkeys by each show's end. 'In one week in Vegas once they collected 5,000 keys,' he said. Ben Segal remembers the rain of panties at his Oakdale theatre: 'By the time his engagement was through, we had three boxes of panties and bras and I called up the Salvation Army to come and get them. But they wouldn't take them so I had to throw them all out.'

The hurled underwear became a huge joke among the Jones touring party. Says Darlene Love: 'I thought ladies were taking off their drawers and throwing them onstage, and I remember we teased Tom about it once. We said, "Tom, how could you wipe your face with them?" And he said, "Oh love, they don't wear these. These are brand new." And in most cases they were.'

The hysteria did not die down when Tom left the stage, of course. In every city they visited frantic female fans tried to gain access to Tom's hotel room by any means they knew. In Las Vegas he was protected by the hotel's security forces and by the capability of those hotels to cordon off entire floors for their visiting entertainers. On the road it was different.

'Tom Jones fans are crazy,' chuckles Darlene Love. 'Wherever we were they'd find the hotel he was staying at. We'd come back and we'd find them waiting in the corridor for Tom. They'd ask which room he was in, and they'd say, "If a security guard comes, can you say we're with you, so we don't get kicked out of the hotel?" Well, we'd go into our rooms and we would have to start closing the doors quickly because they'd come in and start chit-chatting with us and make themselves at home. The aim was to get anything they could, to spend the night with him, to get his autograph, even just to see his face.

'One night we [the Blossoms] were in a hotel going to our room and three of his lady fans grabbed me by the arm and wouldn't let me go and were at the point of tearing my clothes off until I told them which room he was in. That was all so amazing to me. I could see the fans trying to get to him, but trying to get to him through me – you've got to be kidding.'

But if there was a dark side to the touring party it never showed itself publicly. The group were big drinkers, no doubt about it, yet drugs never seemed to be part of the festivities – in part because Tom Jones' own widely known distaste for drugs carried a lot of weight.

'I've never bothered with drugs,' he has said. 'I've been brought up on light ale. I've seen drugs change perfectly normal people into blithering idiots in an hour. I went to a party of Cass Elliott's [the late Mamas and Papas singer] once at a famous London hotel. I was the only one there who was drinking. Everyone else there was smoking pot and I saw their minds go before my eyes.

'Drugs upset me. I remember a bass player I once had in my band – he smoked hashish so much he couldn't play. He got so bad that in the end we just had to prop him up against a wall on stage. He could still play but he couldn't change chords. That shocked me.'

Promoter Ben Segal recalls: 'One night I took Tom out to a nightclub and I ordered drinks for all of us. Suddenly he said: "Let's go." I said, "What's the matter?" And he said, "Can't you smell? This place is reeking of marijuana." And he left.'

However, in the early days of the American touring, Tom was allegedly prescribed amphetamines which he disliked because they affected his sexual potency. But one woman who spent time with him on an early US tour believed he might have been using dexedrine, primarily to lose weight.

Tom Jones has toured tirelessly throughout his career. Roger Wall remembers that eight months of every year were devoted to touring and Tom himself notes that three weeks of those months involved being on the road, followed by one week off. With such a full schedule it was perhaps inevitable that trouble would occur occasionally. It happened in 1974 in Venezuela in a bigger way than anyone would have thought possible.

When the touring party arrived at Caracas Airport and made its way through a milling throng of fans, Tom's bodyguard and old school pal Dai Perry was being severely jostled by the crowd as he tried to protect Tom. Nerves were frayed because there had been word of a possible plot to kidnap Mark, who was then seventeen and a regular member of Tom's touring party. Dai Perry suddenly lost his temper and turned to punch in the face a man who was asking if Tom was losing his voice. Today Dai says: 'They were hitting us and kicking us from behind. I retaliated, I just turned round and let him have one.'

Unfortunately Dai had struck a local newsman, Manuel Olalquiaga, who worked for a Caracas paper called *El Universal*. And he was not about to take this insult lying down. He filed a $65,000 lawsuit against Tom's party and obtained a court order against Tom, who was ordered to appear before a judge three days later and defend himself. In the meantime Tom and the touring party were confined to their hotel rooms. 'There were police outside our hotel doors armed with machine guns,' remembers Roger Wall. 'It was pretty heavy.'

Gordon Mills swiftly arranged for Dai to be smuggled out of the country, reckoning that the Venezuelan authorities were primarily after him. But he was wrong. The local police had clearly determined to teach Tom and the group a lesson and they were prevented from leaving Caracas by customs men. An urgent cable was sent to Prime Minister Harold Wilson but that did nothing to ease the tense situation.

A financial arrangement was finally negotiated, and Tom, who denied throughout that Dai was any kind of bodyguard, was ordered to leave the country within the hour – which he did, after a high-speed drive from downtown Caracas to the airport. 'They were trying to put the fear of God into us,' says Roger Wall now.

Venezuela had been something of a minefield for visiting entertainers around that time. Englebert Humperdinck had been detained on suspicion of drug offences only months previously and Eddie Fisher had also been held.

But the Caracas incident turned out to be the end of the line for Dai Perry, who had also been involved in two other ugly incidents on tour in the previous three years.

In 1971, Dai had hit Michael Maret, a professional boxer, in Madison, Wisconsin, after Maret had tried to enter a party in Tom's hotel room. A fight had ensued which ended in Maret bleeding from a cut over his left eye. Maret later claimed he was held down while Tom hit him but Dai Perry's view of the incident was different. Perry says: 'This guy arrived demanding to come in to the party. When he was told he couldn't come in he started swearing and calling us "a lot of pumped-up Welsh factory workers". Then he announced he was "the next light heavyweight champion of the world". But I think he was mistaken there because he went down after one punch. He wouldn't calm down so I had to clip him one. The next light heavyweight champion of the world didn't really measure up. We found out later he was just the local bully.'

Dai struck again in 1973. After a long tour and some serious drinking the Jones entourage were flying from New York to London on a Pan Am jumbo and, having watched the in-flight movie, Tom was listening to some music on his headphones, loudly clicking his fingers. A woman passenger across the aisle asked him to keep quiet, Tom insulted her and she threw her coffee at him. Tom threw his brandy back at her and a scuffle ensued with the flight crew joining in. Dai Perry waded in as usual, pinning a uniformed man to the ground.

Tom, according to Chris Hutchins the publicity man, brandished a champagne bottle and shouted: 'Come on then. Who wants it?'

The man with Dai's knee on his chest told Dai: 'You'd better let me get up.' Dai retorted: 'You're staying here until the plane has landed.' 'Until I get up the plane isn't landing,' said the man. 'I'm the captain.'

The plane was met by British Airports Authority police, and Tom's party was detained for two hours. As they confronted newsmen on their way out of the airport they clenched their fists a little drunkenly.

Gordon Mills was uncomfortable with Dai's lack of subtlety and after the Venezuela incident he was 'allowed' to leave the Jones organization. The decision was said to be mutual; Dai professed himself sick of travelling. Thus ended a long relationship which had started when the two tearaways used to take rivals up to the Graig in Treforest to pummel them. Dai's life has gone full circle and, having toured the showbusiness world and met Elvis Presley, he now lives back in Treforest in a tiny terraced home. 'It was Gordon who wanted me out,' says Dai bitterly. 'Not Tom. Tom and I, we're still mates, we still have a drink together when he comes home.

'I've seen more posh kitchens than most chefs because that was always the way we'd escape when the fans started chasing. It was a fabulous experience working with Tom, I'll never forget it. I was working nightclub doors in Wales when I got a call to work for Tom. I'd never even had a passport or been out of the country before and then a few nights later I'm backstage at Caesar's Palace in Las Vegas with Elvis Presley, Sean Connery and Sir John Mills. I couldn't believe it.

'They were amazing times. Women were there on tap like hot and cold running water, they were there for the taking and anyone who doesn't take them has got to be off his head. They certainly went wild for Tom. I remember at Caesar's Palace women would be running towards Tom across the tables with champagne and ice buckets flying everywhere. One girl ran up and she only had hot pants on; she took her top off and gave Tom her bra and another came up in a mini skirt and lifted it up, took her panties off and gave them to Tom.

'The most frightening one ran on stage while Tom was at the grand piano and grabbed his balls in a clenched fist and then ran off. Weeks later in Birmingham, Alabama, the same girl was in the front row.

'Tom thought he recognized her and when he asked her if he'd seen her before she just raised her hand and clenched her fist. It nearly brought tears to his eyes all over again. Some of those fans were crazy; they followed us right round the country and would do anything to get to Tom.

'One night in Miami Tom and I were relaxing completely naked in a solarium right in the top of an hotel when two girls burst in. We had to hide behind a wall and grab for towels. It was unbelievable. Wherever Tom was, I was. I had to be to protect him. And every time we moved into a new suite I would search for women hiding in the bathroom or cupboards and often they were there.'

Some of Tom's tours were dramatic in different ways. In 1976, for instance, he became the first white star to appear before multi-racial audiences in South Africa. A total of 75,000 tickets were sold for the historic event, at a theatre called the Three Arts. Gordon Mills had originally wanted all the shows to be open to multi-racial fans but a compromise position was reached: three out of the eight shows would have mixed audiences. The others were for whites only. The situation was not ideal, but even this was a breakthrough for this normally segregated theatre, and Tom's staff professed themselves happy.

Tom, who had always been strongly against racial discrimination, at first refused to go to South Africa unless all the concerts were desegregated, then saw that even the compromise represented progress. 'It was a good gesture,' says Roger Wall. 'It was a start. It said a lot about him, and what he stood for at the time.'

His black back-up singers, the Blossoms, had to be made 'honorary whites' for the occasion. 'It was the only way they could stay at the same hotel and move around like the rest of us,' said Roger Wall. 'If we were all going to a restaurant we had to call ahead beforehand and explain what was going on. It was a little scary.'

As time went on concerts and touring became more important to Tom Jones, for a simple reason. By 1971 Gordon Mills could proudly claim that Tom had sold 100 million

Above: The Pontypridd days – 'Tommy Scott and the Senators'. Some aspects of Tom Jones' stage routine have changed very little over the years. (JMP)

Below: On stage in Paris. Fans show their appreciation. (Barthelemy/Sipa Press)

Above: Tom at his parents' home early in his career. (JMP)

Below: At home with Linda and Mark – just a lad from the Valleys. (JMP)

Above: The star. With Dusty
Springfield, Paul McCartney
and Ringo Starr at a *Melody
Maker* awards ceremony, 1966.
(Popperfoto)

Right: A style is born. Gold
bracelets, fat cigars and a new
confidence all in evidence.
(Rex Features)

Above left: Going up in the world. Tom Jones outside his newly acquired Surrey mansion, 1968. (Syndication International)

Above right: With Steve Marriott of the Small Faces. (Syndication International)

Below: Gordon Mills (centre) with his two star clients, Tom Jones and Engelbert Humperdinck, in 1969. Note the Rolls' registration. (Popperfoto)

At the height of his British television show's popularity, in 1969, Tom poses with Nita, Liz and Donna, who appeared in the show. (Terry O'Neil/Daily Express)

Above left: With Shirley Maclaine in Paris. (Aslan/Sipa Press)

Above right: With Lulu and a new hair-do in London. (Rex Features/Peter Simpson)

Below: With Dionne Warwick and Michael Caine in Las Vegas. (Popperfoto)

Above left: Mr and Mrs Jones dance, 1987. (Syndication International)

Above right: Tom sings at his son's wedding, 1980. (Alec Byrne/Rex Features)

Below left: Proud grandad. Tom Jones with son Mark, daughter-in-law Donna and baby Alexander, 1983. (Syndication International)

Below right: Father and son recover at Heathrow from a gruelling flight in from LA. (Syndication International)

Obviously a present from his biggest fan. (Retna Pictures)

Tom Jones jogs for victory. (Rex Features)

records worldwide, but that same year his American record
sales abruptly dried up. He had enjoyed terrific success in
America with top ten hits like 'It's Not Unusual', 'What's
New Pussycat?', 'I'll Never Fall In Love Again', 'Without Love'
and 'She's A Lady'. But then the hits stopped coming and his
album sales in the 1970s were also way down on his initial
peak period.

In 1976 he left America's London Records, with whom he
had been for eleven years. 'They just weren't very good,' he
said despairingly. He then signed with Epic, a move which
gave him one top twenty hit, 'Say You'll Stay Until Tomorrow',
the following year. But in 1980 he switched to MCA, and in
1981 moved again – to an unhappy five-year commitment to
make country albums for Polygram's Nashville office.

In truth much of the fan fervour at his concerts also
calmed down as the years went by. 'It used to be underwear
and hotel keys. Now I get flowers,' he told *People* magazine a
little wistfully in 1981.

There are those who think Gordon Mills always tried to
push Tom Jones into being a far more mainstream act than
he would have wished, that Gordon tamed the wild Welsh kid
who idolized Jerry Lee Lewis and other rockers. Roger Wall is
one of them: 'Gordon had a pretty firm hand on the creative
side, down to the clothes and the selection of the songs and
the running order of the songs, and I think Tom wanted to do
much more rock and roll, much more than Gordon wanted.

'When Tom and the band finished rehearsal sometimes,
they'd break out into some old Jerry Lee Lewis or Little
Richard tune – it was always rock and roll. And he did
them well. I'd have loved to see him go straight rock and
roll because I think that's where his heart is.'

Still, when Tom was hot he was hot and promoter Ben
Segal loves to reminisce about the shock impact of a Tom
Jones show in those early American touring days.

'We hadn't seen this kind of performer before,' he says. 'It
was sheer magic, what went on. I had a solid ring of security
people all around the stage with locked arms. And still people
got through. I don't think anyone sat in their seats from the

minute he got on stage to the minute he was through.

'The first time he played my theatre, when he got off that stage I was so elated that I went backstage to congratulate him. He was sweating so much that you could take his shoes and wring them out. In forty-eight years I've never seen anyone else perform like that.'

Chapter Eight

THE WOMEN

'I'm honest about the fact that I'm married and it's never going to change. It's putting your cards on the table before you play the game,' said Tom Jones in 1987.

Male singing stars have traditionally been targets of women's sexual advances, and many of them have found an extraordinary number of women willing to accommodate their sexual whims. In his day, Frank Sinatra was notorious for bedding showgirls. In the rock 'n' roll era, Chuck Berry and Jerry Lee Lewis were known for their prodigious sexual appetites. The bed-hopping high jinks of groups like the Rolling Stones and Led Zeppelin have been fully chronicled. And more recently, the members of Van Halen have indulged their wildest fantasies with any number of young, available groupies.

It's fair to say, though, that Tom Jones has continued this time-honoured tradition as energetically as anyone. His need for sexual conquest, of course, pre-dated his singing career. From the time of puberty, it would appear, Tom Jones has been every bit as lustful as his strutting, swaggering stage persona would lead one to believe.

Although he seduced several girl fans (and a couple of female entertainers) in his days touring Britain, Tom's sexual escapades flowered fully when he set foot in America. It was in 1968 and 1969, his first couple of years of superstardom, that the women came flocking to him in big numbers.

Their blatant physical attraction for him was due to two

117

factors. First, Tom was a rugged manly kind of pop star who older women could find appealing in a rough–hewn kind of way. He wasn't remotely effeminate, and didn't look like some long-haired kid, as did the members of the Rolling Stones and the Doors and the Who and the Byrds, to name some of the most popular touring groups of that time. Instead, Tom Jones was clearly all man – and his tight trousers and gyrating pelvis proved the point.

Secondly, in the late 1960s in America, there was a remarkable new atmosphere of sexual liberation. It had been growing throughout the decade, but the enormous influence of the hippies, with their ideals of peace, love and sexual freedom, had a major impact. And after the hippies' 'summer of love' in 1967, a more relaxed attitude towards sexuality started to permeate older age groups. Add to this the fact the millions of American women could now make sexual choices without fear of pregnancy because of the widespread availability of the Pill, and suddenly here was a country teeming with barely disguised lust.

Into this sexual maelstrom walked Tom Jones, boy seducer and professional Lothario. For him, America in those years, with available women everywhere he turned, must, as said before, have made him feel like a kid in a sweet shop – or a drunk in a brewery.

There were a lot of women about, and Tom Jones, in those early years, partook freely. To those who had never seen the Jones boy in action before, the phenomenon was eye-popping. Nick Naff, then advertising and publicity director at the Flamingo, recalls: 'Of all the entertainers I met, Tom Jones was the most insatiable. I mean, there were a lot of women around Elvis Presley's party, but most of them never got near. His band would recruit them, and ask: "How would you like to meet Elvis?" Of course they said yes, and maybe they'd get to say hello. But the band were really aiming to get these women into bed themselves, which they frequently managed to do – even without the women meeting Elvis. But Tom was different. All he had to do was open his door. Which he often did.'

Connecticut promoter Ben Segal, who has booked Tom

Jones into his theatres for twenty years, concurs: 'The man is torrid. He's a man of all men. When it comes to women, what can I say? He's the Rocky of the industry.'

Certainly, Tom Jones seems to know what works on the opposite sex. 'Women, when they pass thirty, are still full-blooded women,' he once said. 'And they like full-blooded men. That's what they get from me. I turn them on, and excitement like that is a good outlet.'

He knew how to work up into a frenzy the women who attended his concerts, too; he played them like an instrument. 'In Vegas, a girl took her bra off and gave it to me,' he recalled. 'As I don't wear bras, I wiped my face with it and gave it back. But she said: "You keep it."

'Another girl who didn't want to be outdone took off her hot pants, gave them to me and stood there in her pantyhose. I looked at her in the pantyhose, wiped my face with the hot pants, and said: "You need these more than I do." '

Few kinds of women, it seemed, were impervious to his animalistic appeal on stage. Nick Naff remembers 'a lady, an entertainment reporter from Denver, who came to see his show three nights in a row. And one night as he was coming off stage, she just leaped at him, and clutched on to him. He laughed it off, and everything was fine, but later I said, "What happened back there?" And she said, "I don't know. I've never done anything like that before. It was remarkable."

'There were a lot of Tom Jones groupies waiting around back then, but the real key to me was the fact that wives of Flamingo executives kept coming back five or six times to see him. They couldn't get enough of him.'

Touring, of course, was a perfect opportunity for Tom Jones to meet many of the women who would be added to his list of brief encounters. At all-night parties after each show, many women would join the collection of musicians, managers and road crew who made up the touring group. This was a predominantly male gathering, and women found it easier to infiltrate than men. At each gig, several local women would be invited to join the party. One of them might spend the night with Tom Jones, and, if he liked her, might stay with him every night for the length of an engagement in one particular town. The other women would pair off with the guys in the band, the road crew – or, if he was around, Gordon Mills, whose charisma and good looks also made him a desirable groupie target.

'I remember Gordon being with a lot more different women than Tom, actually,' says one woman who was close to the touring party in the early years of US tours. 'But it was a major groupie scene after the shows. It was just – boys' time. There were always tons of girls around, and all of them seemed to be blonder than blonde. There were a lot of push-up bras in evidence.

'The men would sit around and play poker and carry on, and the women only really figured in when one of the men needed to have his ego massaged. Or something else.

'The girls always used to be a mix of locals and imports. Sometimes someone in the group would take a girl along for a couple of cities. But it was mostly locals. The band had free rein to walk around the theatre and pick up girls, and Gordon used to do that too. The group used to like to do that, because the women used to say: "Oh my God, aren't you the drummer?" There was a fair amount of that.

'For a while, Gordon had these twin stewardesses. I was never quite sure whether he had one of them or both of them – I never figured out quite what was going on there. The stewardesses seemed to amuse people in the group a lot, and they showed up in several different cities. They were blondes. My recollection is that one of them also went with someone else in the band.

'The Blossoms were treated very well. For this group of guys, there were women you treated well, and there were women you didn't. Not that any women got treated badly, but there were those you didn't pay much attention to, and those were the ones you were just going to fuck.'

The Blossoms were the only women who regularly witnessed these extraordinary going-on, said this same witness. 'They were in a special category. Some days they'd spend cooking big southern meals, which they loved to do. One morning they started off at 7 and all three of them – Fanita Barrett, Darlene Love and Jeannie King – cooked this huge meal. And there were two shows to do that night. They did black-eyed peas, okra, the whole nine yards. And then we all came back after the show and had this fabulous meal. Jeannie had these long, long fingernails and you wondered how she could slice and dice and cook.'

Darlene Love confirms that the Blossoms had a special place in this all-male bastion. 'We had a lot of cookouts for the group. Me and Jeannie would go shopping, because after a while you get tired of hotel food, and we'd buy greens and hams and yams and all those good things, and it was great to do that.'

The anonymous woman who hung out with the Tom Jones touring party in those early days actually had a sexual liaison with the singer which lasted for a few days. She was curious about Tom, she admitted – but he turned out not to be quite the single-minded stud one might have expected.

'My sense of it,' she recalls, 'is that the time I spent with him had much more to do with spending time together than it did with fucking. My sense is that it wasn't just the sexual conquest, that it had a lot more to do with just kind of sitting, talking, sleeping together, holding each other and stuff like that.

'I don't remember getting any pressure from him about that. There were no sexual marathons, or anything. It wasn't anything like that part of his image – I have absolutely no recollection of it being that way. In fact, I'm sure that it wasn't at all.

'And my sense was that that wasn't so unusual for him. I don't remember him as a callous person. There was no sense of being used in the way that a lot of people just discard people.'

But Ursula Alioto, vice-president of his Milwaukee fan club, was a little less enchanted by Tom's attempts to get her into bed. It happened backstage after a concert of Tom's. 'He sat and talked to me for four hours,' she remembers. 'He told me a lot about his life. He told me that when he was three

years old, a woman had told his mother that he, Tom, would
be wealthy. He was smart and interesting. And interested. He
told me he'd give up his money if he could still sing. He liked
singing better than anything – better than sex.

'All this time, we were drinking Dom Perignon champagne
from his private bottles. But I could see that everyone around
us was having to drink cheap wine. He's very cheap, you
know – he wouldn't pass the champagne around.

'I asked him at one point if he had any women friends.
Meaning just that – friends. And he seemed puzzled by the
question. "Why would I want female friends?" he said. "Why
would I need them?"

'And I knew what he meant. After another concert, I
took my husband backstage to meet Tom – and he spent
more time talking to him than to me or all the women who
had gone backstage with me.

'Anyway, on this occasion, we'd talked for about four
hours, and then he started hitting on me. But I said no,
because suddenly the things he was saying didn't seem to
add up, you know? You know how it is when you have certain
fantasies and when they happen in real life, they don't seem
so good as the fantasy? Anyway, I started to hear what he was
saying. So I said no, I reminded him I was married, and that
it was time I went to get some sleep.

'And as I was going up to my hotel room, he gave me
a bottle of wine, and said to me: "Think about what you're
turning down." '

Ursula nearly giggled at this, but kept her composure,
and shot back: 'I'm sorry, but I wouldn't like to walk out
with a number on my back.' He seemed taken aback by that
remark. The next morning, Lloyd Greenfield, Tom's American
tour manager, sought out Ursula, said he had noticed they had
been talking for hours and hours, and asked her if she was
a reporter. 'This was when Gordon Mills was still handling
his career,' she says, 'and there was more awareness of the
problems involved in talking to strangers.'

Since that night, Ursula has met Tom backstage again. 'He
remembers me now, perhaps because of that last comment,

and asks me teasingly if I'm still married,' she says. 'But he's not the same person he was a few years ago. I got taken backstage to meet him recently when his comedian pulled me out of the audience after the show. And Tom was just a total ass. He used to be very sweet and kind. But now, he's like Peter Pan. He won't grow up.'

For all this, no one accuses Tom Jones of being less than candid about what he wants from women to whom he takes a fancy. 'He was very charming with these women,' says Roger Wall, formerly Tom's road manager. 'He was always very upfront with them, and never made any secret of the fact that he was married. He never played any games with them at all, as far as I could see.

'Of course, the women played games with themselves, and persuaded themselves that they could change things with him, that they could be the one. But the man was married and he was very direct about it, yet for some reason they thought they could step in. They were being silly. He was very upfront about his wife – he was a no-bullshit kind of guy about everything.'

One former member of Tom Jones' inner circle, who requested anonymity, describes what he calls Tom's *modus operandi* in approaching a woman in a disco, club or restaurant when he's on tour. If his gaze settled on a woman he found particularly attractive, he would send a bodyguard or maybe a member of his back-up band over to her table. She would then be asked to come over and meet Tom, and join the small circle of friends around him. The night would progress from there. It was a method, allegedly, with a high success rate.

This same ex-associate agrees with Ursula Alioto's assessment of Tom as a Peter Pan figure who will not grow up. 'When Tom Jones is on tour,' says this source, 'all he wants to do is drink and fuck. He seems to have no interest in the world around him. He's a pretty dull, boring guy in that way. If we're away somewhere interesting, he'll never set foot outside the hotel. Like if we're in the Dakotas, he doesn't want to go out and see Mount Rushmore. And that's real history. If we're in Hong Kong, he doesn't even want to go out shopping, or even to look around. He just wants to sit in some dark disco and drink champagne and hope some dumb young broad comes by who he can fuck. That's how he likes them – young and dumb.'

But it's also agreed that Tom Jones' taste in women is catholic. He does not necessarily favour beautiful or elegant women, and indeed has whisked off to bed a number of surprisingly homely partners. Open sexual interest from a woman will give her a head start, people in Tom's circle agree.

His former press aide Chris Hutchins, in a series of newspaper articles which stunned the Jones camp, wrote: 'Intelligence certainly wasn't an essential qualification. He wasn't impressed by great beauty, either.

'He would never play the aggressive role or put himself out to get a girl he wanted. At a party, for example, if there was a super-looking lady he really fancied, but who hung back playing hard to get, he'd make no attempt to win her. Instead, he'd go for the plain girl who was a pushover. Those who didn't ask, didn't get. We used to take bets on which girl he'd end up with at parties, and spotting the winner was never difficult. The girl who made the play for him was the one who won the prize every time. If she was an actress or a model out to make a name for herself, it didn't matter. Tom never gave a damn about their motives.'

Tom also finds black women attractive. His affair with Supreme Mary Wilson is well known, and Hutchins insists he also had an affair with the black American singer Nancy Wilson.

He appeared to have passed on his taste for black women to his son Mark, who was at one point dating a member of a black girl group who opened for Tom at his concerts. One former member of the Jones camp says derisively: 'Donna Woodward was the first white woman who even looked at Mark.'

Still, there were several women whose relationships with Tom Jones were well known to a circle of insiders. All the time he was seeing Mary Wilson, for instance, Tom was also involved with a blonde American model called Joyce Ingalls. She helped bring about the end of their affair by pushing too hard; as Hutchins tells it, Joyce moved into Tom's two-room trailer at Elstree Studios, where he was filming his TV series in January 1970 – and she promptly declared the trailer closed to visitors.

This was clearly going too far, and Joyce was on her way back to New York the very next day. But Hutchins insists Tom was fond of Joyce, and upset by the break-up.

Did he ever feel out of his depth with women? The late actress Diana Dors thinks so. She recalls meeting him early in his career, when 'It's Not Unusual' had just been released. They were together in a London nightclub, with blonde bombshell Diana's jealous boyfriend looking on. As she told it, Tom pulled her on to the dance floor 'and his discretion went right out of the window. Perhaps he thought with the dim lighting no one would see – or perhaps he just didn't care.'

Nothing came of that evening, and a year later Tom invited Diana and some friends to dinner at a hotel near his Shepperton home. He brought Linda along, and they all went back to their house for drinks. On the terrace, he explained to Diana all about his relationship with Linda, at the end of which she remarked: 'A pity, Tom, we would have made a great couple.'

'I know,' he replied, 'but I would always be afraid to make love to you. You always treat me like a child, and I'd be frightened that you would laugh at me.' In other words, Diana's playful sense of humour had made Mr Macho feel insecure about his sexual abilities.

By far the most public of all Tom Jones' affairs was the one which started late in 1973 with the then Miss World, Marjorie Wallace. It was a soap opera starring a world-class beauty queen and no less than four men who were eminent in the sports or entertainment fields, and at the time it became an obsession with London's tabloid newspapers.

At nineteen, Marjorie Wallace, the girlfriend of racing driver Peter Revson, had been voted Miss World in London by a panel of judges which included Engelbert Humperdinck. At the Miss World ball afterwards, Marjorie danced with British heavyweight boxing champion Joe Bugner, to the popping flashbulbs of news photographers. Hutchins urged Humperdinck to do a little more than dance with her if he wanted his picture in the next morning's papers – so on the dance floor, Humperdinck kissed the beauty queen full on the lips.

That started the scandal sheets gossiping, and Humperdinck did actually invite her to his show at the London Palladium a few days later. While Humperdinck was clearly interested, nothing came of the budding romance. But a month later, Tom Jones was at the Palladium, and Marjorie Wallace came backstage to see him. Tom insisted on being left alone with her in his dressing room for a few minutes,, and was obviously taken with her. Later that night, she joined him at his hotel.

Some weeks later, they met professionally, flying to Barbados for a BBC TV special called *Tom Jones on Happiness Island*. Julia Morley from Mecca, who ran both the Miss World competition and Marjorie's life during the year she held the title, was on the set to supervise. Tom was to sing a song to her called 'I Want To Make It With You', before the couple were to get into a romantic embrace, kissing passionately. Julie Morley tried to put her foot down about the kiss, but Marjorie ignored her, and it took place for millions of TV viewers to see later. On Barbados, according to Hutchins, the couple stayed together at Tom's rented house.

On her return to London, Marjorie became involved with the controversial soccer star George Best, and was seen out on the town with him. Tom had flown off to Holland to perform some concerts. Then Marjorie called police to her London hotel and claimed Best had stolen her fur coat and items of jewellery. Some gossip columnists added fuel to the flames, claiming that Marjorie's diary had gone missing – a diary in which she rated her lovers according to their sexual prowess. Tom Jones got a nine, said the gossips, while George Best only rated a three.

In court, Best denied the theft charges, claiming he and

Marjorie were lovers. He claimed that he and Marjorie had had sex in her hotel room, and that she had telephoned her boyfriend Peter Revson in America while Best was still in the room.

All this proved too alarming for Mecca, and Julia Morley announced Marjorie had been stripped of her title after 104 eventful days. Two weeks later, Peter Revson was killed in South Africa in a car crash.

Marjorie now turned to Tom for solace, and though the two rarely came face to face, they stayed in close touch by phone. Then two months later, Marjorie joined Tom for his opening at Caesar's Palace – another development in this astounding saga which received massive coverage. She was staying at his rented house, and the couple were not being particularly discreet about their fling.

But Hutchins arrived to advise them to be more low-key about the affair – and the two men decided Marjorie should leave town. She did, and returned to her parents' home in Indianapolis, taking with her a bottle of sleeping pills from Tom's bathroom. Two days later, she was in a coma in an Indianapolis hospital, having taken an overdose.

For days, she was on the critical list, though the news was initially kept from Tom in Vegas, where he was throwing himself a lavish thirty-fourth birthday bash, with guests like Liberace, Joan Rivers, Sonny Bono, Dionne Warwick and Debbie Reynolds in attendance.

Eventually, Marjorie pulled through. Tom sent a get-well message. Her father Del expressed thanks for Tom's friendship. Both the Jones and Wallace camps denied there had been an affair. Yet Hutchins insists the couple met five months later in Mexico City – and that he saw them again after that in Tom's suite at the Beverly Hills Hotel.

Given his background, one might not expect Tom Jones to hold enlightened or open-minded views on the subject of women and their place in life. And he doesn't. As one writer, Dennis Hunt, once put it: 'Tom Jones' position is that the doctrines of feminism are fine for every woman except his wife.'

Tom was once accused of sexism in a British magazine,but later defended himself against the charge. 'I was asked what type of women I like, and I said it all depended what you want them for. You see a sexy chick on the street in tight clothes and look at her and admire her. But I wouldn't want my wife to walk around like that. The type of woman I want is the type of woman who wants to be at home and be a housewife. As far as I'm concerned, my woman's place is in the home.'

On career women, he added: 'I must say there is nothing wrong with them. I just wouldn't want my wife to be one. Women can do what they want and get men's jobs with equal pay. I'm all for that. There has to be female truck drivers, female schoolteachers, female doctors, female dancers, female strippers and entertainers. They're all fine with me. I just wouldn't marry one.'

But, he was asked, isn't that a double standard? 'No, I don't think so,' he replied. 'That's the way I've always felt. It's a fair approach.'

In fact, his views on the different roles for men and women go far deeper. He once said: 'I think a woman's job is to serve her man. But men have let women go too far. They give them equal rights, and I don't believe in that. You talk to career women today, and they say: "How can I listen to him? I must do my own thing because I have no faith in him." But if a man is a man, a real man, then his woman will want to depend on him. When a woman goes with a guy, she sees something in him. It's not just a sexual need, but something in his character she likes, and she gives herself.

'A man will take any girl to bed, and it has nothing to do with any attraction for her or his love for his wife. A woman may like to think that she is the same, that she is equal, but she's not, because when she loves her man, she'll be faithful to him. You see, a woman's love for a man is greater than a man's love for a woman.'

Such views, of course, were hardly designed to win much respect among feminists. So it was a distinctly tongue-in-cheek gesture for America's National Association of Women to invite him to play at a Washington DC benefit, aimed at

raising funds for the Equal Rights Amendment. Tom played
for free. 'Women have been my greatest fans, and this is
something I can do for them,' he said – even though his
statements on equal rights seemed to contradict the aims of
the ERA.

The benefit concert, with tickets at $100, was prompted
by Midge Costanza, the highest-ranking woman in President
Jimmy Carter's administration. She described him on the night
as 'an international sexist, and talented and wonderful.' Diplo-
matically, Tom chose Tina Turner to open the show for him,
but even at the benefit, he sounded off again about the status
of women. He was all for the women's movement and equal
pay for equal work, he said. 'But I don't like to see women
sitting in bars, using bad language.'

Indeed, his attitude towards women can be rather courtly.
Nancy Eisner, who worked in the Jones camp as US tour
manager Lloyd Greenfield's assistant, remembers taking her
elderly mother to Tom's New York hotel suite to introduce
her. At the time he was surrounded by a group of influential
promoters, agents and bookers. 'Tom was the only person who
stood up to greet my Mom,' says Nancy. 'Afterwards she said:
"I don't care who the rest were. They were all pigs, and Tom
Jones was the only one with any manners." '

Nancy Eisner doesn't accept that Tom Jones is necessarily
a chauvinist. 'I don't believe he would stop a woman from
doing anything, as long as she was capable,' she says.

Tom Jones refused to discuss his affairs for years on the
grounds that such talk would hurt his wife Linda. On stage,
he used to sing the Billy Paul song 'Me and Mrs Jones', and
make it sound as if he was having an 'affair' with his wife. But
in interviews more recently, it has seemed that he is becoming
weary of maintaining the pretence.

In 1987, he told Lynda Lee-Potter of the *Daily Mail* about
Linda: 'She accepts that I'll have affairs, although she doesn't
go along with it, she doesn't say: "Oh, it's all right." She just
tells me: "Be careful." I've never wanted to have affairs, they
just happened, it's better if they don't.

'But I'm always honest about the fact that I'm married and

it's never going to change. It's putting your cards on the table before you play the game. I've always been made aware of my attraction, I can't remember not being aware.'

And similarly, when he was interviewed by music writer Adam Sweeting in 1989, he talked of the fact that Mary Wilson had written about their affair in her autobiography *Dreamgirl*. 'That was like getting caught out twice,' he told Sweeting, who wrote that he was chuckling entirely without embarrassment. 'I haven't had any affairs for a long time – and most of them were brief encounters anyway.'

Chapter Nine

MEGABUCKS

Jo Mills still remembers vividly how the change from rags to riches took place in the lives of Tom Jones and Gordon Mills. It happened right at the point that Tom hit number one in the British charts in 1965 with 'It's Not Unusual'.

'That completely transformed our lives,' she says. 'It was very exciting. Within a couple of weeks of going to the top of the charts, bagfuls of post came in. It was so hectic. Bit by bit I began a fan club. I had a hand-run Gestetner machine. I typed a letter out myself to the first fifty fans. I'd never typed before.

'Eventually we had half a dozen people working for us, and we were deluged with mail. Very soon, Tom had another hit, and it was an unbelievable time as far as the money was concerned. One moment we were absolutely skint, and the next we were able to buy our own house. It was a fairy tale.'

It was also the start of one of the most financially successful enterprises in British entertainment history. And yet just three months before, according to Jo Mills: 'Nobody had any money. Tom had gone back to Wales over Christmas, I had no more earnings from modelling to come, we were up to £1,000 in debt to the bank, and they wouldn't give us any more overdraft. I think that was Tom's lowest ebb.'

But instant success changed everything, as Jo Mills would find. 'Things just got busier and busier. The house was always full of reporters and agents and businessmen. I don't know

how we coped through it. The phones never stopped, sec-
retaries, accountants and business advisers arrived, and the
whole thing mushroomed. More exciting things happened all
the time. And Gordon's friend Gerry Dorsey was always asking
Gordon to do for him what he'd done for Tom.'

At this time, Gerry Dorsey was a struggling singer pushing thirty and wondering whether his career would ever go
anywhere. He had met Gordon Mills when Gordon was still
a member of the Viscounts; Gerry by this time had made a
couple of records for Decca which had flopped, and he
was trying to make ends meet on the working men's club
circuit.

The two men shared digs together in London in the
early 1960's, before Gerry contracted tuberculosis and spent
seven months recuperating in hospital. Gordon assumed his
pal's career was finished, but stayed in touch with him, and
within the space of a few months, they were best men at each
other's weddings; Gordon married a stunning fashion model
named Jo Waring, and Gerry wed a secretary called Pat Healy
from Leicester, the town in which he had grown up.

Around this time, Gordon made what looked like a risky
move by quitting the Viscounts, gambling that songwriting
could be a more lucrative future for him. He did moderately
well, writing 'Hungry for Love' and 'I'll Never Get Over You'
for Johnny Kidd and the Pirates, and 'Three Little Words' for
the Applejacks, all of which were hits. Even so, Gordon knew
the competition was fierce, and reckoned that managing other
artists might be his forté. At this point, of course, he had not
met Tom Jones.

But in the first year that Tom's career assumed whirlwind
proportions, Gerry Dorsey's was languishing. He believed his
best bet was for Gordon to take control of his affairs, and
hope for the magic touch which had worked for Tom Jones.
So meteoric was Tom's rise – with an American tour and
two follow-up hits in 'With These Hands' and 'What's New
Pussycat?' in 1965 alone – that Gordon literally had no time
to devote to Gerry Dorsey.

When he did, and when he agreed to manage him, he

shocked Gerry by announcing he wanted to change his name – to Engelbert Humperdinck.

Gordon had seen the intriguing name on an old classical record, the music to *Hansel and Gretel* by the oddly named nineteenth-century composer. Gerry balked at first, but finally conceded Gordon might know what he was doing. Gordon for his part insisted that Engelbert Humperdinck was a name no one would forget.

He was right in that regard. Engelbert got a recording contract with Decca largely because executives there were so intrigued by the idea of someone with such a name. Two singles were released which aroused mild interest, and then Gordon pulled a stroke of genius for Engelbert by insisting he record a soulful ballad called 'Release Me', which had been an American hit for Little Esther Phillips, but which was virtually unknown in Britain.

At the beginning of 1966, the record was released. It was helped by a terrific TV plug – Engelbert got to sing it on *Sunday Night at the London Palladium*, deputizing for Dickie Valentine, who was ill with flu – and it reached number one in the charts, where it stayed for five weeks and sold a million copies.

So Gordon now had two singers under his control, both with skyrocketing careers. Some critics charged that Engelbert was an attempt by Gordon to clone Tom, but Gordon kept the image of the two separate in his mind. Tom was a hot, sexy rock 'n' roller, while Engelbert was a more sensitive, romantic balladeer. The fact that both men wore tuxedoes on stage was the only common denominator.

The year 1966 gave Gordon Mills' two artists two of the biggest hits of the year – Engelbert with 'Release Me', and Tom with 'Green, Green Grass of Home', a song Tom had heard on a Jerry Lee Lewis country album. The melancholy melody had homecoming as its theme, as does that Welsh anthem 'There'll Be A Welcome In the Hillsides', and somehow it seemed quite appropriate for a Welshman to be singing it. The record moved quickly to the top of the British charts, and stayed there seven weeks.

Jo Mills has another theory for the song's success. 'It coincided with the Aberfan disaster (in which a slag heap had collapsed on top of a small mining village, engulfing the community's tiny school and killing scores of children). It hit home at the heart of the people.'

Jo gives Gordon the credit for finding the song for Tom, though Tom claims he heard it first himself. Either way, Tom and Engelbert and Gordon were off and running.

By 1969, the three men were raking in so much money through record sales, concert appearances and American tours that it became almost impossible to know how to spend it. Gordon determined that each of them should live in accommodation fit for high-earning pop superstars. He moved his own family into a house in the elite St George's Hill area of Weybridge – once home to Beatles John Lennon and George Harrison as well as Cliff Richard. With typical Welsh sentimentality Gordon re-named his huge mansion on seven acres of terraced gardens 'Little Rhondda'.

Tom and Engelbert also moved to St George's Hill with their newly acquired Rolls-Royces, and the three men and their families were all now living within a mile of each other. It reinforced the notion of an exclusive club, with just three members.

Tom moved into a mansion which he named Torpoint, which was guarded by iron gates, and hired a security patrol to keep inquisitive fans away. Immediately, he started to build a fitness complex in the house, with a sauna and swimming pool.

By 1971, Gordon's house had become the nerve centre of their business empire. He ran it from a surprisingly small ground-floor room. The airy, rambling house had four garages with Rolls-Royces and Mercedes cars in them. Rather eccentrically, he also had a small zoo of exotic animals on the grounds.

An article in *Life* magazine from this time depicts the three men as brothers, with Gordon the eldest. He chose every song his artists sang, supervised every arrangement, approved every booking and made all the business decisions. 'He'll decide on something and say: "That's it!" ' said Tom with a shrug. 'It's open and shut.'

How firm was Gordon's grasp on the two men? Gordon, on the phone from America, once got Engelbert to stop a recording session in London. 'Engelbert,' said Gordon by transatlantic phone, 'I don't like the way you're doing "My Marie". Put more guts into it.' Click. Engelbert put more guts into it.

The money that was now pouring in was of quite extraordinary proportions. By the start of 1970, the *Los Angeles Herald Examiner* could report that Tom was receiving $150,000 for a single appearance. *Life* magazine noted that no entertainer before Tom ever got $100,000 against 75 per cent of the gross for a single concert.

The only trouble in this paradise was Britain's Inland Revenue, which took huge chunks of the three men's incomes. Gordon asked for a solution to this dilemma, and his chief accountant, Bill Smith, came up with the idea of forming a company.

It was to be called MAM, which stood for Management and Agency Music, and Messrs Mills, Jones and Humperdinck were its three directors. MAM now launched itself on to the stock market, with the initial share price of 66 pence.

'That was the first time it had ever happened,' recalls Sylvia Harrison, who worked for American tour manager Lloyd Greenfield. 'The first time stock was ever traded when the assets were singers. Under this arrangement Tom and Engelbert didn't get fees for appearances. Instead, they were shareholders, the money went into the corporation, and they got dividends. I'd pay the boys the expenses, the travel, whatever came out of their account, and the balance would go into the main company.'

Obviously, now that MAM was a public company, its main assets had to be insured. Its main assets, of course, were Tom and Engelbert, who were initially insured for $2.4 million, then for $4.6 million. Annual premiums on the two stars' lives were a staggering $50,000 each.

Jo Mills reflects: 'Gordon was not a businessman. He

was a music man, but he had to become a businessman as chairman of a public company.' And MAM was effective – it meant a tremendous amount of tax relief for Gordon, Tom and Engelbert. City investors were keen to get into the act; initially Tom's shares were worth half a million pounds, but within weeks of the first stock offering, they had tripled in value.

Later, MAM would be an entity which owned hotels, a marina and an agency which leased fruit machines and jukeboxes to pubs and clubs. MAM also became a record label in its own right, and its first single, 'I Hear You Knocking' by Welsh rock singer Dave Edmunds, went to number one on the charts. Mickey Gee, formerly one of Tom's Squires, played rhythm guitar on the record.

At this point, a third protégé of Gordon Mills arrived on the scene. He was a young Irish-born art student and singer-songwriter named Raymond O'Sullivan, who had written to Gordon, enclosing some tapes of his songs. Gordon liked the material, and determined that Raymond would be groomed as his next big star. He seemed unlikely material. Unlike Tom and Engelbert, who were both ruggedly attractive, Raymond was pale, baby-faced and shy to the point of mumbling when he talked. Clearly, Gordon couldn't put him in a tuxedo and send him out on the road to woo audiences of mature housewives.

Instead, Gordon decided to make the most of Raymond's limitations and exploit his awkward boyishness. He dressed him like a scruffy Depression-era schoolboy, in baggy three-quarter length trousers, a flat cap and a striped tie, with long socks and hobnail boots. He looked a little like an overgrown version of the hero of Richmal Crompton children's book, *Just William*.

Still, Raymond was a Gordon Mills protégé, which meant that, like Tom Woodward and Gerry Dorsey before him, his name would have to change. Gordon re-christened him Gilbert O'Sullivan, and after a year of coaching him, unleashed him on the world.

The first reaction on the part of the public was amusement. Gilbert O'Sullivan did not look like a rock star. He didn't have long hair, or glittery eye make-up or tight pants, like most performers in that era of 'glam-rock'.

But he could sing, and he could certainly write songs. 'Alone Again, Naturally', 'Clair' and 'We Will' were big hits for him within months. The unlikely Gilbert O'Sullivan was further proof of Gordon Mills' Midas touch.

Gordon treated him like a young son. For the first year, he kept him on £10 a week pocket money – a gesture which would later come back to haunt him. Gilbert baby-sat for Gordon's children (the song 'Clair' is about one of Gordon's daughters) and generally kept a low profile. But he too moved from his Notting Hill flat to St George's Hill, Weybridge, to a house smaller than those of his older singing colleagues, but luxurious nevertheless. He also bought a car from Tom, a Mercedes that had hardly been driven.

The money kept rolling in. Between them, Gordon, Tom and Engelbert at one time had eight Rolls-Royces and four Mercedes. They shared a £750,000 custom-built jet, which turned out to be a waste of money; all three men commuted mainly between England and America, and the jet could not hold enough fuel to cross the Atlantic. Its maintenance costs were astronomical, and after MAM tried leasing it out to wealthy businessmen, it was sold.

Tom, meanwhile, was discovering that there was no way to escape the British taxman. As his earnings grew, he found himself being increasingly squeezed as a high earner. Things came to a head when the Labour government returned to power in 1974. 'I was out of the country at the time,' he recalls, 'and in February of that year, I got a call from my accountant Bill Smith, saying: "You will have to seriously consider not coming home, because they're going to kill you with the tax." '

By this time, he was making in the region of £5 million a year, and reckoned that from the beginning of his career he had paid the British government something like £7 million in income tax. The situation was clearly only going to get worse for high earners like himself; something had to be done.

'I thought to myself: I'm coming to America every summer

for seven or eight months, going home for the winter and then paying a lot of tax in the process. It wouldn't have made much sense to keep doing that. The tax was 98 per cent on unearned income, 84 per cent on earned income, and 15 per cent with-holding tax in the States. So for two years, I just kept on the move until I got my Green Card [a permit to work full-time in America].'

These were a bizarre couple of years in Tom's life, in which he carefully had to calculate how many days each year he could stay in the United States without being severely penalized by America's Internal Revenue Service.

His entire work schedule revolved around these critical factors. Essentially, even a brief return to Britain was ruled out – and his tax problems would keep him away from his native country for almost a decade.

'When the exile began, I was touring America, and Mark and Linda were back home,' he said in 1983. There was another strange twist: 'I'd just bought a 1,300-acre farm in Sussex with Gordon and Engelbert, which I'd never even seen and couldn't go back to see.

'I was in a position that I couldn't go back to Britain, or I'd get clobbered by taxes, so there I was, touring and doing very well in America. And yet that was a problem too, because I also faced getting hit for American taxes. So I was quite homeless, and I was dodging around all over the place. I couldn't spend more than six months any year in America, and I couldn't go home. Any time I wasn't working, I'd shoot down to Mexico, and stay in Acapulco. A real exile.' He flashed a sheepish grin. 'Yeah, I know, stuck in Acapulco, sounds terrible, right? Hearts and flowers stuff. But it was a time when nothing felt permanent.'

This uneasy period wasn't without its amusing times, though. 'Sometimes in order to keep working,' he recalled, 'I'd cut the timing in getting out of America very fine. One time, I'd come to the end of a concert tour, and I had to be out of America that same night, by midnight. If I stayed over, I was easy pickings for the taxman. I was playing in Long Beach, California, that night, and John Wayne had lent me his yacht to sail out of US waters. I finished the show, dashed right offstage into a waiting limo, changed my clothes in the car as it raced to the harbour, and there was John's yacht, waiting with engines running to get me out of the twelve-mile limit.'

On the whole, though, this strategy of living like a fugitive took its toll. In order to see Linda, he had to meet her and Mark on 'neutral' territory in France or Belgium. But during this period in exile, Mark came out to America and spent time on the road with his father. 'I didn't like doing all that,' said Tom, 'but it did save me a lot of money. The move was made for all the right reasons.'

The next step, though, was to find a permanent residence in America, so that his family would have a single base. In 1976, he paid $1,000,000 for a house on the prestigious Bel-Air estate in Los Angeles – $200,000 below the asking price.

The house had belonged to singer Dean Martin, and it is situated on a street named Copa de Oro. One has to be a multi-millionaire in order to live in Bel-Air – it may be the most expensive neighbourhood in the world. The sixteen-room house, completed in 1940, is an anomaly on this exclusive street, where Spanish-style architecture predominates; it is built entirely in red brick, which is highly unusual in southern California. It has been reinforced to offer protection against a possible earthquake. But the house's uniqueness is not apparent from the street – it is completely walled off, and one must pass through high electric gates emblazoned with Welsh dragons in order to enter.

This manor house is built in the style of the eighteenth-century architect Adam. The red brick was what first caught Tom's eye – if anything in this decidedly non-British corner of southern California could remind him of home, this house could. He even saw similarities between this house and his Weybridge mansion, Torpoint. He was also taken by the house's pool – at 45 feet by 25 feet, large even by Bel-Air standards.

Now he had a Green Card, Tom could afford to make this his permanent residence, and pay US taxes, which are structured to favour higher earners. He persuaded the reluctant Linda to make Bel-Air her full-time home, and had their furniture from Torpoint shipped out to America.

To one of the authors who visited the house on Copa de Oro, it seems very much a man's home. Outside, you park your car next to a spotlit fountain. Inside, there is a lot of wood panelling, high-beamed ceilings and chandeliers. The TV room/library has mahogany panelling, and brass and pewter ornaments abound. The dining room seats twelve, the breakfast room six. The living room, with its Victorian-style furniture and deep blue sofas and chairs, seems large enough to contain four or five of those squat little Welsh corner pubs in which Tom spent his adolescent years. A spiral staircase takes you from the broad hallway to the four upstairs bedrooms. In the house's basement, Tom has had a fully equipped gymnasium built. Inside what looks like a medieval turret attached to the house, there is more fitness equipment. There is a screening room with projection equipment, a fireplace and a well-stocked bar.

One reaches the pool by passing flower beds lavishly filled with exotic plants, like oleanders, hibiscus and bougainvillaeas. There are also red roses – which are not easy to grow in this climate and are an uncommon sight. The pool itself is extraordinary, a massive expanse of sparkling blue water surrounded by terracotta sculpture, statues of Roman maidens, and little open-mouthed fish at all four corners. A therapy pool bubbles nearby.

The personal touches in this mansion seem to be nearly all his, and betray a deep attachment to his earlier days in Britain. In the hall hang his gold records, and awards from music papers. In the library are pictures of him with the rich and famous. In the living room, on a shelf, perches a British bobby's helmet. There are mugs with Union Jacks on them. And in the garden there is an old-fashioned British phone box, for which he paid £250, and imported. 'When I was a kid, I used to phone my missus from a box like this one on Tower Street,' he said. The box still has the Button A and Button B box inside, and dates from the time when a phone call used to cost fourpence.

Minor inconveniences cloud this palatial lifestyle. Tour buses, filled with gawping tourists hoping to catch a glimpse of Tom, stop by at the front gate. The house is easy to find – as Dean Martin's abode, it was already a scheduled stop for the tour buses.

'People were always stopping by with cameras,' recalls Tom. 'They'd hang around and wait for you to come out. One couple spread a blanket out on the front lawn and ate their lunch! So I had to put the fences and gates up. And that means I can't go out much any more.'

Still, the megabucks kept coming, and Tom Jones persisted in a pattern which had characterized his rise to fame – he was always very generous to his parents, Tom and Freda Woodward. He bought them a succession of houses to ensure their comfort and to keep them near to his own home base. Back in England, when Tom had sold his first house in Shepperton, and bought a place in nearby Sunbury-on-Thames, he gave his parents the Shepperton house. When Tom moved on to St George's Hill, Weybridge, he bought his parents another house in Weybridge to keep them close. He also had his sister Sheila and her husband Ken Davies live in a lodge on the grounds of Torpoint, and employed Ken as a groundsman.

And now he had moved to Bel-Air, he did precisely the same thing – he bought his parents a house in the very same neighbourhood. His sister Sheila came to live with them; she had divorced Ken Davies, who had left her for another woman, something which made him distinctly unpopular with Tom and his father.

Freda Woodward can actually look from her terraced garden, with its magnificent views of Los Angeles, and point to nearby houses belonging to superstars Sylvester Stallone and Barry Manilow. Her million-dollar property is light years removed from 44 Laura Street, Treforest, where her husband used to come home from the pit and take a bath in a zinc tub in the kitchen. But inside, the same down-to-earth hospitality that one might find in the Rhondda still exists. In the afternoon, tea and biscuits are served to guests; the teapot has a patterned wool tea-cosy. Undeniably, Tom Jones and his tight-knit family have retained some fundamental values.

Tom's permanent move to Los Angeles had been Gordon's idea, and both he and Engelbert also moved to southern California. Jo Mills persuaded Gordon not to sell Little Rhondda, and she stayed there. Gilbert O'Sullivan, who was not in the same earnings bracket as the other two singers, stayed in Weybridge.

Unhappily, Gordon had to dismantle the private zoo he had kept at Little Rhondda. He had started it when he saw that his friend, gambling club owner John Aspinall, had one in the grounds of his house. Gordon decided to emulate John, but then animals became an obsession for him. 'From the day we met, Gordon went to bed with a book on animals,' jokes Jo Mills. 'How we had five children, don't ask me.

'We had a wonderfully kept private zoo at Little Rhondda. Over the years, we had a lot of different animals but his main thing was tigers, gorillas and orang-utans. Once a jaguar got out, just after my daughters had been going round the drive on their bicycles. Nobody realized it had escaped. We managed to lure it back with bait; we didn't have to dart it.'

In southern California, the climate was too harsh for Gordon's animals to be cared for privately, so he donated seven orang-utans and five gorillas to the San Diego Zoo. One of them fathered the first baby gorilla born there in twenty years; the baby was named Gordon.

Now that the three main protagonists in MAM were uprooted and living in America, the pressure on their relationships began to show. Engelbert Humperdinck was becoming increasingly restless about his role in the organization, and genuinely believed that he was playing second fiddle to Tom Jones.

In some ways, he had some justification in feeling this way. Tom had become a star before Engelbert, if only by a year, and Engelbert always felt he was playing catch-up. Tom had had a number one record before Engelbert, Tom was a star in Las Vegas by the time Gordon had managed to secure for Engelbert a lucrative contract at the Riviera Hotel and casino. Tom was a little younger than Engelbert, his act was more dynamic, and when critics compared the two men (which they inevitably did) Tom was usually held in higher regard.

But in the 1970s, Engelbert's attitude hardened. He was a little more cautious with money than Gordon or Tom, and he believed they were needlessly extravagant in their lifestyles – which were paid for with company money. Another bone of contention for Engelbert was Gordon's obsession with getting Tom into movies. This was a project which took up much of Gordon's valuable time – time which Engelbert believed could have been spent on him.

'Gordon fancied Tom more than he fancied Engelbert, and that's all there was to it,' says Sylvia Harrison. 'Gordon regarded Engel as a meal ticket, and that was it.'

She tells a story which accurately reveals the delicate balance in the relationships. 'I was working for Lloyd Greenfield [Gordon's right hand man in America and Tom's US tour manager] in New York, and whenever Engelbert came to play in the vicinity, I'd be the one sent out to look after him. When he was out at Westbury [near New York City], I had to go out there and listen to Engelbert's shit. He complained a lot.

'When he was in New York one night, he wouldn't go on stage and Gordon called me at home and said: "Go over there, you're the only one who can persuade Engelbert to go on." I went over there and sat in his dressing room, and listened to him rabbiting away for half an hour, then I said, "Come on, put your knickers on, and let's go."

'He said he didn't like the room he was playing, and he didn't like the people. Eng's rather melodramatic. He needs to feel that he's important, he needs a little bit of "Come on, Eng, do it, do it for me."

'And he said: "It's not that I don't love you, Sylvia, but why do they always send you instead of Gordon coming out here?" He knew that had it been Tom complaining, Gordon would have been there like a shot.He felt like the poor relation.'

Even back in the 1970s, says Sylvia Harrison, Tom and Engelbert did not get on particularly well. 'If they were in the same room, they would treat each other coolly. I think someone was in the middle, mixing it up a little – and I think it was Gordon, trying to keep them away from each other. It was a case of divide and rule.'

Jo Mills adds: 'Tom and Engelbert had periods of speaking and not speaking – they'd get back together and at the end of a good night, they'd both get roaring drunk and have a fight again.'

In 1977, Engelbert split from Gordon and Tom, and branched out on his own. He stressed that his problems were with Gordon, and denied that there was any rivalry between him and Tom. He simply wanted to have a greater say in his own career.

Since the split, he has continued to make a good living from concerts and personal appearances. Like Tom, he plays Las Vegas and Atlantic City, and continues to have an enthusiastic following abroad.

After Gordon's death, he and Tom made a sort of uneasy peace with each other. In 1987, Tom said: 'We are talking again. When he fell out with Gordon, he went his own way. We never kept in touch because I think he felt awkward about it. He did not want to call, because he thought Gordon would intervene. If I had met him on the street or anywhere, I would have spoken to him, but we never had any contact. I think he felt more that we were not talking, whereas I did not.

'When Gordon died, Eng said that he felt awkward going to the funeral because he was worried about how others would receive him, like Gordon's mother. So he stayed away rather than cause an upset. I said to him: "Why didn't you give me a call?" And he said: "Why didn't you give *me* a call?" I said, "For Christ's sake, let's not start all that over again." He also said that he had wanted to see Gordon in hospital, and he said he was told not to go. He said that it came back to him that he would not be welcome. I said, "Well, that's up to you, it's not for somebody else to tell you." Obviously, I had gone to see him right away, but then again I was close to Gordon all the time. There were never any differences between us like that.'

Still, as Tom tells it, Gordon's death left Engelbert with a lot of unresolved feelings. 'He called me up and said: "Let's get together again," and I said, "Fine." It's never been any other way with me. He came to see my show in Vegas, and then we had dinner afterwards. He said, "I want to be friends again." I said, "Come on, there was never any animosity on my side. You were the one who split from Gordon. Whatever your idea was about Gordon it was your own. It was nothing to do with me. Let's leave Gordon at rest, and leave it at that."

'Then a few weeks later, I did the same thing – I went to see his second show and have dinner. And we talked about the old days when we all went on holiday together, and when we all lived on St George's Hill in Weybridge.'

Still, those close to the two men agree that the relationship between them has remained cool. Engelbert, says one source who worked with him in the late 1980s, remains embittered by the whole experience, and still harbours resentment for what he regarded as Tom Jones' preferential treatment by Gordon. 'I heard that they had dinner together a couple of times,' says Sylvia Harrison, 'but that they don't see that much of each other. The fact is, they don't have an awful lot in common. They're very different people.'

After Engelbert's departure, it was Gilbert O'Sullivan's turn to become disenchanted. Though he had never sustained as successful a career as Tom or Engelbert, there was a period when he was selling as many records as any artist in the world – and he had made a substantial contribution to swelling MAM's coffers. In 1982, he sued Gordon and MAM for half of the estimated £14.5 million he had earned over the years, and a judge ruled in his favour, noting that Gilbert had been fleeced and exploited.

Clearly, the heady days of the 1970s were over for MAM, which would eventually be swallowed up by the larger Chrysalis entertainment group. After the O'Sullivan affair, Gordon, clearly chastened, went back to his obsession – searching for the right movie script for Tom Jones, the only major artist he still retained.

Chapter Ten

THE INNER CIRCLE

It often happens that when an entertainer becomes wealthy and famous, he draws round him a tightly knit circle of friends and co-workers who socialize with him, and also form a kind of protection from the world outside.

Some of these people are little more than hangers-on. They're glorified errand boys, really. They laugh a little too loudly at the boss's jokes even when they're not that funny. They fetch and carry. They act as part-time chauffeurs. They accommodate the star's smallest whims, as well as his most outrageous. They say 'yes' a lot.

The most obvious example of this phenomenon is the Memphis Mafia, the crowd of good ol' boys who used to hang around with Elvis Presley in Las Vegas and at his Tennessee home, Graceland. The Memphis Mafia, according to a number of books written about Presley, became his entire social life; they stayed within sight of the King like so many shadows. Essentially, of course, most of them were leeches without a real job function. But if Elvis was prepared to have them around, why, they'd stay, and enjoy the perks of the job – free food and drink, tons of available women, a glimpse of a genuinely glamorous lifestyle, and very little honest toil. If one can believe the stories, being around Elvis and the Memphis Mafia for a while was the height of boredom, since none of them was intelligent or made decent conversation. Of course, the Memphis Mafia had a high tolerance for boredom.

Frank Sinatra did things slightly differently when he surrounded himself with his Rat Pack. For a start, he was in his forties when he started carousing with this wild bunch of compatriots. And Sinatra handpicked his buddies not from the ranks of old school-age friends, but from other entertainers who shared a taste for high living, fast women, extravagant spending and slightly bad behaviour.

When Tom Jones first started touring regularly in America, he kept a tight-knit group of friends and co-workers around him. But this did not mean he had succumbed to the flattery implicit in having a big group of buddies around him wherever he went; rather, it was a sign of a slight insecurity, of feeling like an unsophisticated stranger in a strange land.

There was another big difference between Tom Jones' retinue and those of earlier stars. Sinatra and Presley were unquestionably the acknowledged leaders of their respective packs. Elvis was the King of the Memphis Mafia; the Rat Pack referred respectfully to Sinatra as the Chairman of the Board. There was no mistaking who deferred to whom.

And while he was on the road, Tom Jones was the boss to his entourage for most of the time. Until, that is, Gordon Mills came into town. And at that point, everyone – Tom Jones included – deferred to him.

Quite where Gordon Mills established his strength of personality is not clear. Having a singer as successful as Tom Jones, and then another as successful as Engelbert Humperdinck, can certainly do wonders for a man's self-image. But those who know him insist that Gordon had remarkable self-confidence even when he was broke. The fact is that when Gordon Mills arrived to join the tour party, he called the shots, and everyone picked up on his cues.

Gordon tended to join the tour party for the most glamorous big-city engagements. 'Vegas, maybe New York, Chicago, Los Angeles,' remembers Roger Wall, who was road manager for Tom Jones from 1973 to 1980. 'Sometimes in Vegas, he'd stay for the whole engagement. There, he oversaw the show. It seemed to me he set the show up. He had a pretty firm hand on the creative side.'

Gordon had a pretty firm hand on the self-indulgence side, too. He could party with the best of them, and enjoyed the company of the women who hung around the tour party as much as the next man. Maybe more than the next man. 'Gordon was a philanderer, just like Tom,' says his ex-wife Jo Mills flatly. 'Linda could live with that, but I couldn't.'

One woman who hung around the tour party on the early American tours remembers: 'The group were very good fun. I remember Tom as being OK, but everyone around him as being much more fun. Gordon without question was in control. I firmly believe much of this [party scene] was Gordon living vicariously. On a personal level, being able to score women, he was right up there with Tom. He was bright, very bright, and he had more charisma than any of them. He could be tough, but he did it with a lot of charm.

'My recollection is that he played Tom very well. He knew just how much lead to give him, but on some subtle level, he was always in charge.'

It's an intriguing notion, this balance of power. On stage, the dynamic, sexually aggressive Tom Jones whipped his fans into a frenzy – but at parties backstage, it was Gordon Mills who drew people like a magnet. You couldn't exactly imagine old Colonel Tom Parker butting into Elvis' parties and taking over. As for Frank Sinatra – well, who even remembers who managed him?

The key to this strange imbalance may lie in the contrast between the two men. Whereas everyone agrees Tom is a simple, straightforward character, Gordon is widely perceived as complex.

'I felt he was moody,' says Roger Wall. 'He'd have mood swings. He was a Taurus, and I'm a Taurus, so I think I understand that part. Tom's a Gemini, and they're often split characters, but I've never seen that stuff. If he had a double side, I was never privy to it. He was always one way to me.

'Gordon always seemed preoccupied. There was always something going on in his mind. There were thoughts going on. He seemed to find it very hard to relax. Tom, on the other hand, could relax anywhere, anytime.'

Tom himself endorsed this view of Gordon. 'He can't relax,' he once said. 'He keeps saying he's got to get a holiday, but when he gets one he can't relax. I was down in Acapulco, you know, and Gordon calls me up and says: "What are you doing?" And I say: "I'm just sitting by the pool, relaxing." The next thing you know, he's saying to me: "Yeah, but what is there to do?" '

Jo Mills also saw her ex-husband in the same light. 'One thing about Tom that I always envied was that when he was with Linda, he was loving and caring. I think in his way he did love her. But when Gordon was with me, after just as much separation, his mind was on so many other things, and he was just as busy. Tom could cut off when he was home.'

Another factor that made the inner circle respect Gordon was that a certain reputation preceded him. Roger Wall remembers: 'I was a bit intimidated by him in the beginning. I heard these things about him months before I met him, about how tough he was, and you start to wonder – what is this man about? But he was very pleasant. I never had any problems with him.'

Roger Wall doesn't buy the theory that Tom Jones was a sort of surrogate for Gordon Mills' fantasies. 'They're two completely different people,' he adds. 'But I can see how the combination of Gordon and Tom worked, especially in the early years. I can see how one worked off the other. But I don't think Tom has any desire to run a corporation. All he wants to do is sing.' And Gordon? 'Well,' says Roger Wall, shaking his head in a puzzled manner, 'I've never really understood Gordon.'

Nor has Nancy Eisner, who worked for Gordon in New York, then Los Angeles. 'Gordon knew a lot,' she says. 'He was difficult, remote, and hard to read. He had an artistic temperament.' Alluding to his obsession with wild animals, Nancy adds: 'I don't think he exactly loved human beings.'

Still, she thought he could have been a performer of some distinction. 'I remember him singing a song he'd written for Tom, called "Hey, Mr Man in the Moon', and I had to tell him that though I thought Tom had a great voice, I liked the way Gordon sang it better. It's often the way when you hear composers – like Hoagy Carmichael – singing their own material. It just had a lot of heart, the way Gordon did it.'

The relationship between Tom and Gordon set the tone for the entire entourage. Gordon's daughter Beverly says: 'Tom trusted Dad implicitly to do everything for him. They used to argue, sometimes long into the night, but not about anything to do with work. Dad was in charge there, and that was the beginning and end of it. They would sit up and argue about politics or history until 6 a.m.'

Annie Toomaru, who was Gordon's girlfriend right up until his death, remembers: 'Gordon was a great person to be around, and I loved his sense of humour. He was very sporting, very outgoing.' The two men, she says, were both fun to be around. 'Tom couldn't go to bed before 6 or 7. Every night was a party. It was like a big family. Tom likes to party, and Gordon did too. When they were together, he was drinking a lot. I taught him to cut back on drinking; when I first met him, he drank a lot of wine every night, and after that, cognac.'

Several people who were interviewed for this book expressed the opinion that Gordon Mills was a more intriguing story than Tom Jones. 'If you're writing a book about the Tom Jones story, you're really writing the Gordon Mills story,' said one ex-member of the tour party, who declined to be interviewed.

Gordon Mills, then, was clearly the man with the leadership qualities, the most ease in social situations, and the more forceful personality. It's intriguing to speculate what might have become of him had he tried his hand in other fields. Politics? Industry? Gordon gave everyone the impression that no matter what he had done, he would have done it supremely well.

At first the touring group in America – the musicians, the road crew, technicians – were at least half British. 'They were a very loyal group of people,' says the woman who joined the touring party in 1969. 'All the band, the first road manager. They were all real party people. I can't remember ever meeting anyone's wife. They would show up more at Vegas than on summer tours.

'After the shows, they'd stay up all night long, drinking, playing poker, playing pool, sitting around and talking. And there was plenty of screwing around. A lot of drink was drunk, and I remember some of the guys being very crude. But I don't remember Tom ever being rude or being a bad drunk. He did drink gallons of Dom Perignon and was sometimes the worse for wear afterwards. Certainly if anyone spends eight hours drinking champagne, it's going to have its effect.'

One of the people closest to Tom in his touring group at this time was Big Jim Sullivan, formerly an accomplished session guitarist, who had joined the Tom Jones back-up band. Sources describe the popular Big Jim as one of the nicer people in the entourage. 'He would spend time to talk to people at the parties after the shows,' said one. 'He wasn't always looking over his shoulder to look for girls. He had time for people.'

When Tom was not around, Lloyd Greenfield was left in charge of sorting out the logistics of the tour. Lloyd was essentially Gordon's man in the US, and until the mid-1980s was based in New York City. He was a Jewish New Yorker who, say those close to the Jones camp, had none of Gordon's charisma or charm. One source described him as being like 'some guy in some small agency, representing the Catskills – and suddenly he lands on his feet with the hottest sex symbol in the world.' Still, Lloyd is bound by marriage to the Jones camp – he married one of Tom's back-up singers.

But if Lloyd was nominally the most important member of the management team on the road, then 'Gog' Jones was Gordon Mills' eyes and ears. In part, this was because he and Gordon went back a long way, all the way back to the Rhondda Valley, in fact.

Gog had been a schoolfriend of Gordon's, back in Tonypandy. Gog had also been a friend of Johnny Bennett of the Bennett family with whom Gordon had played harmonica as a youngster. Gog had also arrived with Gordon the night Gordon dropped in to the Top Hat Club in Cwmtellery, and first seen Tom Jones performing. Gog had also worked with Gordon as a bus conductor for a spell. By the time Gordon and Tom arrived in America, Gog had known Gordon for twenty years.

It was Gog who now accompanied Gordon when he went on safaris to Africa to gaze upon the wild animals he loved so much in their natural habitat.

But in the end, Gog tired of life in America and life on the road. He was homesick, and he wanted to go back to the Welsh valleys whence he came. Unhappily, once he did get back to Wales, his life apparently seemed dull and unexciting to him, and he could see no future. Neither could he go back to Gordon. Tragically, he died, in circumstances that suggested he had taken his own life. 'He was very quiet,' recalled Sylvia Harrison, who worked for Lloyd. 'He never seemed happy in America – but when he went back home, he found he had nothing.'

Another safari partner of Gordon's was Johnnie Spence, Tom's musical director when he first started touring America regularly. Spence had made a name for himself as an orchestral arranger in Britain before going to America with Tom and Gordon.

Johnnie was quite a character, a strong forceful personality with a dramatic presence one did not easily forget. He sported fashionably long hair, even though he was in his thirties. And he walked with a pronounced limp.

But he was an extraordinary showman. The sight of Johnnie brandishing his baton, his long hair flailing around his head, used to astound audiences. And when he was musical director fffor singer Paul Anka, Johnnie was given a couple of instrumental numbers to perform – which regularly brought the house down. He led the Johnnie Spence Orchestra on Tom's successful TV series, too.

A talented film composer, he scored the movie *Panic in Echo Park* and was working on another movie, *Spiderman*, in 1977, when he collapsed suddenly and died at the age of forty-one. His death was a great shock to Gordon, Tom and the entire Jones camp. On the strength of Tom's American success, he had settled in America, and had bought a house in the fashionable Los Angeles suburb of Encino, where he lived with his wife, daughter and son. He was a major loss to the entourage.

Another important person in the early days was Tom's publicist, the controversial Chris Hutchins. In 1966, he was working as a pop journalist, as news editor on the *New Musical Express*. But it was a limited line of work, with indifferent pay, and Hutchins wanted out. He saw in Tom Jones a vehicle that would transport him to an entirely better style of life.

Hutchins had noted with some disdain a picture in a women's magazine showing Tom Jones, wearing an apron, washing dishes at his kitchen sink, while his wife Linda dried up. He knew that Tom Jones badly needed an image-making publicist, so he called Gordon Mills, who he had met before, and asked him to lunch.

Hutchins proposed to Gordon that Tom's availability to the press should be limited. Henceforth, his marriage should be played down, and his sexuality should be played up. And Tom Jones should be publicized and promoted as a superstar in the same mould as Presley or Sinatra, as a kind of self-fulfilling prophecy.

By the time lunch was over, Hutchins had talked himself into a job with Gordon – and because Gordon managed Engelbert Humperdinck, Chris Hutchins became his publicist too.

It's fair to say that he kept his part of the bargain with Gordon. After Chris Hutchins joined what he would later call the Family, Tom Jones did indeed become perceived by the public as a glamorous superstar. He would not look like a homebody again for another twenty years, when he cheerfully posed for pictures with his new baby grandson.

Hutchins also played a part in orchestrating the publicity campaign that made Tom a big star in America. But he was generally unpopular in the Jones camp, and in 1976 Hutchins quit Gordon Mills' organization – but he had an unpleasant surprise up his sleeve. He wrote a sensational series of stories about his experiences with Tom, Gordon and Engelbert for *The*

Daily Mirror. He called the series 'The Family', and some of his memories were vicious indeed.

Hutchins accused Tom of being virtually illiterate, and expounded on his extra-marital affairs in detail. He portrayed Gordon as ruthless and arrogant, someone who never uttered the word 'please', because he regarded it as a weakness. But he was probably hardest on Engelbert Humperdinck, who had split from Gordon only a few weeks earlier. Hutchins sneeringly painted him as someone desperately trying to keep up with Tom Jones in every respect, even down to the cars and houses each bought.

'Engelbert's enormous following and success were matched in size only by his vanity, his insecurity, his hypochondria and his insufferable ego,' Hutchins wrote, nastily. 'In person he is a difficult man to like. He is one of life's losers, and by no amount of success or hard-earned wealth could he ever conceal it from those around him.'

The fury that the first day of Hutchins' series for *The Daily Mirror* unleashed in the Mills organization was a sight to behold. From California, Gordon ordered an injunction to be served on the newspaper, to try and prevent it from running further instalments. *The Mirror*, probably not too upset at the free publicity the injunction would give the Hutchins series, fought the order in the High Court. And three distinguished judges, Justices Denning, Lawton and Bridge, ruled on the side of *The Mirror*, giving the newspaper free rein to continue publishing the revelations.

Hutchins now claimed that he had received a death threat from America – a threat which Gordon dismissed, while claiming he would seek redress against Hutchins within the law even if it took him ten years. But a couple of days after the series had ended, Gordon flew in to Heathrow, on business in London, but threatening vengeance on Hutchins. 'I may attack him,' he shouted at newsmen. 'I may take a swing at him.'

The singers were more measured in their responses. Humperdinck commented that he had nothing to hide, Gilbert O'Sullivan said he had done nothing of which to be ashamed, and Tom admitted he felt betrayed, and it would be better for him not to see Hutchins again. 'I don't know whether I could contain myself.'

Clearly, the Hutchins incident had shaken everyone's confidence in the Jones camp. Gordon now issued rules for his employees – all of them now had to sign what amounted to a 'loyalty clause', stating that they would not write or reveal in the press anything about the organization.

In the meantime, some fences badly needed mending. No single replacement for Hutchins was immediately obvious, and Gordon hired Rogers and Cowan, the largest entertainment publicity firm in Los Angeles, to handle Tom. The Rogers and Cowan executive given Tom's account was George Kirvay, a tall, lean man with a mournful expression who talked in a world-weary drawl. Kirvay was shrewd, skilled and experienced – a sensible, professional publicist whose calmness provided the badly needed antidote to the Hutchins fiasco.

Still, Kirvay also had other celebrity clients demanding his attention, and in the long term, Gordon wanted a publicist within his own organization who would handle Tom's publicity the way he wanted it handled. While retaining George Kirvay for a transitional period, Gordon brought into the fold John Moran, whose experience had not been in showbusiness at all.

Instead, John Moran had toiled in politics. He had been a worker for the Democratic Party in the state of New York, and he knew a lot of very important people. Moran had worked as an aide to President Kennedy, and then for his brother Bobby Kennedy; at the drop of a hat, Moran would tell anecdotes about his heady days, filled with promise and optimism, around the Kennedys. Moran was a mature adult, and Gordon liked him; he had been close to sufficient numbers of truly influential people to be able to put the entertainment industry in its proper perspective. But Moran also knew that the selling of a pop star to the public was not unlike selling a politician; it was a sophisticated, subtle, yet manipulative business.

Gordon hired Moran on the understanding that he, Gordon,

was the boss, and not Tom Jones. Moran's allegiance must always be to Gordon. Moran got the picture, and executed Gordon's demands to the last detail. He made no secret around other employees that his allegiance was to Gordon Mills. Shortly after Gordon's death, this loyalty would cause him to be summarily dumped from Tom Jones' inner circle.

Two Welshmen completed this small circle of friends. There was Dai Perry, Tom's old friend from Treforest, who had watched Tom getting into fist fights as a reckless teenager. Dai was installed as Tom's bodyguard in America, and proved himself useful in protecting Tom from hysterical – and potentially dangerous – fans. But Gordon thought him oafish and too quick to make trouble, and after the incident in Venezuela in which he struck a newsman, Dai went back to Wales.

Chris Ellis, who also came from the Pontypridd area, had been with Tom since the touring days in Britain, as a kind of unofficial driver and road manager. When Tom went to the States, the wirily built Chris Ellis went too – but the transportation problems with equipment were vastly bigger and more complex, so Chris was kept on as a personal assistant to Tom.

Road manager Roger Wall remembers: 'Chris Ellis was there when I started, in 1973. He took care of the clothes, and things like that – he was a kind of valet. Then I don't know what happened. Chris was just not around any more – and Tom's son Mark started looking after his dad.'

The rise and rise of Mark Woodward is one of the most intriguing facets of Tom Jones' career. He started off by joining his father's tour party on trips through America when he was only thirteen or so. He was a shy boy, who seemed to have inherited none of his father's athletic grace, social ease or charm. Instead, Mark was pale, overweight and awkward. It was almost hard to believe this was Tom Jones' son, and several people who worked with his father now admit they used to make cruel comments about the unfortunate boy behind his back.

Of course, Mark had had a sheltered upbringing. From the time he was seven years old, his father was off on the road somewhere, and as a young child he was raised mainly by his mother Linda. This had strange consequences, too, because from the moment Tom Jones first hit big in Britain, Linda and Mark were not officially supposed to exist. Even after 'It's Not Unusual' reached number one, and the secret that Tom was a married man with a child leaked out, Chris Hutchins came along and ordered that Linda and her son should stay firmly in the background.

It is widely agreed that Linda never quite came to terms with being made a non-person in this way, and she and the boy lived a quiet existence, first in Pontypridd, then Shepperton, then Sunbury-on-Thames. They stayed close to their immediate family, but Linda was not a social animal, and Mark's contact with other adults was limited.

But it was decided that he should join his father on an American tour. The crowds, the excitement and the sheer pace of a Tom Jones tour in the early 1970s must have been an eye-popping experience for this retiring Welsh boy – and he simply didn't seem to fit in at all.

One Tom Jones fan remembers Mark from those days in this way: 'He was thirteen, maybe fourteen, and looking lost, lonely and forlorn. He was very fat and unattractive in those days. I remember sitting with him in a bar in Las Vegas, when he was that age. There was me, a girl friend, Dai Perry, Pat Henry who was the comedian on that tour. And we were laughing and joking, and having a real good time. He was drinking vodka even then. And he didn't say more than two words the whole evening. We always felt very sorry for him. He seemed very sad.'

There were times, too, when Tom seemed to those around him to be embarrassed by the boy's presence. Ursula Alioto, vice-president of Tom's Milwaukee fan club, vividly remembers a comment by Tom which shocked those who heard it. 'It was after a concert in Green Bay, Wisconsin. I had gone backstage to meet Tom, there were a lot of people around, and Mark, for some reason, was running down a hallway.

And Tom yelled angrily: "Hey, fatso, why don't you slow down!" He often said things like that, putting Mark down.'

Still, Mark Woodward must have seen something about his father's life that he liked, because he started to yearn to be a part of it. Tom remembers when Mark was sixteen, 'I was travelling a lot, wasn't seeing him much. I got home, took him out to dinner one night, could see that he was moody and asked him what the matter was. He said he wanted me to be with him more. I talked to his headmaster and he said: "Let him leave school and take him on tour with you." He's been with me ever since.'

Mark certainly did not have a great education, or a lengthy one – but most people around the Jones entourage regard him as savvy and intelligent. Roger Wall remembers: 'After Chris Ellis left, Mark just sort of started, because he was always around his dad. If Dad stayed up till 8, Mark stayed up till 8 – he sort of took that role over.

'Mark's very bright. I watched him watch everybody and what everybody did, and ask a lot of questions. I had a feeling he would start running the business one day, which he should. He knows his dad, he knows how everything works, he knows the cast of characters.

'He's an amazing guy. I think he could have been an actor. On the road, he used to do these amazing impersonations of people. He could capture absolutely anyone. He's basically lived on the road since he was fourteen, fifteen, sixteen, and it's been the best possible experience for him.'

Mark graduated from being his father's 'minder' to the position of lighting director. And Tom said of him in 1980: 'He's the best lighting director I've ever had. Having had him with me all the time has made us very close – almost like brothers. Best of all, he has never found reason to rebel against me the way most sons do. And I like to think I set a good example for him. That's why he doesn't take drugs like so many young people.'

Nevertheless, Mark did start to gain a reputation in his late teens that was the exact opposite of his image when he first joined the tour party as a shy, insecure fat boy. Now he was a party animal, a fast-living pleasure-seeker rather like his father. Mark became known as a heavy drinker, which was hardly surprising, considering the example passed down to him by both his parents. And he started chasing girls, showing a distinct preference for black girls – including members of the Jones tour's opening act. At one point, Mark lived in a two-bedroom apartment over the huge garage in his father's Bel-Air mansion – and used to throw wild parties there. His metamorphosis, it appeared, was complete.

Still, Mark's fast lifestyle did not seem to interfere with his duties for Tom, and he continued to work diligently for his father. In any case, by the time he reached his mid-twenties, Mark was preparing to settle down. The object of his affection was a young woman living in New York named Donna Paloma. She was dating Barry Morgan, Tom's drummer, and the brother of Michael Morgan, Tom's musical director, who had succeeded Johnnie Spence. Donna was regarded with some suspicion in the Jones camp. Four years older than Mark, she seemed to be not so different from any number of good-time girls who had latched on to members of the band over the years. And she had been flirtatious, to say the least, with other members of the band besides Barry.

But Mark fell for Donna in a big way, and she moved to Los Angeles. Eventually, they became an established couple, and married. In typical style, Tom bought them a Beverly Hills house as a wedding gift. Mark and Donna lost no time in starting a family, and Tom's grandson Alexander was born in June 1983.

When Gordon Mills died, Mark took over as Tom's manager, and installed Donna as publicist for Tom Jones Enterprises, ousting the departed John Moran. In 1987, the couple had a daughter, Emma Violet. And the brief for that shy, awkward boy now grown into a confident, self-assured man is to maintain his father's career into the 1990s.

Tom's family must be counted part of his entourage. They show up faithfully at his concerts near to the home he bought them in Bel-Air – when Tom plays the Greek Theatre in Los

Angeles, say, or Vegas or Tahoe. His parents and his sister Sheila were often on hand when Tom was being honoured with some showbusiness award. Unhappily, Tom Woodward senior died in 1981 at the age of seventy-two, a victim of pneumoconiosis – the dreaded 'black lung' disease that afflicts all too many miners.

Tom could at least reflect that his own extraordinary wealth had enabled him to get his father to retire from the pit earlier than he might have done – a move which may have added extra years to Tom senior's life.

As it was, he grieved at his loss. His father had often accompanied him on social occasions in America, and had been tickled to meet celebrities like Presley and Sinatra. Phil Elwell, owner of a British-style pub in Santa Monica called the Dirty Duck, recalls that when Tom dropped by for a pint, Tom senior was often with him.

The only other people regularly close to Tom Jones over the years were the Blossoms, his trio of black back-up singers. One of them, Fanita Barrett, has been with Tom almost since he started touring in America. Others have fallen by the wayside. One Blossom, Jeannie King, died in 1981 of heart problems after bypass surgery. She was in her early forties, and had married one of Tom's sound technicians, Larry Richstein, and moved to Seattle to start a brand new, peaceful life.

The mortality rate among this entourage is alarmingly high – and was a subject over which Tom Jones has been known to brood. Darlene Love, formerly one of the Blossoms, recalls reuniting with Tom backstage on the David Letterman TV show in 1988. 'And we ended up talking about all the people who had died,' says Darlene. 'He was very gloomy about it. We went down the list. Gordon Mills. Gog Jones. Johnnie Spence. His father. Jeannie King.

'Finally, he turned to me with a sad little smile, and said: "It's you and me, kid. We're the only ones left." '

Chapter Eleven

HOLLYWOOD

'It's this country where the money is, so I'm going to work around the country. I want to do films, I want audiences to recognize me,' said Tom Jones in Las Vegas in 1968.

By this time, Tom Jones had got a batch of million-selling singles under his belt, and a career which was hitting dizzy heights. Both he and Gordon Mills recognized that the best strategy now was to concentrate on cracking the American market, with its wide variety of possibilities.

The logic was obvious. America had four times the population of Britain, which meant four times as many potential record buyers. Then again, every sizeable city seemed to have a massive concert hall which could be filled with his fans – an enormous contrast to the town halls and cinemas in Britain, with their small capacities of 2,000 or 3,000. America also had Las Vegas, where a man could earn a small fortune for a mere week's work performing in one of the glamorous casino hotel lounges.

And, of course, America had Hollywood.

Even at this early stage of his career, getting into movies seemed like a natural move for Tom Jones. He was a singing star with massive sex appeal to audiences of a wide age range. He had dramatic good looks, and his live performances confirmed a charismatic stage presence. True, he had never acted, but then Elvis Presley was no actor either – his limitations were similar to those of Tom Jones when he embarked on his Hollywood career, yet he had survived. Admittedly, no

one would ever remember any of Presley's films as classics –
but the King had kept his fans happy and made a fortune for
himself and his manager, Colonel Tom Parker, even from
forgettable movies like *Fun in Acapulco* and *It Happened at the
World's Fair*.

Hollywood, then, seemed ripe for the taking. And even
after Tom Jones had enjoyed just one hit single, 'It's Not
Unusual', film studios were enquiring about his availability.
Paramount Pictures was ready to discuss a possible deal with
him. But at this stage, Gordon Mills rejected Hollywood's
overtures, feeling it was too early in Tom's career for such a
big departure.

By 1968, though, he was prepared to consider offers.
Mills had a two-pronged plan for Tom Jones in the USA –
he would make him king of the lucrative casino and concert
hall circuits, and he would make him a movie star.

In his first aim, he was wildly successful, and Tom Jones
even today pulls in huge crowds to casinos in Las Vegas and
Atlantic City, and to concert halls across America. But as for
Tom Jones' Hollywood ambitions, the result was two decades
of miserable failure – a catalogue of frustration, bad luck, poor
timing and questionable choices.

At first, he and Mills could afford to take their time.
In the late 1960s and early 1970s, the Tom Jones legend
was sweeping America. His records went gold with amazing
regularity. He had a successful TV series on ABC. He could
pack any concert hall at which he was booked to play. And
Mills was determined to hold out for the right movie and the
right kind of studio backing before Tom made his move in
Hollywood.

There was also some reluctance on Tom's part. Singing
came naturally and easily to him, but acting was another
matter altogether. Still, after three years of spectacular success Stateside, it finally looked as if he was ready to take the
plunge. In June 1971, he told columnist Earl Wilson in New
York: 'I make a film in October. I've stayed away from films.
I've been a bit frightened. I don't want people to say "he's not
such a good actor".'

Though Tom did not tell Wilson, he and Mills had bought the rights to an intriguing novel called *The Gospel Singer*, by southern author Harry Crews. The book had attracted favourable reviews and a kind of cult following when it was published in 1968.

Two months later, the grand plan for Tom Jones' triumphant entry into Hollywood was unveiled. In August 1971, Herb Jaffe, a vice-president at United Artists film studio, announced that Tom had been signed to a three-picture deal. He also announced that *The Gospel Singer* was being adapted for film by the respected screenwriter Robert Thom.

The United Artists announcement was an extraordinary opportunity for Tom Jones. It was the sort of deal for which many leading actors might have given their right arm, and it was being offered to someone who had never done a day's serious acting in his life. The studio was saying it would agree to pay him a certain (large) amount of money to make three movies, which they would help him find, and which he would promise to make for United Artists exclusively – United Artists, a Hollywood institution, founded by silent movie legends Charlie Chaplin, Mary Pickford and Douglas Fairbanks. It seemed incredible.

And had things gone differently, the United Artists deal could have catapulted Tom into a Hollywood elite of movie superstars so highly regarded by their studios that they can command huge, lucrative future commitments which allow them the freedom to make the movies they wish. Even today, few in Hollywood enjoy this sort of luxury – Clint Eastwood with Warner Brothers, Eddie Murphy with Paramount, Woody Allen with Orion, and virtually no one else.

As it was, Jaffe's announcement was the last optimistic word to be uttered publicly about the movie plans for *The Gospel Singer*. More than seven whole years later, after legal problems and lengthy, acrimonious wrangling, Gordon Mills was still trying to get the movie off the ground – but to no avail.

On the face of it, *The Gospel Singer* was promising material. It would have provided a substantial first role for Tom, certainly

more meaty than the fluffy nonsense which constituted Elvis
Presley's movies. There was singing in it, too, and in October
1971 Hollywood columnist Hank Grant wrote that Paul Anka
had been approached to write the songs for the movie.

The story is of a golden-haired young man with the
voice of an angel whose fans come to regard him as
God's messenger, and fall to their knees before him at
massive gatherings in places like New York's Carnegie Hall.
But when he goes back to his hometown, a small, backward
farming community in south Georgia called Enigma, the singer
decides he cannot handle all the adulation, and tries to get
his followers to regard him as a flawed human being. To this
end, he starts to behave in a wicked and corrupt manner. But
instead of understanding his plight, his followers turn against
him, and ultimately lynch him.

Obviously, this was far from being a light-hearted story,
and both Gordon Mills and Tom Jones had their doubts.
Would Tom's fans accept the decadence of his character
and the violence of such a film? Might it offend his millions
of followers in the southern Bible Belt states, where you didn't
criticize evangelists, or those who brought the word of God to
ordinary people?

Harry Crews, the author of *The Gospel Singer*, wrote an
early version of the screenplay, as requested, and went to see
Tom Jones to talk about his script. Crews is an outspoken type
with a taste for colourful obscenities, a self-confessed wild
man who once was a heroin addict and even now indulges
in drinking sprees when he isn't working for days on end at
his latest novel. When he caught up with Tom Jones, it was
clear to him that the singer had cold feet about tackling *The
Gospel Singer*.

'He loved the goddamn book, but he didn't want to die
on camera,' recalls Crews. 'He loved it that the guy dies in
the book, but he didn't want Tom Jones to die in the movie.
He didn't want that audience to see him hanging on the end
of a rope. He wanted to change the ending so his character
didn't die, which is easy to do, but it does hideous violence
to the story.'

Tom admitted his plans at the time. 'I think we may change the ending,' he said. But he insisted he was enthusiastic about the rest of the script.

Given his reluctance about being strung up on camera, was Tom Jones the right actor for the role? Crews admits he had his reservations. 'You never know about people until you get them on the set,' he admits. 'But for instance, what would Tom Jones have done about his hair? In the book, the boy is blond, and much is made out of the fact that the boy is blond. That had to do with the American notion of what being blond is all about, you know – a kind of clean-cut purity. This character had an image as pure as the driven snow, but underneath it all, he was one of the most dirty, rotten people you'd want to meet.

'Anyway, Tom Jones is obviously not blond, and he made it clear that he was not enamoured of being blond.'

Crews met Tom under strange circumstances. Tom was performing in Jacksonville, Florida, near Crews' own home, and a meeting was arranged between the two of them at Tom's hotel. 'He was in the biggest suite you ever saw,' Crews recalls, 'which took up probably the whole top floor of this hotel in Jacksonville. And he was eating dinner alone in this huge suite, with just one other guy – a middleweight boxer who it seemed both Jones and [American football superstar] Joe Namath used to drag around and take care of. At his show that night, this boxer comes on stage and wipes Jones' face with a towel. It was all part of the act. He wasn't a bodyguard, exactly. He looked too old for that. And judging by the scars on his face, he didn't look like he'd been much of a boxer, either. But Jones just seemed to like having him around.'

Despite what he saw as the drawbacks of having Tom Jones playing his title character, Crews admits he had two things going for him. 'He's got this great voice, for one. And for this character, he can also fake this southern accent. He can do this down-home, southern, 'grits' dialect as good as you'd want to hear it. It's a hard thing to do, and I couldn't figure where he got it from.'

The answer was Elvis Presley. Tom admitted that Elvis

had been coaching him with his deep south twang. 'I told Elvis I wanted to play it and he said he'd help me with my southern accent,' he said. 'He even considered playing the part himself.'

Still, Crews believed that Tom had no real feeling for his book or his script. He remembers that he tried to get Tom to consider filming *The Gospel Singer* just as he had written it. 'I wasn't trying to sell him anything,' Crews says now. 'But at one point I did say to him – hey, man, you're listening to me with half an ear. Now I don't care if you listen with half an ear or no fucking ear at all, but you really ought to try and hear this, because it might give you another career. A career you haven't got now, and one that you'd like a lot. If you don't want to hear it, that's all right with me.

'He gave a sort of low-energy shrug of the shoulder, which was the way he always acted around me, and said: "No, no, boss man. I'm listening." And so I went ahead talking. But he really wasn't listening.'

Crews thinks that ultimately Tom Jones could not see himself, 'one of the most glamorous male entertainers in the world, in this movie, set in rural south Georgia, surrounded by a lot of pig farmers. I know what was going through his mind – they're gonna put pigshit on the shoes of Tom Jones? They can't do that. That was the way he read it.'

Still, Crews had his story bought by the Jones organization and they paid his asking price. 'And then,' he says disbelievingly, 'they were going to change it so it wouldn't be anything like what they bought.'

The years dragged by, and nothing happened. At one point, May 1975 was set as the shooting start-up date for *The Gospel Singer*. In September 1974, Mark Tan, the Las Vegas columnist for the *Hollywood Reporter*, disclosed that Tom and Gordon Mills had been 'spending all-night sessions at Caesar's Palace, working over script, music and casting'.

So much time elapsed that Jones and Mills temporarily lost their rights to make a movie of *The Gospel Singer*. Those rights went to producer Larry Spangler and a company called Global Productions. Jones and Mills sued them for breach of contract, asking $100,000 in damages, claiming that they had agreed to buy the rights for $35,000, but that their offer had been rejected and the rights sold to another party. It was now seven years after Herb Jaffe's optimistic announcement, and still *The Gospel Singer* was no nearer to being made.

In 1976, two film offers came Tom's way, but neither of them came to fruition. The first was for him to star in a movie version of Jackie Collins' novel *The Stud*, which would star her sister Joan, in her pre-*Dynasty* days. The movie's co-producer Terence Deane took Jackie's script to Tom, and watched him read it. But apparently the subject matter was again too hard for him to take.

In *The Stud*, Tom would have played the kept lover of Joan Collins, whose character was married to a rich Arab emirate. Scenes in the movie involved bisexuality, drug-taking and orgiastic sex. Four-letter words were sprinkled throughout Jackie's script. Tom would have none of it.

'I wouldn't like my Mum and Dad to see me in this sort of film,' he explained – rather primly for a thirty-five-year-old man accustomed to having underwear thrown at him on stage. 'It's just short of being pornographic.'

Tom applauded the fact that his character was not into drugs, but was appalled at the language in *The Stud*. In one scene, his character wanted to get back to London, but hadn't got the money. 'He asks his rich lady for a ticket, and she tells him: "Fuck your way back," ' he complained.

After having gone over the script with Tom, Deane noted: 'He isn't what people think. He's quite a shy guy. He was like a little boy reading the script – really embarrassed.'

Jackie entered the fray by stoutly denying that her script was pornographic. She said she was 'flabbergasted' that Tom would turn down the role for those reasons. 'What on earth is he scared of?' she added. 'He's made a name for being a sexually aggressive stage performer. In fact, his whole image is that of a great big hunk of man.'

One associate of Tom's at the time thinks the verbal slanging match between Tom and Jackie was a publicity stunt, arranged to draw attention to Jackie's movie and to Tom's plans to move into films. Certainly the two have become friends over the years – and Jackie Collins' fascination with Tom is evidenced by her novel *Lovers and Gamblers*, which deals with a sexually prodigious rock star rather like Tom Jones. She has maintained that her character was a composite, but certain elements about him are interesting. The character sleeps with any women who make themselves available to him, even quite plain ones; he has a young son, awkward and bumbling, who travels with him on tour; and there is an amazing sex scene involving the rock star and twin teenage girls, which recalls Gordon Mills' notorious stewardesses.

After *The Stud*, there was Tom's projected movie *Yockowald*. If the progress of *The Gospel Singer* became mired, it was plain sailing compared to the disaster of *Yockowald*. His role in the film was first announced in June 1976, and at first it looked as though this was a solid movie which would certainly get made. Tom was to play 'a flamboyant, extroverted character, who is hired as a paid assassin'. It was to be a non-singing star role.

What added further credence to *Yockowald* was that the two men who had written the script, and who between them would direct and produce it, were both established Hollywood veterans. Producer Clarence Greene and director Russell Rouse had been working as a team since the late 1940s, and had made a string of well-received films. Their 1950 movie *D.O.A.* (which was recently re-made, starring Dennis Quaid) made an instant star out of Edmund O'Brien. *The Thief* from 1952 with Ray Milland was a bold, critically acclaimed experiment – a film without dialogue, just sound effects. And *The Oscar* from 1966 had been a popular hit. It seemed as though Tom Jones was in good hands with Greene and Rouse.

He threw himself enthusiastically into the business of learning his lines, and put everything else in his career temporarily to one side. He and Mills cancelled eleven weeks of lucrative concert bookings, including dates at Caesar's Harrah's in Nevada. By doing this, he incurred the wrath of some promoters. The owner of the Colonie Coliseum Arena Theatre in Albany, New York, lost a week's worth of performances by Tom, and complained that fans and promoters were being let down by the sudden cancellation. He had taken $100,000 in advance for 8,000 seats.

But acting in a movie was by now the most important thing in Tom Jones' professional life. It had been five years since one of his singles, 'She's A Lady' had gone gold, and his record career was starting to look shaky. He still sold out concert halls, but in truth his career needed a new boost that only a splashy entry into Hollywood could now give him.

In July 1976, the cameras started rolling and *Yockowald* was under way. After eight years of trying to make it happen, it finally looked as though, in addition to all his other achievements, Tom Jones was about to be a movie star too.

But it was not to be. Less than three weeks later, shooting on *Yockowald* was halted. Suddenly, no money was available to continue the film. It was a nightmare for all concerned, the kind of awful experience that occasionally happens in Hollywood out of the blue, for no apparent reason.

To this day, Clarence Greene grieves at the loss of *Yockowald*. 'It kills me just to think about it,' he says. 'I think Tom Jones woould have been a big movie star had we been able to make *Yockowald*. He was absolutely great in the part.'

What happened? Greene still isn't clear. He and Russell Rouse (who later died of a stroke) had written an off-beat script and were happy with it. 'Tom was to play a character who the CIA picked to assassinate somebody,' Green recalls. 'He was an unusual character, who had a lot of kindness in him, basically. There was a girl in the picture who he tries to help. She was written as a fat girl, which is unusual in itself. But his heart went out to her. He wasn't really a killer, but he was forced into a position whereby he had to assassinate somebody.'

The role, says Greene sadly, 'fitted Tom Jones like a glove.'

He and Rouse secured financing through an American bank from a Canadian investor. *Yockowald* was to be distributed through a major company, Embassy Pictures.

Everything seemed set. 'There was a party before the

picture,' said Greene, 'and the bank representative was there, and said we could go ahead, the money was in the bank. But after we started to shoot, the money wasn't there for payroll. Then the bank was sold to a Japanese owner. Things just went down and down, and all of a sudden there was no money in the bank. There was a point where I was prepared to say to the bank, "Let's make a deal, just let us finish the picture," but it didn't happen.'

Rouse and Greene were not even able to sue to recover their own costs. 'We didn't have the money for legal depositions to sue on our own behalf,' Greene recalls, 'and we certainly couldn't afford the legal expenses for the actors, the crew and some other merchants who were involved. There was no way of getting the film back on track, and I don't even know what happened to the Canadian who was supposed to be putting up the money. We had to let it go.'

Greene stresses to this day that none of the financial problems which finally overwhelmed *Yockowald* were related to Tom Jones' ability as a movie actor. 'He'd been in front of the cameras before we pulled the plug, and he had been excellent,' he said.

He also remembers the singer seeming bewildered by the financial disasters which beset *Yockowald*. 'I don't think Tom was too aware of that end of the business.' Greene, Rouse and Gordon Mills held a series of long urgent meetings to explore ways of saving the movie, but they were all in vain.

For Greene, the whole affair still rankles. 'This was a terrible thing in my career, because I just knew, I was positive, that I could have made a star out of him. He would have been as big as anybody.'

After the *Yockowald* fiasco, it would be two whole years before Tom Jones would again step before movie cameras.

Time was by now running out for him. He was thirty-eight years old, which is late in life for anyone to make their movie debut – especially a singer whose glory days were seven or more years behind him. John Hawkins, the New York-based literary agent for Harry Crews, thinks that one reason *The*

Gospel Singer never got made was that Tom became too old to play the lead role.

However, Gordon was becoming frustrated by Hollywood, and the apparently enormous difficulties in getting films made. By this time, Tom was also struggling to find the best material available to record. So Gordon decided that he and Tom would take matters into their own hands in the fields of records and films.

They built Britannia Recording Studios on Cahuenga Boulevard in Hollywood in 1978 as part of the plan. It would be a place for Tom to record, and also a state-of-the-art facility generating income from other artists cutting their own albums. (Part of the hit Eagles' album *The Long Run* was recorded at Britannia.)

At the time Gordon said he was 'trying to develop a really big music publishing company. I'm trying to find new songwriters who will write for the company, so that Tom and I can have the first choice of anything they write. But finding these people isn't easy. Most songwriters today seem to be recording their own material, or giving it to people who are on top of the charts.'

If this was a frank admission of how far Tom's star had fallen, Gordon stressed that his main priority was to land Tom in a feature film. To this end, along with Britannia, he and Tom had also started a production company to buy and develop scripts for movies, and to create special TV shows starring Tom.

Without their own production company, Gordon said, breaking into Hollywood was too tough. 'Film producers and directors are totally unaware of our business,' he complained. 'They don't even know one singer from another – and they couldn't care less whether they could act.'

Gordon insisted that Tom could make it as an actor; all he needed was the experience and the exposure. This time around, it was decided to attach Tom to a film of more modest expectations, but one which at least would end up being completed and seen by audiences.

So it was that Tom signed up for a part in a television

movie for America's NBC network, called *Pleasure Cove*. He would play a singer in a tuxedo – a role close to his own life. But his character was also a charming rogue who indulged in a little smuggling.

Pleasure Cove was a variation on two successful American TV shows at the time – *Love Boat* and *Fantasy Island*. The film was written as a 'pilot' or a tryout for a new TV series, though Tom was written in as a guest star and would not have stayed with the show had it become a series. (It didn't.) The interweaving stories in *Pleasure Cove* were about holidaymakers at a posh California beach resort, one of which featured a nude beach.

But what Tom would quickly find was that movies shot for American TV are shot much quicker, and at a much lower budget, than feature movies which play in cinemas. *Pleasure Cove* had a breakneck shooting schedule, and none of the cast were given the kind of luxuries they might expect if they were making a feature movie.

Lou Shaw, the writer and producer of *Pleasure Cove*, remembers Tom being 'a great trouper' – despite some less than favourable working conditions.

'We hadn't finished all the beach scenes on time, and the next day, we had to shoot a scene in a disco in downtown Los Angeles, where Tom was singing,' Shaw remembers. 'So I brought out a truckload of sand to the disco, and dumped it all in the parking lot outside. It was very cold that day, I remember. Tom shot a scene inside the disco in his tuxedo, went outside, changed into a bathing suit, did the scene on the sand in the cold,then immediately took a shower, went back inside, got back into his tux and finished the disco scenes. I don't know how many other guys would have done that. In fact, we were all rather worried about how he'd react when we asked him to go through this for us, but he just said: "OK, anything I can do." '

Bruce Bilson, who directed *Pleasure Cove*, remembers another embarrassing scene which must have brought home to Tom that making movies isn't all glamour.

'There was this one beach scene with Tom and an actress called Barbara Luna, and when we showed it to our executive producer David Gerber, he felt it wasn't quite right, and asked us to shoot it again.

'We had to move our location to a place called King Harbor at Redondo Beach, and we used a little piece of sand just below a beachfront restaurant. The sun was starting to go down, and people were leaning out of the restaurant and drinking margaritas. Barbara was wearing a little flesh-coloured nothing of a bikini, and Tom was in the briefest pair of bikini briefs. And it was getting colder, and all these people were getting more and more drunk, and yelling at them. I have to say he was a wonderful sport about the whole thing.'

Shaw remembers that the disco scenes had to be stopped a couple of times, because adoring girl extras were looking at Tom singing rather than looking at their partners, as requested. Both he and Bilson think he acquitted himself well in *Pleasure Cove*. 'I don't know why he hasn't done more movies,' says Shaw, 'because he was fine in this.' Bilson adds: 'He wasn't the world's greatest actor, but essentially he was playing himself, and he plays Tom Jones quite well. He was better than adequate. He was a very nice guy to work with, and without putting on any bullshit, he did a good job.'

The two men even insist he was a good sport during a scene on a nude beach, which (because this was for prudish American TV) had no nude people. 'I had to shoot people behind beach balls, or partially hidden by bushes,' recalls Bilson. 'It was difficult.' In one scene, actress Constance Forslund had to walk fully clothed across the nude beach to where Tom Jones was sprawled, supposedly naked. Because hers was a strait-laced character, she kept her gaze aloft – and consequently tripped over a series of naked bodies before she reached the broadly smiling Tom. 'He did the whole thing with a charming grin,' says Shaw.

But the reviewers were not smiling when they saw *Pleasure Cove*, and in retrospect, being part of such a fluffy, trivial film did Tom's career no good. Nothing that he did made the critics sit up and take notice. Indeed, *Variety*, the trade magazine read by Hollywood's movers and shakers, only listed his name as one of a gang of smugglers in its review, and nothing was said about his acting abilities – or the lack of them.

Instead, *Variety*'s respected critic Tony Scott, writing under his usual pseudonym 'Tone', wrote of *Pleasure Cove*: 'A trite, lame exploitation of resort life . . . it could give vacations a bad name. The hotel has a nude beach . . . the scene in which it's used could make an adolescent cringe. There's even a shark to chase the folk who fall haplessly into the water. Things are bad when the viewer starts pulling for the shark.'

In short, *Pleasure Cove* was an ignominious debut for Tom, a TV film which was probably forgotten by most of its viewers the morning after it was broadcast in January 1979.

Still, it was a start, and six months later, in Atlantic City, where he was playing a casino called Resorts International, Tom announced plans to make another movie.

This one was called *When the Lion Feeds*, and it was to be an adventure period film, set in South Africa in the nineteenth century. No singing was to be involved, just straight acting. But nothing happened. The film never got off the ground, another instance of Tom's inability to carve out a film career.

Oddly, he took to acting with tremendous enthusiasm. He liked the rhythm and the pace of moviemaking, and after *Pleasure Cove* was completed (but not seen by critics) he was full of his plans to do more acting. *Hollywood Reporter* columnist Hank Grant noted in December 1978: 'Tom Jones is so excited over the results of his . . . role in the *Pleasure Cove* telemovie, he wants to launch a new career with straight acting roles. It'll be a neat trick if they let him do it on his next pic *The Gospel Singer* . . . '

But by this time, people in Hollywood weren't holding their breath any more.

A sad little postscript to Tom Jones' Hollywood career occurred in June 1989, when the singer was awarded a star bearing his name on Hollywood's Walk of Fame. The ceremony took place on Hollywood Boulevard, and a crowd of well-wishers and fans gathered to applaud when the star, laid into the sidewalk, was unveiled.

Johnny Grant, the mayor of Hollywood, made a short speech to the assembled gathering, and introduced Tom Jones, whose own speech was brief. Noting that he had lived and worked in Hollywood for many years, Tom said the Walk of Fame star was 'the biggest honour Hollywood can give. Once the star's in the pavement, it's there for ever,' he added. Within half an hour, the ceremony was over, and Tom joined the ranks of almost 2,000 celebrities – like Greta Garbo, Charlie Chaplin and Bob Hope – to be so honoured.

On the face of it, this looked like a worthy tribute to Tom's long career. But the reality was very different.

Though Tom described the star as being 'the biggest honour Hollywood can give', this is far from the truth. The Walk of Fame ceremonies are actually a thinly disguised promotional venture, aimed at creating publicity for the now shabby and decaying area of Los Angeles known as Hollywood, which has been in decline since the 1950s. Hollywood Boulevard is today filled with tourists, but its regular inhabitants are tramps, down-and-outs, winos, runaway children and teenage prostitutes of both sexes. It isn't a street to walk down after dark.

Hollywood is not even a city in its own right, and Johnny Grant's title as mayor is strictly self-imposed. The tiny bespectacled Grant, a former TV quiz show host and entertainment reporter, uses his unofficial position to preside over the Walk of Fame ceremonies – and somehow keep his face before the media and TV cameras.

So how did Tom Jones get his star on the Walk of Fame? He wasn't elected by a jury of his peers, as with the Oscar or Grammy awards. The truth is far less glamorous. A celebrity gets a star by paying a sum of $3,500 to the Hollywood Chamber of Commerce, which organizes these ceremonies. Typically, a movie studio or record company puts up the money for a celebrity's star, and the ceremony is timed to coincide with the opening of that celebrity's new movie or the release of their latest record. (Dustin Hoffman, Paul Newman and Clint Eastwood are among the superstars who neither want nor need a Walk of Fame star.)

When Tom Jones got his star, the $3,500 was duly paid on his behalf, but came mainly from contributions from his fan clubs. His publicist and daughter-in-law Donna Woodward wrote in a press release: 'It is important to note that Tom is one of the very few celebrities to be nominated and supported solely by his fans. The applications and necessary fees were handled and raised by the members of the many Tom Jones Fan Clubs throughout the United States.'

It was a touching, loyal gesture by the fans, but it obscured a sad fact – that in the last two decades, Tom Jones has never been with a record company who thought it worth spending $3,500 to give him a star on the Walk of Fame – a testament to his inability to sell large numbers of records for almost twenty years.

Then there was the ceremony itself, which took place outside Frederick's of Hollywood, a store which sells skimpy, suggestive lingerie. Frederick's has a flourishing mail order business, but many of the customers who browse, giggling, around its Hollywood Boulevard store are tourists – unsophisticated (and frequently overweight) housewives from the Midwest who think Frederick's push-up bras and see-through panties are the last word in sexiness. Frederick's, whose owners had requested that Tom's star be placed outside the store, was decked out in gaudy mauve flags for the day; afterwards, Tom and his party adjourned inside the store for a private reception.

The crowds this June day were pitifully thin – between 200 and 300 people watched, and fully half were the boulevard's regular down-and-outs, pausing awhile to feast their drunken or half-crazed eyes on the proceedings. In the crowd, the smell of urine, and cheap wine from the vagrants' breath polluted the air. An open double-decker bus passed by slowly, and from its top deck, a handful of fans in orange T-shirts applauded. 'You're still the best, Tom!' shouted one, a little faint-heartedly. But the crowds this day did not even stop the traffic on Hollywood Boulevard.

The resulting publicity was pitiful. *The Los Angeles Times* did not even mention the ceremony. Mitchell Fink, gossip columnist for the *Los Angeles Herald Examiner*, merely noted in a sneering tone: 'How fitting that Tom Jones should get his star on the Walk of Fame in front of Frederick's of Hollywood.' *Entertainment Tonight*, America's nightly showbiz news show on TV, showed a clip of the ceremony lasting only ten seconds. It was hard to escape the notion that America's press didn't care about Tom Jones any more.

Jones had ended the ceremony by reaching into a small white bucket and tossing into the crowd cheap black and blue garters with his name and a tiny golden star sewn on them.

The biggest honour Hollywood can give? No. The Oscar and the Grammy would claim that award. But Tom Jones' inability to get into movies has denied him an Oscar, and his only Grammy was awarded long ago in 1965, when he was voted best new artist. Instead, this hot June day was indeed his biggest moment in Hollywood – hurling shoddy, sleazy-looking garters into a crowd of down-and-outs in a phony ceremony designed to drum up publicity for purveyors of saucy lingerie.

Chapter Twelve

THE FANS

In 1983 Tom Jones said, 'My fans are just terrific. They're absolutely terrific.' The point can be argued over and over, but it is probable that Tom Jones has the most fiercely loyal fans of any British entertainer in history.

They have sustained him in his career for a quarter of a century. They have bought his records, attended his concerts, avidly watched him on television. They have joined his fan clubs, done charity work or raised money for the greater glorification of his name, called in to radio deejays to play his records. In short, they have been his boosters.

It almost goes without saying that the overwhelming majority of these fans are women. They're women who have adored Tom Jones from the first time they heard his voice, and cast their gaze on those legendary swivelling hips of his.

And they come to his shows, slip the maitre d' a twenty to ensure a seat in the front row, and sit through his performance with rapt, glazed smiles. In pauses between songs, they will offer up the gifts they have brought with them this particular evening, like pagan worshippers to an idol. And Jones in his turn knows and expects this; indeed, he uses the gifts from fans as a way of giving himself breathing space between numbers.

'Hello, darlin', what's this, then?' he will say, crouching to pick up a gift box slipped on to the stage. Typically, the present will be a box of cigars (his favourite Monte Cristos), or an item of sexy underwear – men's bikini briefs in gold lamé,

181

for example. The present will probably be accompanied by a card which Jones will read out loud, stopping abruptly with a make-believe blush if the message is too risqué. He will then bestow a passionate, long kiss on the mouth of the wide-eyed donor.

This is a routine, a harmless, mildly sexy piece of showbiz ritual. It's also a useful, economical way for Tom Jones to acknowledge the fans who have helped him endure as a highly paid entertainer for twenty-five years.

But behind this bit of light-hearted stage banter, the truth is that Tom Jones and most of the people surrounding him in his management team have had uneasy, uneven relationships with his fans since Tom first became a success. One might say that these loyal fans have, over the years, been a direct source of income for all those working in the Jones organization – yet they have been tolerated at best and treated with open contempt at worst.

To understand why this should be, it must be remembered that Tom Jones from the outset attracted a wide variety of female fans. Teenage girls loved him and his records, especially so in the earlier years of his career, but so did their mothers – and even their grandmothers. Many of the people still active in Tom Jones' fan clubs across the world have been members for twenty years or more.

These women, to be brutally honest, don't look as good as they once did. To be even more candid, some maybe never looked that good at all. At a 1989 Tom Jones concert at Bally's Grand, in Las Vegas, the audience was slightly more than half women; most were there with their husbands. The median age was perhaps forty, and most of these women were clearly working class. Many were a little overweight; polyester and other man-made fibres were the fashion statement of the night.

While these fans are undoubtedly good people, their image is at variance with the image Tom Jones has sought to promote for himself as a singer. Think of the song 'Delilah' – how are we to envisage the woman in that song? Probably as an olive-skinned, slim-waisted beauty with long dark hair and flashing eyes. Think of the women being described in 'She's

A Lady' or 'Daughter of Darkness' – what do they look like? One's imagination could run riot, but obviously they are not forty-five-year-old housewives from Arkansas with a weight problem, bad skin and dressed in shapeless shift dresses.

In short, most Tom Jones fans have never been as glamorous as the women in his songs; maybe they're just not as glamorous in real life as his songs make them feel. And this is an awkward fact of life which has seemed to embarrass the Jones organization throughout Tom's long reign.

Joyce Sacks, a vivacious suntanned blonde, who assuredly is attractive, was a founder member of Tom's Los Angeles fan club, the Jones Girls, in 1969. 'Even in the early days,' she remembers, 'the fans weren't all young women. And they weren't all glamorous, either. But it wasn't minded then, because Tom Jones was able to get what he wanted out of his fans at that time.'

When fans did get to meet Tom – backstage after a concert, or at a fan-organized charity event – they would find him courteous and affable. But many of them also found his closest colleagues rude and dismissive.

Disgraced press aide Chris Hutchins was one Jones organization man who had a bad relationship with Tom's American fan club 'girls' – which is how they describe themselves. 'He was a tyrant,' says Joyce Sacks. 'He was a very nasty, rotten man who seemed to hate the fan clubs. He showed that by treating us with contempt. He talked down to us.'

Whenever relationships between Tom's management team and a fan club president became stormy or even ruffled, word would spread like wildfire. The American fan club presidents operated an informal grapevine – which even extended to Britain and other countries – which carried the latest hot gossip. Sometimes imagined slights became real slights in the mind of a fan club president, who would then fan the flames of dissent by reporting some brush with Tom's inner circle. The stories would circulate from Texas to New Jersey to California to Florida by phone in a matter of minutes.

And some of the 'incidents' were probably over-inflated, in part because of who the fan club organizers were. Says one, who wished to remain anonymous: 'A lot of these people are lonely women with nothing else to do. Tom Jones is the biggest thing in their entire lives. They travel all over the country to see him, they write their newsletters, they have their meetings, and their friendships come out of the fan clubs. It can be a little sad.'

Still, the relationship between Gordon Mills and Tom's fan club girls was no figment of anyone's imagination. Gordon, who seemingly never relaxed or switched off from work, often seemed to the fan club presidents to be impatient with them. If anything, this was probably a function of Gordon's character – he constantly had business ideas ticking over in his brain. He also felt that he personally should not have to deal directly with Tom's fan clubs: that was work to be handled by an underling in his office. Whatever his real feelings, he struck many of the fan club founders as distant and unfriendly. One day, Joyce Sacks cornered George Kirvay, a public relations executive with the firm Rogers and Cowan who represented Tom in the late 1970s, and talked about the Gordon problem.

'I asked George, "Does Gordon hate us?" ' she recalls. 'Does he think we're idiots? We're doing all this work for Tom and not getting paid for it. Surely he must respect us for the amount of money we raise – but he's never made himself accessible to us.'

Gordon's stand-offish attitude was particularly troubling to the fan club presidents, because they were close enough to the Jones organization to be familiar with Gordon's mystique. His good looks and charismatic presence made him almost as intriguing a figure to those fans in the know as Tom Jones himself.

George Kirvay relayed the fans' concern to Gordon, who soon afterwards sat himself down next to Joyce Sacks at one of Tom's Vegas shows. 'He asked me what he could do to help,' she recalls. Within a few days, Gordon had responded publicly. He sent a letter to all the fan clubs in the US, noting that it had come to his attention that some fans thought he did not appreciate their efforts on Tom's behalf; he confirmed that he genuinely did. 'The next few years,' recalls Joyce Sacks, 'were bliss.'

Gordon never again made the mistake of risking alienation among the fan clubs; he actively ensured that they were kept happy. In 1983, he pulled a master stroke on their behalf; he was dissatisfied with the performance of an office worker whose job it was to co-ordinate with the fan clubs, so he fired the woman and replaced her with his own girlfriend, a beautiful Tahitian-born businesswoman called Annie Toomaru. He persuaded Annie to give up her job as owner of a travel company to join his organisation.

'Annie was fabulous,' says one fan club president. 'The fans loved her, and she got along just great.' Gordon's talent for placating had worked again.

Through the years, Tom Jones' fans have demonstrated their allegiance to their hero in a multitude of ways, some of them bordering on the extreme. You'd be hard put to find a more loyal fan than Leslie Lawrie, a Solihull housewife, whose semi-detached house is like a church in which to worship the Jones boy. She has a collection of press cuttings about Tom Jones, numbering over 30,000 and spanning twenty-six years. She owns all his albums, and has tapes of him on TV shows from all over the world in her videocassette library.

Then there are those fans whose behaviour seems to cross the boundary of what would be normally acceptable. What are we to make, for example, of the gay male fan at one of Tom's Vegas shows, who joined the line of adoring women fans at the front of the stage to give Tom a gift, and get a big kiss in return?

George Kirvay remembers the incident well. 'I was sitting in a banquette with Gordon Mills, watching the show, and this guy goes down to the front of the stage with the women. And I thought "Oh, my God." I'd always wondered what would happen in this event – how Tom would handle it. But he handled it beautifully. He kissed all the women in line, like he always does, and when he got to this guy, he just stuck out his hand and shook hands with him. Didn't make a joke out of it, didn't try to put him down. He took it in his stride.'

Then there was Carol Holtzer, truly one of Tom's most fanatical followers. She organized his first Los Angeles fan club in 1968, which she called Gemini, after Tom's astrological sign. The ranks of Gemini swelled considerably when Tom's TV show, which was only a marginal success in the US, was cut back by the ABC network; originally a weekly show, it was later broadcast only once a month. Carol Holtzer immediately placed an advertisement in a Los Angeles newspaper, calling on women to picket ABC's L.A. headquarters. 'The response was overwhelming,' recalled Joyce Sacks, who joined the picket. 'Carol was outrageous. She should have gone into public relations.' Indeed, Carol Holtzer was photographed at the head of the picket line, brandishing a sign with the mildly suggestive slogan: 'Happiness is Tom Jones once a week.'

Carol's enthusiasm for Tom Jones was a wonder to behold. 'She talked of erecting buildings, putting up hospitals in his name, all sorts of outlandish things,' says Joyce Sacks. Unfortunately, Carol overstepped the mark. She allegedly wrote a letter to Tom's wife Linda, which caused tremendous consternation in the Jones household; it was said to detail affairs that Tom had been having. Carol's Gemini colleagues were agreed she was madly in love with Tom, perhaps to the point of obsession. Chris Hutchins disliked Carol, possibly because some of her more outrageous activities infringed on his own public relations function, and the letter gave him an excuse to get rid of her. He and Gordon confronted Carol, and told her she had to disband Gemini or resign.

Carol called together the other women in Gemini and explained the situation, though vehemently denying she had done anything wrong. 'She was absolutely hysterical,' remembers Joyce Sacks, who offered to carry on the Los Angeles fan club along with a friend, Ruth Montiel. 'But we carried on. We re-named ourselves the Jones Girls. Chris and Gordon didn't want anything that smacked of Gemini.'

But even Carol Holtzer's wild exploits seem tame compared with those of Barbara Anderson, of Rochester, New York, who deliberately broke the law to indulge her Tom Jones fixation. Barbara seemed to be able to attend every Tom Jones concert in a tour. She invariably had the best seats – and whichever cities she visited, she always stayed in the best hotels, and dined in the finest restaurants. 'We couldn't figure out how she did it,' said Ruth Brooks, a Canadian fan club president. 'We figured she must have a real good job.'

But Barbara Anderson didn't. Nor was she an heiress, or a woman of independent means. In fact, she was a lowly bookkeeper, earning a mere $17,000 a year at a company called Lockwood, who made aerial maps. Barbara made her money the old-fashioned way – she embezzled it. In 1982, police established that she had falsified 300 cheques over a thirty-month period, totalling $100,000. This was all to keep Barbara in money to follow Tom Jones across the country. The consequences of her fanaticism were troubling. Her embezzling caused such a drain on the company's profits that some travelling salesmen had to be laid off, and others had to take a cut in wages while being ordered to stay in cheaper hotels or even humble YMCA hostels. For all Barbara Anderson's trouble, Tom Jones never got to know her.

Although relationships between Tom Jones' management and his fan club girls fluctuated over the years, things went generally smoothly. Tom and Gordon did just enough to make the fans feel appreciated in the long term; the fans on their part laboured tirelessly on Tom's behalf, boosting his career, and raising money for charities like cerebral palsy victims. Sometimes the peace was an uneasy one, but it was at least a peace.

Things changed abruptly in July 1986, with the sudden death of Gordon Mills; Tom's son Mark Woodward took over as his manager. How abrupt was the change? Some fan club members report phoning the Los Angeles office of Gordon Mills Enterprises the day after his death to express condolences; the people who answered the phones said 'Tom Jones Enterprises, can I help you?' The fan club girls were stunned by what they perceived as the coldness of this small detail.

But that was only an indication of things to come. Within two weeks of Gordon's funeral, the popular Annie Toomaru, who had worked hard to improve relationships with the fan clubs, was fired. In the subsequent shake-up, Mark's wife Donna became publicist for Tom's organization, with the ultimate responsibility for liaison with Tom's seventy-five US fan clubs.

Under Donna, the fan club girls sensed a new attitude on the part of Tom Jones Enterprises toward them. Gone was Annie Toomaru's easy, friendly approach. In its place was a new atmosphere – one of impatience and faint contempt. Gradually, the fan club girls came to think the new policy of Tom Jones Enterprises was to phase out certain of the local fan clubs, and take over the running of the clubs themselves in a kind of national network run from the management's Los Angeles offices.

A sign of the new contempt towards the fan club girls showed itself when Tom Jones was awarded the star on the Hollywood Walk of Fame, at a cost of $3,500 to be made payable to the Hollywood Chamber of Commerce. Florence Coleman, a long-time Tom Jones fan from Margate, New Jersey, who works as a vice-president of administration in an Atlantic City casino, decided in 1987 that it would be a nice gesture for the money to come not from Tom's own management company, but from the fan club girls themselves.

Attempts to get Tom a Walk of Fame star had been broached before by the girls. The Los Angeles fan club had tried to persuade Gordon Mills to agree to a campaign for a star. But Mills had urged them to wait, saying that he wanted Tom to have a hit record that could be promoted at the Walk of Fame ceremony. Because this was the early 1980s, and Tom's record sales were at a low ebb, this could have meant a long wait.

On another occasion, fans asked Tom's then publicist John Moran to ask Tom if he would agree to a campaign for a star. Moran was enthusiastic, but urged caution, saying that he did not want Tom to know about any such attempts; if the Hollywood Chamber of Commerce rejected his application, he argued, Tom's feelings might be hurt.

Still, after Gordon had died and John Moran had been removed from his job, it occurred to Florence Coleman that the time was right to renew efforts for a Walk of Fame star. She wrote to Mark Woodward, and outlined her proposal to raise the $3,500 for the Walk of Fame Star from Tom's US fan clubs; each of them in turn would hold fund-raising events. Donna Woodward responded, and gave the idea her blessing; Florence was put in charge of raising the money.

She thought that if each club could raise $65, that would cover the Hollywood Chamber of Commerce fee and some additional costs for the star. And indeed, many of the fan club girls energetically set about organizing raffles and car washes to raise the money. But the response – perhaps a reflection of the state of Tom Jones' fortunes by this time – was disappointing. In a rather melancholy letter to other fan clubs in 1988, Florence noted that of seventy-five fan clubs, only forty-eight had committed to raise money for the Walk of Fame Star. A mere thirty-three had actually sent in money, but in some cases less than the requisite $65. In the same letter, Florence announced a raffle for a pair of black boots actually worn by Tom on stage. Things were looking decidedly grim.

Still, Florence's energy and persistence eventually got the money raised, and Tom was scheduled to receive his star in June 1989. It could have been a joyous day for Tom's fan club girls, many of whom would have travelled the length of the country to see their idol get his award. But Tom Jones Enterprises did nothing to encourage the girls to come. 'You don't need to be there,' they were told by phone. 'It's only a brief ceremony – it's not worth travelling a long way to be there.' To make their feelings quite clear, Tom Jones Enterprises invited no fan clubs to attend the ceremony. One fan club member remarked bitterly: 'The press was at the event that day, and the management didn't want the press to see that so many of Tom's fans are forty- and fifty-year-olds.'

Florence Coleman was invited to the ceremony by the Hollywood Chamber of Commerce. She flew 3,000 miles to be there, and attended the brief reception inside the lingerie store Frederick's of Hollywood after Tom was awarded his star. Other fan club members would later report Florence had felt ignored, that no one at the reception talked to her, she felt completely isolated, no one from Tom's management introduced her to anyone present, and none of Tom's management team had the presence of mind to halt the proceedings and mention her contribution to the day's events.

In fairness, Florence Coleman says publicly that she had a great day, that she was warmly received, and even though she and Tom exchanged few words, she could see the extent of his gratitude from the expression on his face throughout the ceremony. 'He thanked me, and he was very gracious,' she said, and denied any feelings of being snubbed or isolated.

But the gossip surrounding Florence Coleman was merely an indication of the relations between Tom Jones Enterprises and his fan clubs, which by early 1989 were at their lowest ebb ever.

This showed itself in his appearances at the Bally Grand casino in Las Vegas. Ursula Alioto attended one of his shows there in July 1989, and recalls: 'I had seats right up against the stage and I noticed there weren't as many seats as usual up front for the fan club. The maitre d' told me that several ringside seats are saved for what they call the "bimbettes". The members of the band go out into the casino and they recruit young, very pretty women so Tom can look out during the show and see a lot of young attractive faces. Then after the show, they had Chris come out and recruit some of these young girls to go backstage and meet Tom, and do what they do. And all this happened right in front of the fan club ladies.'

Seeing this was enough to force Ursula to quit working for a Tom Jones fan club. She asked the older women around her in Vegas: 'Have you no pride? Are you just going to sit back and let this happen?' The whole experience, she said a few days later, made her feel 'crummy'.

Massive discontent among the fan club girls broke out over a letter from Tom Jones Enterprises, which was unsigned, but was generally believed to have been penned by Donna Woodward. Donna was by now widely unpopular with the fan club girls, who regarded her as an upstart, a newcomer who was indistinguishable from a groupie, really. Through her friendships with members of Tom's backing band, the fan club girls thought, Donna had wormed her way into Mark's affections – and now, as his wife, was enjoying the fruits of a big share of Tom Jones' substantial fortune. Another little habit of Donna's infuriated the veteran fan club girls – her insistence that they refer to Tom as 'Mr Jones'. After all these years, Tom was to be 'Mr Jones'. It seemed intolerable.

The infamous letter, headed 'To all fan clubs', declared that it would 'outline our new policies'. But its tone was quite extraordinary – reminiscent of a scolding Victorian governess, admonishing wayward children.

Paragraph 1 of the 'new policies', regarding backstage visits, was enough to provoke widespread furore on its own. It read: 'It is not a Fan Clubs [sic] natural right to demand a backstage visit with their performer. If your motivation for being a club is based on a personal moment with the artist, then your motivation is wrong. Contrary to what you may hear, very few artists ever visit with their fans, due to a tremendous demand on their personal schedules, of which you have no knowledge, nor should you speculate in this area.

'Your main function, should you chose [sic] to continue in your endeavours, is to support the artists in his endeavours, by word of mouth, by radio station call-ins, and record purchases. This is what matters to Mr Jones, and it is your efforts in these areas that he appreciates most.

'It is nobody's business who gets backstage for what reason. The decision on backstage visits is entirely the prerogative of Mr Jones and his Management.'

The undiplomatic tone of the letter shocked the fan club girls. It was bad enough that they were suddenly being denied backstage access to Tom when he played concerts in their area, something they had previously been granted as a courtesy for their efforts on Tom's behalf. But this letter looked as if Mark and Donna were hell-bent on getting rid of the fan clubs. How else could they read the phrase 'should you choose to continue in your endeavours'? Did Mark and Donna want them out? And was this what Tom himself wanted?

Worse was to come in the letter's second paragraph, which detailed the new regime's policy on the decorating of dressing rooms. This read: 'Access to Mr Jones' dressing room before and after the show has created a variety of problems that have increased in occurance [sic] in all areas of the country. These incidences [sic] have affected many people, from Mr Jones to his staff to the venue itself. Mr Jones does appreciate your thoughts and efforts, and welcomes any messages or items left with the theatre manager. It is in your best interest to know that gifts more appreciated and used are fruit, homemade food items, towels and champagne.'

News of the astounding new policy reached Britain soon afterwards, and *The People* ran a brief commentary headlined 'Fruity Welsh squelch'. 'What a damned cheek!' said the commentary about the champagne gift suggestion. 'If anything, the drinks should be on Tom – to toast the long-standing loyalty of his admirers. As for fruit, may I hand this big-headed boyo exactly what he deserves – a large raspberry.'

For some reason, the news was slower to be leaked in the US, but in July 1989, Mitchell Fink, the acid-tongued gossip columnist of the *Los Angeles Herald Examiner*, ran a brief item about the new policy. 'From our Department of Gall comes word that singer Tom Jones has made members of his fan club aware of the kinds of gifts he prefers receiving,' wrote Fink, who briefly outlined the gift suggestions and the new backstage rules.

Fink's nine-line item got the jungle telegraph working. Fans from Los Angeles who read it called others from across the country, and many of them called Fink with their comments the very same day the item ran. 'I was amazed,' said Fink. 'Of all the items I'd run in the last year, nothing provoked a reaction like this one.'

Phone calls to Fink came not only from the *Herald*'s circulation area in Los Angeles, but from as far away as Atlanta and Miami. Fink, taken aback by the response, duly printed some of the angry fans' comments the very next day. This was the sampling he published:

This is a slap in the face. It's horrible. Give me a break.

Maybe it's a phase he's going through. Maybe he'll come to his senses. He's survived for twenty years but he won't survive for another twenty years acting like this.

It is downright degrading to the women who have spent thousands of dollars trying to keep him from becoming a has-been.

He wants to cut loose his older fans because he no longer wants to be reminded how old he is.

In a pointed footnote, Fink added: 'These are the very people, by the way, who chipped in and made it possible for Jones to get his star on the Hollywood Walk of Fame. Some payback.'

Indeed. But the fan club girls sensed from the infamous letter that trouble lay ahead. In its closing, the letter stated: 'We are now in the process of reorganizing the fan clubs to create a more cohesive and effective group.' That was news to most of the fan club organizers who had toiled for years, promoting the name of Tom Jones – they had certainly not been consulted about the matter.

A little defensively, the letter from the management went on: 'We do pay attention to your letters and calls, and we take many of your comments and suggestions into consideration.' But even this attempt at conciliation was tinged with more than a hint of disdain: 'To all those who keep the right perspective, we thank you for your many efforts . . . ' Perspective? Some of the girls had worked tirelessly for Tom for twenty-four years, and no one had ever lectured them about 'the right perspective' before this team of management newcomers.

But the crux of the whole letter was saved right until the end: ' . . . we thank you for your many forms of support. But there are also criticisms that have come to us that reveal pettiness, selfishness and a warped sense of "understanding" of Mr Jones' business, and it is most annoying for the management staff to have to spend time with these "issues". In our restructuring of the clubs, we will try to help you focus on what is important, and what is most appreciated by all involved.'

Many of the fans see the new policy as a form of age discrimination – a move on the part of Mark and Donna to weed out the veteran fans, now in their forties and fifties, from the fan clubs, supposedly to replace them with younger women fans. The widespread taunt from these older fans about Tom is: 'We're making him look old.'

'I've seen a big change in the way he handles fans,' says Ursula Alioto. 'A lot of them are Tom's age or older, and the way he treats them now is just terrible. Ten years ago when you went backstage he would kibitz with you, he was a human being. He seemed like a down-to-earth person, who thought his macho stage image was funny, and nothing more, but that it wasn't really him. Now he seems to believe the whole bit.

'These days, he's stiff and cold. Going backstage to meet him now makes you feel like a child, getting your picture taken with Santa Claus. His eyes are sort of glazed, he seems bored, and he doesn't seem to want to meet the fans now. Chris Montgomery doesn't let the women talk to him for more than a couple of minutes before he makes them move on. There's no warmth there any more.'

Then there's Karen and Adele, two women who work in a travel agency and also run the New Orleans fan club, Tom Jones' Old-fashioned Strutters. The new backstage policies brought them to the brink of quitting their activities on Tom Jones' behalf. 'Here's a man,' says Adele, 'who hasn't had a hit record in a long time, and their fans devote themselves to him. And now they get this terrible discourtesy from him – it's a terrible shame. We've always gone backstage to meet him after shows, and now we can't. Now we can't even get in the first four rows of his concerts. Me, I'm just interested in how I get treated when I spend so much money on him.'

The two women think the change in attitude towards the fans happened around the time the letter was circulated.

'We went to see him in 1988,' says Adele, 'and he was friendly enough then. That's changed, and here's a man we would wait for outside of a theatre after a show till 2 or 3 in the morning – not to act stupid towards him, but because we're fans. It's a complete turnaround.'

They wonder if he feels he can ignore older fans because of the success of one hit record, 'Kiss'. 'Is he on that much of an ego trip?' asks Adele. 'Teenagers won't keep him up on top. If that's his choice, fine, but I won't spend any more of my hard-earned money on him. Why should I spend money on airfare, hotels, rental cars? I've travelled to see him since 1972. I've raised money for muscular dystrophy, for multiple sclerosis, for various telethons, all in his name.'

Adele has seven cameras in her home, each equipped with zoom lenses, wide angle lenses, telefoto lenses – the works. And predictably, her devotion to photography is limited to her devotion to taking pictures of Tom Jones. 'I have thousands of pictures of him,' she says, a little sadly.

'What's so sad,' she continues with a sigh, 'what's so degrading, is that we'll probably still keep doing this. I don't know why – because we wouldn't take this kind of treatment from our husbands.'

Florence Coleman, though, has another point of view. 'It's something that Tom has done for so long, letting fans backstage,' she says. 'We've been so privileged that Tom has seen so many fans. If you just look at it in that perspective, you get to see that the man has other things to do.'

The veteran fans photocopied and mailed from state to state a 1989 interview with Tom from the magazine *Elle*, in which he told music writer Adam Sweeting that he was aiming at younger audiences. Noting that his then upcoming album *Move Closer* was on the hip, small eclectic label Jive Records, Sweeting wrote: 'His association with the label will, he hopes, encourage new listeners to look beyond the stereotype of the middle-aged Lothario and discover the diversity that has always hallmarked his live performances.'

Innocent words, perhaps, but they were like a red rag to a bull as far as Tom's older fans were concerned. So was another

colourful Sweeting sentence from the same article: 'Chances
are if you stop people on the street and ask them about Tom
Jones, they'll mention Las Vegas and swarms of blue-rinsed
ladies in horn-rims, scuffling in an unseemly fashion for scraps
of the singer's clothing or even lumps of his flesh.' The words
weren't Tom's, but the impression conveyed was that he might
endorse them.

The sense of alienation between Tom's management and
his fan clubs, then, had never been greater than in the first
half of 1989. Many of the diehard fan club organizers were
so shocked at the downward turn in relationships that they
considered quitting; but they were torn by a long-standing
affection for Tom's sex appeal and artistry.

It was an upsetting time, and two of Tom's earliest fans in
Los Angeles, Ruth Montiel and Joyce Sacks, wrote an angry
letter to Donna Woodward, which asked: 'Can Tom Jones
really afford to discard his "old" fan club members, some
of which have remained loyal since the late sixties? It seems
to us that he has empowered his management to discourage
and distance his fans . . . we are appalled at the deterioration
of co-operation and professionalism which is now evidenced
between Tom's management and the fan clubs. Is it really
is his best interests to continually alienate members of the
clubs? . . . Your stand regarding fan club attendance [at the
Walk of Fame ceremony] is a slap in the face for all those
who have remained loyal to Tom.'

The day after the letter was mailed, Joyce Sacks received a
call, not from Donna Woodward, but from one of her assistants
at Tom Jones Enterprises. 'All she wanted to know,' recalls
Joyce, 'is who these fan club members were who claimed they
were discouraged from attending the Walk of Fame ceremony.
I wouldn't tell her – but I did add that many fan club members
were terribly upset at the way things were going on. The woman said they were "menopausal". And she hung up on me.'

Menopausal? Quite an insult from the office of a man who
once described his fans as 'absolutely terrific'. And a sad sign
of ingratitude to thousands of fans who have maintained Tom
Jones' career.

Chapter Thirteen

AFTER GORDON

Tom Jones has thousands and thousands of loyal fans all over the world. But don't count Annie Toomaru among them.

Annie is a stunningly attractive woman in her mid-forties, with deeply golden skin and long straight black hair. She was born and raised in Tahiti, but has lived in Los Angeles for several years. In July 1982, she met Gordon Mills, and the couple fell in love.

Annie was hardly Gordon's first excursion outside his marriage to Jo Mills, but she was by far the most serious, and sometime in 1985, with his divorce from Jo pending, Gordon told his mother Lorna of his plans to wed Annie.

By this time, Gordon had brought Annie into his organization, and had given her a job which would allow her to spend more time travelling with him and Tom. On the road, Annie joined an elite circle around Tom which included Gordon, his American tour manager Lloyd Greenfield, his assistant Nancy Eisner, public relations director John Moran and Tom's son Mark Woodward. 'I felt like a respected part of the organization,' she says now.

But Gordon's death from cancer in 1986 was the occasion for massive changes in the Tom Jones organization, and what Annie failed to realize was that she represented part of a past regime to young Mark Woodward, the boy who would be king, the son who stepped into Gordon's shoes as his father's manager.

After Gordon died, Annie was out, cut from the organization

by means of a phone call from New York City from a company accountant, Shelly Phillips. She was fired less than two weeks after Gordon's funeral, and Tom Jones, who she believed was a friend, never once picked up the phone to call her.

She was part of a limited but ruthless purge which rocked Tom Jones' management team that year. A month after she was dismissed, John Moran, who liked and openly admired Gordon Mills, was relieved of his duties as public relations director. Significantly, it was Donna Woodward, Mark's wife, who took his place – even though she was without any apparent PR experience. Bill Smith, Gordon's top man in London, relocated to Los Angeles to run the financial side of the organization. Within a year of Gordon's death, Nancy Eisner quit, telling close friends she did not like the direction the organization was taking. 'Things were just not the same,' Nancy says now. 'Gordon created something most people just dream of creating, and I felt very angry and pissed off that he was dead. Even if someone like Colonel Tom Parker had taken over, I couldn't have handled it after Gordon. I was on Tom's payroll, but when your son and daughter-in-law come in to run the business, it's easy for them to feel they're a unit.'

The personnel changes put Mark firmly in the driver's seat, with the ability to call the shots about his father's career, and make whatever suggestions he wanted in terms of Tom's stage act, album material, even clothes. With a charismatic figure like Gordon gone, it was inevitable that the organization would undergo some changes. But the changes around Tom Jones that year of 1986 were radical, even cruel. And no dismissal was more cruel than Annie Toomaru's.

'For three years, I had co-ordinated the fan clubs,' she says now. 'I answered all his fans' letters, sent out itineraries for the fan clubs, worked with charity organizations. I got letters from fans saying I was doing a great job, and I kept those letters.'

During the phone call that dismissed Annie, Phillips said she was Gordon's private secretary, and she was no longer needed in that capacity. But Annie insists: 'All the time I was in that office, I was working for Tom Jones.' She travelled with him, too – to Lake Tahoe, Honolulu, Las Vegas, and even to England in 1983. When Tom's mother or sister joined them on the road, Annie would be part of the dinner party. 'We'd hang around together, all of us,' she remembers.

But the very day of Gordon's funeral in Surrey, she suspected something might be wrong. 'After the funeral, we all went back to the house. John Moran had already taken me on one side and advised me to go up to Tom and tell him that when I flew back to L.A., I would go straight back to work in the office. Tom was getting ready to leave, he was saying his goodbyes, and he was about to walk out the door without saying goodbye to me. So I walked up to him and told him I would go straight back to work in L.A., and he said: "I can't think about that right now." It made me feel very uneasy. That was the first time I saw anything different in Tom.'

Since her dismissal, she has had no contact with any member of the Tom Jones organization. Nor, she says, has Gordon's mother Lorna, or most of his five children. 'The last time I went to stay with them, I know they were very disappointed.'

What does she make of her sudden fall from grace? She lays some of the blame with Mark Woodward. 'Tom's son always had a little animosity towards Gordon,' she says. 'When Gordon was alive, he asked Mark to come over to our house to spend time with him and learn the business. But Mark never did. Gordon actually wanted Mark to take over eventually, which is why he invited him over. But I guess Mark had his own views of what he wanted to do for his father. Gordon used to say that Mark was still young, but it felt like he didn't care about what he, Gordon, had done for Tom.'

But she reserves her most savage criticism for Tom Jones himself. 'My feeling is that Tom is a very self-centred person, and when you do something for him, there's nothing in return.' She insists that had Jones simply called her after Gordon's death to explain that cutbacks were necessary but regrettable, she would have understood. But the call never came.

'Gordon talked about Tom in a fond manner,' she added. 'He never put Tom down. The only critical thing he ever used to say about him was that Tom was selfish, someone who wouldn't take the trouble to send flowers to someone who had helped him, little things like that. But then Gordon used to say that it was his fault, because he had trained Tom to be like that. He had told him to get on stage, do his act, and let Gordon worry about everything else.'

By contrast, Gordon didn't forget. In his will, he left money to his mother, to his four daughters and one son, to Annie, and to a former mistress who had preceded her.

Lorna Mills, Gordon's mother, is equally bitter about the way Tom seemed to ignore Gordon's memory after his death. She remembers an appearance by Tom on Michael Parkinson's talk show, in which, as she says: 'Parkinson praised my son to the skies. He told Tom in front of the audience – Gordon made you what you are, he was your Svengali, and he was a legend in his lifetime.

'But the only reaction that got from Jones was a shrug! It was as though he didn't even want to acknowledge Gordon.

'My son made him what he is – but he has never once had the courtesy to see how I or Gordon's family are doing.

'There has never been a phone call, or a visit. It seems as though he doesn't want to know the Mills family now Gordon has gone.'

Annie Toomaru came close, almost cruelly close, to being Gordon Mills' second wife. 'Gordon's divorce became final in 1985, and the following year, they were working out the settlement for the estate,' she recalled. 'Everything was going to be final by the end of July 1986. In June 1986, we were looking for a smaller house in Los Angeles, and at the end of July, Gordon and I were going to fly to England to repossess the house where his ex-wife had been living. We were going to leave L.A. on 28 July; I know, because I booked the tickets.'

The trip would never be made. While Tom was in the recording studios in Los Angeles earlier that month, Gordon, who was with him, complained of stomach pains. At first, he attributed it to food poisoning, but when the pains persisted,

Annie took him to Cedars-Sinai Medical Center on 11 July for a series of routine tests. Meanwhile, Tom flew to Vegas to fulfil a casino engagement.

At first, the doctors could find nothing wrong with Gordon. Nancy Eisner recalls: 'They took the IVs out of his arms, and told him he could go home. That was good news, and to celebrate, we got Adriano, the proprietor of Adriano's restaurant, one of Gordon's favourites in L.A., to bring some gourmet food up to the hospital. But when it came, Gordon just couldn't eat it. "It's hurting,' he said." '

Finally, the doctors discovered cancer, and performed an operation on Gordon in the vain hope that it might prolong his life.

Gordon's entire family came to Los Angeles to be near their father. Annie slept in Gordon's room all through the eighteen-day vigil, while she in turn was comforted by his daughter Beverly and by Nancy Eisner. Even Jo Mills came to Los Angeles with her new boyfriend to lend moral support to her children. Annie and Nancy Eisner spent long hours at Gordon's bedside, playing cards and watching Gordon lying in bed, heavily medicated. In his slumber, Nancy remembers, 'he would wave his arms around a lot. The doctors reckoned that he was dreaming about reaching for something – but I used to say it looked as though he was conducting.'

Tom Jones was deeply concerned too. 'I spent a lot of time talking with him on the phone, and talking to Mark,' Annie remembers. When it became obvious that Gordon was deteriorating, Beverly Mills called Tom and suggested he should come to Cedars-Sinai. So Tom visited Gordon in hospital in his eighth-floor suite. 'He saw how bad Dad was,' says Beverly, 'and then we went into the smoking room.' After he had viewed his unconscious body, Tom adjourned to a nearby waiting room where smoking was permitted. 'It was the first time I have seen Tom break down,' says Nancy Eisner. 'He wept like a baby.' Beverly Mills remembers: 'He sobbed, and cried: "What am I going to do?" He said it over and over again. He wailed and cried: "Oh God, Bev, what am I going to do?" We all cried our hearts out.'

Gordon died on 29 July – the day after he had been due to fly back to England with Annie and start a new chapter of his life with her. His body was flown over to England, where he was buried, according to his wishes, beside his father at St Peter's Church in Hersham, Surrey. Tom cancelled all his engagements and flew back for the funeral, at which he was one of the pallbearers.

This was another tearful occasion for Tom. He was red-eyed during the entire service. Beverly Mills remembers: 'I remember at the house, Little Rhondda, before the service, we all picked a rose to put into the coffin And it became terribly important to Tom to choose just the right rose. We all shared a lot of pain that day.'

But by the time Gordon Mills' funeral came around, Annie's fate was sealed. Changes were inevitable, and people had to be swept aside to make room for Mark – and anyone else he wanted in the new-look Tom Jones team. It is still unclear whether Tom himself took the initiative in naming Mark as Gordon's successor, or whether Mark pushed himself forward to fill the vacuum at the top of the organization. Most people close to the Jones camp favour the latter theory, citing Tom's passivity and lack of interest when it came to business decisions.

Whichever way it happened, Tom Jones' career took a more radically different direction than at any time in the previous eighteen years – since he had first set foot on a Vegas stage, in fact. Mark, who had been travelling consistently with his father on the road since he was about thirteen, had had ample time to make up his mind how he would change things if his big moment came.

Mark first determined that his father's image needed a major shake-up. He could see no reason why Tom, with that extraordinary voice of his, could not appeal to people in his own age group. Mark was twenty-nine, and a serious pop fan. Roger Wall recalls: 'He used to do the tapes for the dressing rooms. He had a great ear for new sounds, and when new wave music started coming, he latched straight on to that.' Wall feels that Mark was directly responsible for getting Tom to include in his act the Prince song 'Kiss', which gave him a massive hit in 1988.

Under Mark's management, Tom's entire look underwent a big change. His frizzy curls were cut much shorter and tighter, and any pretence at a pompadour ended. From his wardrobe, out went the tight, lacy shirts and the fitted flared suits. In came an array of hats, and some looser, garish leather outfits, some of which might have looked more acceptable on a twenty-year-old. For Vegas, Tom now started to wear dark, double-breasted suits and black shirts; combined with his new hairdo, and longer sideburns, they gave him the appearance of a gangster from London's East End.

During the next year or so, Tom Jones would once again undergo plastic surgery to change his appearance. A surgeon's scalpel removed bags from around his eyes. Youthfulness was the order of the day in every detail of his new image, and Mark's influence was clear.

The son had persuaded his father to listen to newer material by younger artists – like Prince, INXS, Wang Chung and Billy Idol. And sure enough, songs by these artists started to creep into his stage act. 'Kiss', with its irresistible rhythms and suggestive lyrics, seemed tailor-made for Tom's concerts.

But a turning point for Tom came when Anne Dudley and J. J. Jeczalik, the duo who comprise the eclectic, avant-garde pop group Art of Noise, saw him performing the song on British television. The pair, who specialized in reworking classic pop (they had already had a single hit with Duane Eddy), immediately approached Tom to ask if they could record the song with him. Mark was enthusiastic, so Tom went into the studios with the Art of Noise; his catchy little phrase before the instrumental break, 'Think I better dance now,' helped the record stick in listeners' minds.

Although it narrowly failed to make the US top twenty, 'Kiss' marked something of a come-back for Tom in America, where, remarkably, he had only had one top forty hit in the previous seventeen years – 'Say You'll Stay Until Tomorrow' from 1977.

For 'Kiss', Tom shot his first video, which at least showed he was keeping abreast of the times. For the video, in keeping with his new image, he donned a baggy, oversized suit, reminiscent of those worn by Talking Heads' David Byrne. Suddenly, Tom was hip.

'Kiss' also paved the way for a new album on a new label. Tom signed with Jive Records, a London-based subsidiary of RCA, which specializes in soul and rap artists. On Jive's wildly varied roster at the time was soul veteran Millie Jackson, rap artists D.J. Jazzy Jeff and the Fresh Prince, and disco pin-up girl Samantha Fox. None of these artists were Tom Jones' style, in truth, and neither was Jive – it was the first time in his twenty-four-year career that he had been signed to anything but a major record label.

Still, the move to Jive allowed his publicity machine to trumpet his first pop-rock album in almost a decade, after years in the country ghetto at Polygram. And his office tried to play up his new hip credentials by stressing the vibrant young producers Tom had worked with on his new album, *Move Closer*. These included Barry J. Eastmond, who had worked for Billy Ocean; and Timmy Allen, who had written R&B hits for Millie Jackson and Stephanie Mills. But in the end, this all counted for nothing, and *Move Closer* failed to make even a dent on the charts.

However, the album did at least establish that Tom Jones was determined to breathe new life into his career, by accentuating a more youthful image. But some of the ways he and Mark chose to enforce this were unfortunate, to put it mildly.

Around the end of 1986, less than six months after Gordon's death, at least three of the older, long-serving musicians from Tom's backing band were fired without explanation. Their musicianship was not in question, and they felt that they had been fired because they looked too old on stage.

One of the musicians, Jimmy Nuizo, filed a lawsuit against Tom Jones, alleging age discrimination. But it was impossible to make the charge stick. Gordon Mills had protected the Jones organization before his death by ensuring that all the musicians were on one-year contracts. And these older guys were simply released when their contracts expired.

Still, the firings came as a shock, as Steve Romanelli, a sax, oboe and English horn player, explains. 'We were like a family. I'd played with the band for seven years. There was no warning.'

Steve, who was fifty-six when the axe fell, adds: 'I imagine a change of management had a lot to do with it. I had vibes that there would have been problems earlier than that if Gordon hadn't been around. Gordon kept us on a little longer, I think. But had it been left to Michael [Morgan, the musical director who did the firings], I think we would have been gone a couple of years earlier.'

Steve returned to his native Pittsburgh, but his prospects were bleak; three years after his dismissal from the Jones' band, he had not worked regularly. 'I think they wanted a younger image,' he says wearily. 'And even though we did a good job musically, I guess we didn't present a younger image.'

However, he has no feelings of bitterness towards Tom Jones personally. 'As long as I played with him, Tom was a prince, a beautiful guy. He visited my home every time he came to Pittsburgh. He met my mother, he was very close to her, he met my whole family. He supped with us, we had a good time.'

And did this 'beautiful guy' repay this hospitality by picking up the phone to wish Steve well after he was fired? 'No, not really,' admits Steve. 'I think he's pretty busy. I don't think he makes a practice of trying to call people.'

Indeed he does not – as Dave Swan will quickly tell you. Dave is a Vegas comedian, who was born around the same time as Tom in a South Wales mining village close to Treforest. He first met Tom way back in the early 1960s, through their mutual friend Bryn Phillips, the singer-comedian who shared the bill with Tom that fateful night in 1964 at the Top Hat Club in Cwmtellery, the first night Gordon Mills saw Tom performing.

Some fifteen years later, Dave arrived in Vegas and carved out a good career for himself, doing stand-up comedy in some of the desert resort's smaller lounges. He and Tom would get together when Tom was playing in Vegas; Dave and his wife would get free seats for Tom's shows, and go backstage afterwards.

'Once,' Dave recalled,'I said to him, "How about the chance to have me be the opening act for you?" But he passed the buck, and said decisions like that were up to Gordon. He said that he'd once insisted that Gordon book this one comedian, but he'd failed dismally. After that, Gordon told him to stay out of those kind of decisions.

'Still, I got a call from Gordon when I was in Reno, asking me to come down and audition for him in Vegas. I did a showcase for him, and he said, "Well, you're a very good comic, but I've heard all your stuff before." He was being real facetious. Gordon could be a real asshole, you know. But he told me he wanted to see more of my material. So I flew down a second time, at my own expense, and showcased again. And in the end, all Gordon could say was that he thought my being Welsh and Tom being Welsh would detract from Tom's uniqueness, because I'd be on first. I couldn't see it at all; I think it would be a unique situation to have two Welshmen on one bill. But that was that.

'Then Gordon died, and I thought I'd take the bull by the horns and have another shot.' He and his wife went to see Tom at one of his Vegas shows, then went into his dressing room backstage. 'There were quite a few people piled in there,' says Dave. 'There was his mother, his sister, Mark, the actor Greg Morris and his wife.' Initially, according to Dave, he was harassed by Tom's big blond burly bodyguard, the former SAS man Chris Montgomery. 'Very zealous, he was. Tom never had a bodyguard in the old days. Never needed one. Now this Chris appears on the side of the stage when Tom's kissing the women in the front row. Totally ridiculous.'

Dave managed to dodge round Chris, and was in the middle of reminding Tom of their old plans to work together as a team. 'Suddenly, he turns around and shouts: "Let's have dinner!" And everyone troops out, leaving my wife and me just standing there. Very embarrassing, it was. And humiliating.

'The sad part,' continues Dave Swan, 'is that I could have been part of that team, if I had been given a break. And what really hurts me is that I'm a fellow Welshman.' He does not claim that he was ever a close friend of Tom Jones, but he's annoyed now when his phone calls to Tom are not even returned.

His story would have a familiar ring to Tracey and Beverly Mills, two of Gordon's daughters, whose memories of Tom are remarkably similar. 'Tom was always very selfish,' says Beverly, 'not in an unkind way, but he always thought of himself first. He would never think to send a birthday card or a thank you note – he just wouldn't think. But partly that was because Dad took care of everything like that.'

After Gordon's death, there was a long legal wrangle over the business. Tom wanted to buy Gordon's half of what was now Tom Jones Enterprises, and Gordon's children wanted him to buy it. 'But then the lawyers got involved,' recalls Beverly. 'We had to get the best price for our two youngest sisters and brother. We never fell out with Tom during this time – but he never called. At least it's settled now, but it's taken a long time.'

Tracey is the one Mills kid to have seen Tom Jones since the funeral. 'I wanted to see him, so I went to the Royal Albert Hall to see his [spring 1989] concert,' she says. 'I was going to send a note backstage asking to see him, but then I saw a musician I knew and he took me back. First I met Mark, who was pretty cool, and then went to talk to some other people. After ten minutes, I went up to him, and made him talk to me. He took me in to see Tom and Tom was lovely. It was a great meeting. He was really nice.'

To this day, all the Mills family members seem bewildered at the rise of Mark Woodward. They watched him growing up as an overweight, pale, unattractive, awkward kid, and they seem incredulous that he has succeeded Gordon as Tom's manager.

The year 1989 was a decidedly mixed one for Tom Jones. Although the relationships between him and his fan clubs were stormy, and although his briefly revived record career seemed once again to have stalled, he could still point with satisfaction to a hugely successful European tour, which at least seemed to confirm he was as big a draw as ever close to his native Britain.

Then came the Katherine Berkery affair.

She was twenty-four when she met Tom in a fashionable New York disco. She claimed that Tom was waiting for her when she came out of the ladies' room at the club, and she agreed to join him. He took her back to his hotel suite that night, and, as they listened to his records on a stereo, they made love in his king-size bed.

The next evening, she had front-row tickets to one of his New York concerts. They spent the next five nights together, and were never apart for more than a few hours. At one point during the tryst, she claimed, Tom asked her to persuade a friend of hers named Alicia to join them for a threesome, but she had refused.

After he left New York, Tom did not call her again. But after three months, she found she was pregnant – and tried to call him. But he did not return her frantic calls.

Katherine's son Jonathan was born in the autumn of 1988, and Katherine, feeling she had been wronged, approached prominent New York divorce attorney Raoul Felder. Felder, who handled Robin Givens' messy divorce from Mike Tyson, took on Katherine's case with enthusiasm, and urged the Manhattan Family Court to award Katherine child support.

At first, the Jones camp reacted defensively. Donna Woodward issued a statement saying: 'Mr Jones has been a victim of an irresponsible and scurrilous allegation.'

But this turned out not to be true. Tom was ordered to take a blood test to establish whether he was the father, and the results showed it was more than 99 per cent probable that indeed he was.

In July 1989, Judge Judith Scheidlin told Tom's lawyers in court: 'Gentlemen, you have lost your case.' And as a result, Tom Jones was hit with an immediate court order to pay Katherine £200 a month to care for Jonathan.

This was an interim figure, and Felder immediately

announced plans to increase it to £2,000 a month until Jonathan is grown up.

After the court had ruled in her favour, a jubilant Katherine, holding Jonathan on one arm, told reporters she had been offered £50,000 by the Jones camp to drop the paternity suit. 'But I refused,' she said, 'I'm damned determined that Jonathan will carry the name Jones on his birth certificate.

'What Tom did was deplorable, low-down and downright outrageous. Now I realize I was nothing to him. I was just another chick on the road.'

Some former Tom Jones associates were frankly amazed that he would have left himself vulnerable to a paternity suit. 'I can't believe he isn't using precautions,' said one source. 'You have to figure that Tom Jones could have gotten an awful lot of girls pregnant.'

The publicity about the case devastated some of his fans, many of whom still prefer to regard him as a world-class flirt rather than a philanderer. And it struck another nail into the coffin of his extraordinary thirty-three-year-marriage.

Chapter Fourteen

LINDA

'When you're in the process of making love,' said Tom Jones in one of his franker moments, 'the woman seems everything to you. After you've made love, she is one of two things. Someone you want to keep with you. Or someone you want to crawl away from. A wife must be in the former category.'

Tom Jones has certainly crawled away from many, many women in his libidinous lifetime but he has always kept his wife of thirty-three years, even though these days she is rarely with him.

Melinda Rose Woodward, née Trenchard, lives today in splendid isolation in the stylish, seven-bedroomed mansion Llwynddu House, set in ten acres of beautiful Vale of Glamorgan countryside. On a clear day she can look across the valleys towards the terraced home in Pontypridd where she grew up.

But only very, very occasionally can she look at her husband because he lives in even greater opulence in California where he insists his career keeps him. The remains of one of the most remarkable showbusiness marriages adds up these days to a bizarre 'arrangement' whereby Linda lives in her beloved homeland and her philandering husband resides with the rest of his family – mother, sister, son, daughter-in-law and grandchildren – 7,000 miles away.

In 1989 the two partners in what publicists love to call one of the happiest of all showbiz marriages spent only a handful of days together.

Linda stayed on in Wales after enjoying Christmas 1988 and Tom flew back to Los Angeles. When he arrived in Britain for his highly successful European tour in April Tom's description of the marital set-up then was: 'We had a big family get-together at Christmas and Linda hadn't seen her sister for so long so she said, "Do you mind if I stay here until you come over for the tour?" And I said, "If you want to stay with your sister, go ahead." '

But even after Tom arrived and installed himself and his entourage at London's Inn on the Park hotel the couple took their time to get together. He said: 'I said on the telephone to her, "I'm here" and her answer was, "Yes, but how busy are you going to be?" I had to admit I was very busy so she decided to stay down in Wales.'

The purchase of £575,000 Llwynddu House with its leisure and entertainment wing and grounds full of sweeping lawns, idyllic woods and even a duck pond was Linda's means of escape from the empty life she grew to loathe in Los Angeles.

It was certainly not the appeal of the all-weather tennis court that brought her to the lonely new home in the exotically named village of Welsh St Donats, but a chance to return to her roots after tiring of sitting at home in unfriendly, unfamiliar Los Angeles waiting for details of her husband's latest sexual exploits to reach her.

Tom explains the move: 'She doesn't like to travel with me very much any more. She gets fed-up of that and if I'm away she doesn't really like being there without me because she hasn't made any friends or anything in L.A. She is not a showbusiness person so she said, "When you go on the road I'd rather be in Wales." At least she is with her people, people that she grew up with and she feels more kinship towards.' But despite his frequently professed enthusiasm for the land of his fathers Tom has no plans to join Linda on a permanent basis. 'I will keep my American residency. I have a British passport but I have a Green Card to work in the United States. I will keep all that because I work there so much,' he says.

Friends in Wales insist that even rattling around in her country house, frequently alone apart from the ever present security guards, Linda is happier today than for years. She spends her time with her sister Rosalyn. They shop for bargains in Pontypridd market and even enjoy caravan holidays at the seaside resort of Porthcawl just as she and Tom once did half a lifetime ago with baby Mark. She has discovered her personal peace of mind as far as possible from the endless showbusiness razmatazz, in rural tranquillity just ten miles from where she grew up. But she has reached her solitary situation by a most remarkable route.

Tom Woodward was the only man she ever loved. When she found herself pregnant at just fifteen years old by her school sweetheart, she was bewildered and frightened but she never insisted that he must marry her. Yet Linda was wildly delighted when that was the course he chose. Even if she did have to wait until after her sixteenth birthday only a month before their son Mark was born.

But long before Tom Woodward gradually metamorphosised into the figure of female fantasy known as Tom Jones, Linda Woodward learned that fidelity was not exactly her ambitious young husband's strong point.

Second cousin Billy Russell insists: 'Tom's brains always were in his balls. He chased women from being a boy and he caught plenty.'

As a young girl Melinda Trenchard was undoubtedly a local beauty, claimed widely in the Rhondda by contemporaries to be a dead ringer for Kim Novak. Dai Perry, his boyhood pal and subsequent bodyguard, recalls: 'Linda was a lovely girl, a real beauty of a lass, she was real handsome. She was always Tom's girl, never interested in nobody else. I used to take out a friend of hers and well before Tom and Linda married we used to go in the pubs and have a few flagons. Lots of fellas would have taken Linda out but she never wanted to know about anyone else than "my Tom" as she always called him.'

Certainly Tom's charm worked wonders, even on those who might have been expected to resist the match. His mother-in-law, Vi Trenchard, far from resented the swarthy young man who got her older daughter pregnant. Gerry Greenberg recalls Vi, who died in 1987. 'She was a waitress in a café which was right next to the White Hart where we used to drink. She was a very nice woman, Vi, very chatty. She could not talk about anything but her Tommy – it was as if he was her own son. With Tom's track record with the ladies and the way he treated Linda you would have thought she would have been anything but. As it was she absolutely doted on him; she treated him like God.

'And this was before he was famous, she must have been euphoric when he actually made it.'

In fact chirpy Vi remained one of Tom's greatest fans until her death. Even after his money meant she could happily retire from waiting on tables she would go back whenever the café owner was short staffed. 'He was good to me when I was desperate for a job,' Vi would say. 'Now if he needs me I go back to help out.' Linda went to work up the street from the café as an assistant in a draper's shop after she left school and it was a very sober establishment whose management frowned on any visits form her tearaway Teddy Boy boyfriend during shop hours. Linda never minded about her young lover's wild reputation. Courting one of the toughest guys on the scene carried a certain cachet and even if the police came to visit, Tom's streetwise explanations and the squeaky clean family home usually prevented further investigation. As Tom said many years later: 'When they came to see my mother with the brass nicely polished in the front room and pictures of Grandad with his medals they went away saying, "No ruffian could live here."

'In my teens I used to wear a sky blue suit and black suede crêpe-soled shoes. We were all very aggressive. Teddy Boys were men with big shoulders.

'Our girls were aggressive too. They wore lots of make-up and were very tough. That's the kind of thing I grew up with and it's left its mark. Teenagers don't have to be aggressive today because older people aren't fighting them.'

By the time they approached their mid-teens Tom and Linda were inseparable and while the early pregnancy was an enormous jolt to both families it was no real surprise. After the simplest of wedding ceremonies the young couple moved into the cramped basement of her parents' humble home, 3 Cliff Terrace, and hurriedly prepared to become parents. But South Wales mining villages did not swiftly accept the notion of women's equality and Linda frequently found herself bringing up baby Mark while Tom was singing, drinking and socializing around the pubs and clubs of Pontypridd and Treforest.

Gerry Greenberg says: 'You very rarely saw Linda out with Tom but that is par for the course in that part of the world. The wives wait patiently at home for their men and as long as they come home eventually they're happy. Linda is on to a good thing. She knows it and she accepts it; she used to accept it in the old days. She must have been aware that he was never 100 per cent faithful. Even before he became famous, she knew what he was like. I never saw her out at any gigs with him.

'But for all Tom's running about Linda is his backbone, she always was. She was his shoulder to cry on; the pillow that he would always fall back on; and I think if you took her away he would be lost. Even today I think she is part of his life, she is absolutely vital to him. Although he likes to play the field he has got to have her behind him. I think he would be absolutely devastated if she left him.'

As Tom's solo singing switched course when he joined the Senators, the other group members frequently sympathised with Linda's situation. When the group was struggling and starving in their grimy London flat in 1964 lead guitarist Mickey Gee felt desperately sorry for the young bride who was by then reduced to working in the hated glove factory to make ends meet.

Mickey Gee says: 'Linda used to keep her distance, she always knew her place. Tom was very, very macho. His word was law to her. While we were living in that squalid flat she was working in the factory and she used to come up to London to see him now and then. We would often have to smuggle other women out before she arrived and occasionally she used to get pissed off and there were squabbles. And sometimes Tom was singing so I would take her for a drink. I always liked her.

'People ask me if I am surprised they are still married and I don't know what to say. I was surprised Tom stayed married in 1964. It amazed me then, but for it to have lasted another twenty-five years, wow, words fail me.'

But bass player Vernon Hopkins who knew Tom and Linda for longer believes he knows the reason for the survival of the strange relationship. Hopkins says: 'People say it is amazing that they have stayed married because he must have had more other women than almost any man on earth, but it does not amaze me. Tom is scared to face life without Linda, he wants her safe at home and out of the way. It's his security if you like, they live apart, together. They live completely separate lives, they always have. They were married at sixteen, remember. Tom Jones is very insecure in lots of ways, very insecure indeed. He couldn't take the actual break, a divorce that is so final. He just couldn't take it.

'At the beginning Linda was very good for him, they were good for each other. But they grew apart, that's what this business does to you. It's not a 9 to 5 job. But in some way or other they will always be together.

'Linda is a Welsh wife, they don't run screaming for their lawyers when their husband plays around. They grin and bear it. You've made your bed, now lie in it is the attitude. Tom always goes home in the end and Linda knows that.'

But if the years of obscurity were hard to take, so the years of fame were even more difficult. The ludicrous lie dreamed up by manager Mills to pretend that Tom Jones was a single man when he burst to stardom certainly made it a painful introduction to the spotlight for the shy young wife. She went along with the deception because Tom told her to but she confided to friends afterwards that it upset her greatly.

'Everyone knows we are man and wife and Mark is our son,' she said at the time. 'Even if we hid away for ever people would still remember and tell the newspapers. It just made us all look silly.'

To Tom that was simply part of the business which Gordon controlled. He trusted Gordon completely. But success was

important, perhaps the most important thing to Tom. He said:
'I had a good life in Wales, a very happy time, and it is not
something I want to forget. When I started in this business I
did not have a car and we did not have a house.

'We lived with my wife's mother in Wales. So when I
moved to London, to get the record going, when I got "It's
Not Unusual", I had a house I could share with my wife and
son for the first time. It was something I was very proud of,
to have a nice house at Shepperton and be together. It was
not just for me; had I been single it would not have been the
same thrill. It was great for me that I could share that with
my wife and son.'

Linda always found the publicity surrounding her husband
hard to take. It was less that Tom's appeal was always so
earthily basic than that people perpetually pestered her for her
reaction to his seemingly irresistible sex appeal. And matters
were not helped by the arrival in the Mills team of publicist
Chris Hutchins. The truth was always a moving target as a
campaign was constructed to bury the cosy married image of
Tom Jones and resurrect a racy, man-about-town style which
fitted the singer's various appetites perfectly.

All of which worked wonders for Tom's career but it left
Linda very much on the outside looking in. Not that Tom
ever did too much to help her cope. Much of the time he was
concerned with getting on, getting laid, and being masterful.
He was always firmly in charge. Keyboard player Vic Cooper
recalled picking Tom up from his Surrey mansion on the way
to a recording session.

Cooper says: 'Tom was late, which was par for the course. I
was waiting downstairs for him with Linda. Suddenly he burst
into the room and shouted at her, "I told you to press these
trousers, you haven't done it properly, bloody press them
again – now." And he hurled the trousers across the room
at her.

'She blushed, upset at being bawled out and embarrassed
that I was there. But Tom didn't seem at all put out. I got
the feeling that it was a pretty normal conversation as far as
he was concerned.'

Equality in the Jones household was simply never an issue. Wives were there to serve their husbands, that was the way it was where Tom was brought up and that was the way he intended it to be in his home.

Back in Treforest Tom had sat and watched as his mother waited intently for the squeak of the backyard gate that indicated his father about to return home from the pit. That squeak was her signal to leap into action and have his dinner out of the oven and on to the table ready for him – not a second early in case it went cold and not a second afterwards in case he had to wait.

That was normality to Tom, and Linda's background was very similar. To them a woman's job was to serve her man. Whether or not the man played around with other women did not alter the arrangement.

Tom said: 'I tell my wife she is the boss in the home, not me. That's right, isn't it? When I was a kid, if I came home from school it never worried me if my dad wasn't there, but at the pub or the miners' club. My dad was quiet and traditional and strong. He spent his life down the pits until he died from the dust and the smoke embedded in his lungs. I didn't want to end up that way. Singing and fame were important to me but I still wanted what he believed – a man should be the boss in his own home. My father did a job of work and my mother was a housewife. It was the tradition. That's what she wanted, that's what he wanted. That's why if my mother hadn't been there when I got home as a kid, why, it would have been the end of the world. And my wife is always there, she is someone to come home to.'

Of course, before he came home Tom had frequently climbed out of bed with another woman. Vic Cooper recalls: 'We could never really understand why Linda put up with Tom's treatment, all the other women and everything. I remember one of my girlfriends asked her about it and she just said, "As long as he tells me he loves me when he comes home then I'm happy." '

Linda was always the retiring kind and as Tom's fame grew she was pushed more and more into the background.

She never liked being pointed out in public by fans squealing, 'That's Tom Jones' wife.' And when she did go out sometimes her lack of worldliness let her down.

She once attended a glittering fund-raising gala for the World Wildlife Fund at London's Talk of the Town nightclub wearing an extremely expensive full length fur coat. Gordon Mills had a great interest in wildlife. Everyone saw the joke but Linda, and the gaffe became one of Tom's favourite anecdotes in later years. He used thoughtlessly to delight in telling the story, roaring with laughter about it. Linda just didn't think.

But incidents like that helped to erode her fragile ego. The lack of self-confidence is something which has grown over the years. Jo Mills, Gordon's wife, was in many ways the complete opposite. A successful dancer and model, it was her income which helped Gordon to bankroll Tom and the Squires in the early days.

Jo met Linda the night her husband first saw Tom sing and although their backgrounds and their attitudes to life could scarcely have been further apart the women became good friends. Jo recalls: 'I remember meeting Linda and being introduced at the start of the evening. Then she somehow disappeared.

'She told me later that she had been so anxious about Gordon's visit that she had drunk much too much and spent most of the night locked in the loo sobering up.'

Watching Tom sing is something Linda has rarely done but when you consider how he describes it that is hardly surprising: 'My act is the closest thing to sex that I do. The adoration from the fans is very sexual,' he says.

Jo Mills and Linda Woodward had a great deal in common. As their husbands' remarkable partnership hurtled to ever loftier heights of success that was something they came to realize only too clearly. 'Tom was a philanderer and Gordon was a philanderer,' says Jo Mills today. 'But the big difference between them was when they came home. I always envied Linda that, because when Tom was with her he was really with her.

'He was loving and caring and I think in his own way

he did love her. But when Gordon was with me, after just as much separation, his mind was so often away on other things, he was just as busy because his work did not stop at the end of the concert.

'Tom could cut off when he was at home. When he was fooling around he was elsewhere, when he came home she got his undivided attention. I don't know how Linda has coped with all Tom's philandering over the years. There has been so much of that, so many other women that I don't know what is left of the marriage, she has become more and more of a recluse. I haven't been in touch with her now for several years.

'I know Tom's family is very important to him, a close family relationship is his life. But the pressures on any relationship during our sort of lives is colossal, we all have our own ways of coping with it, of getting a release from the situation. Mine was booze for a time, but I haven't had a drink now for six years. But I know what Linda has been through, the pressure can ruin your life.

'Tom and Gordon both chased after other women. Linda must have decided she could live with that. I couldn't.

'Our marriage was really over in 1976 but I went out to America to try and rescue it and it was not a happy time. We staggered on for three more years and then I came back in 1979 and filed for divorce.'

But while Jo Mills was a forceful, independent woman, Linda Woodward was not. And Linda had the added handicap of being married to a sex symbol. As Tom's fame grew so did Linda's problems and she withdrew more and more from public life.

She shunned Tom's shows because watching hundreds of women scream their lust for her husband deeply embarrassed her. She stayed away from the backstage mêlée of hangers-on because she felt overwhelmed by smart company. In fact most of the time Linda sat quietly at home. Alone.

In a rare interview in the late 1960s she said: 'Perhaps in the beginning I could not help feeling jealous. There were so many glamorous girls around Tom that I didn't feel I was good

enough to be his wife. I was frightened to go to the front door
without first putting on my make-up. Tom understood my fears
and helped me through it. Now I never worry. I always know
that Tom is coming home.'

But Linda was not always the quiet mouse. She would
always be incensed at hotel operators who blocked calls from
'Tom Jones' wife' with wisecracks and after every indiscretion
reached the newspapers she rowed angrily with her lecherous
husband.

Once a burly bodyguard watched in open-mouthed disbelief
as the man he was protecting was chased around their home
by Linda armed with a shoe, furiously lashing out at Tom after
a gossip column photograph of him with yet another young
girl. 'I know you,' she shouted. 'Don't think I don't know
what you're like.'

In those earlier years Linda was always able to pull
Tom down to earth. Tom recalls: 'Once I had a friend of
mine from New York staying at Torpoint while I was at
the London Palladium. We used to have a snooker room
at the top of the house with a jukebox. We were playing
and talking about things from America, he was talking in a
New York accent. And I was beginning to talk just like him
until my wife said, "Who the hell do you think you are? What
are you talking about?" I thought, "Jesus Christ! What am I
talking about?" This fellow could not get over it. He said, "I
have never seen anything like that before." But my wife can
talk to me any way she likes. It helps me to keep my feet on
the ground.'

'I have had my flings – Linda knows that. When she
has found out I have had a fling she's given me a right
rollicking. When I went with Mary Wilson, Linda gave me
hell. But the flings have never been important enough for
me to want to end my marriage. She's packed her bags a
few times but always stopped short of walking out because
she says, "Where would I go?" '

One of the attractions of buying Dean Martin's Tudor-style
Bel-Air mansion for one million dollars was its similarity to
Torpoint. Tom said: 'We were able to take the furniture from

Weybridge and put it straight into Bel-Air. It's like being in Britain. If you don't put the television on you wouldn't think you were in America.' But the truth was that Linda always hated living in Los Angeles. Tom said: 'She cried for twenty-four hours when we first moved from England. Oh, man, you don't know . . . I said to her, "It's too late now – you saw the house, you liked it, everything's final." Gardeners were instructed to grow roses, a rarity in southern California, but even with Welsh dragons installed on the gates it still did not feel like home to Linda. Tom tried to explain Linda's situation: 'We have known each other for so long, we knew each other at school, we were children together, to change that would be like changing a member of your family. It would be pointless. And we get on great together, when we are together.

'She just does not particularly want to be part of what I am when I am at home. That is why she nevers bothers with interviews or photographs. She is scared stiff of other people in showbusiness, but I have never got close to them in Los Angeles because of my wife. I could not go out to someone's house for dinner without inviting them back. She would not like it. She would get nervous, you see. She is a nervous person.

'She wouldn't want to know unless she was taken by surprise. Then it is fine. Once we were over at the house of film producer Robert Evans which I was thinking of buying and he showed us a new movie and Jack Nicholson and his girlfriend turned up. And my wife was fine. She did not get all uptight because it was on the spur of the moment. But if I had said, "Let's go over to Bob Evans' house to watch a movie with Jack Nicholson," she would have said, "No way".

'She looked at other people like that as if they are stars. To her I am not a star. We were kids together, we knew each other from ten years of age. But she has become a bit of a recluse. She doesn't like strangers. She didn't really ever settle in America. She doesn't drive and she wouldn't get into a minicab.'

Tom has frequently been frank about his long relationship with his wife: 'Somehow I have always managed to keep the marriage together. Linda knows damn well I have to flirt around on stage. It's part of my act and she doesn't question it, but not many women would put up with that nonsense.'

Tom has become increasingly relaxed about his extra-curricular sex life. Before the headline-hitting paternity suit of 1989 Tom was cheerfully talking on late night British television with interviewer Emma Freud and admitting: 'Marriage keeps me single, it keeps me from getting married again. If I'd come into showbusiness as a single man I might have got married six or seven times by now but I was already married so I couldn't.

'Linda knows I love to sing, she could do without the adulation from women but she knows I couldn't do without it, so she goes along with it.

'She lets me have a free rein. She says, "Whatever you do don't let me know about it, and especially today don't do it, because you might kill yourself and me along with it." '

The highly publicised Marjorie Wallace affair was another low point in the marriage. Tom admitted afterwards: 'When I went out with Marjorie Wallace a couple of times and Linda found out there was hell to pay. She was frightened that I was going to run off with her but when I assured her I wasn't it was all right. Not that she ever let me forget it. Even later, whenever Marjorie came on television in America, Linda went on about it. But the only thing she's really bothered about is that maybe one day I'm not going to come back. As long as we stay married then she's OK. She doesn't want me running off with some young girl.

'I tell Linda that I must love her because although I get all these approaches I always go back to her. It's a simple matter of not wanting to lose what you've got – and I wouldn't want to lose Linda. She's been a part of my life almost as long as I can remember. Getting married so young was all part of trying to prove that you were a man as early as possible.'

But from Linda's point of view the outside world has become an increasingly threatening place. Tom's frequent description of his wife as a recluse is every bit as accurate as it is insensitive. When their son Mark married she at first refused to go to the ceremony, and only twenty minutes before it began did she relent and agree to attend.

Some of the gaps caused by Linda's shyness in America were filled by Tom's mother and sister. Interviews, for instance, were sometimes conducted in their nearby home, rather than at Tom's house, so Linda would not have to hide away in her own home from inquisitive journalists. And in some ways Tom's close relationship with his mother has also helped to put pressure on Linda. Like most Welshmen Tom regards his mother as perhaps the most important other human.

When one of the authors asked Tom Jones what was his most precious possession his answer was: 'My health, because although I love my mother, I love my sister, I love my wife, I love my son and daughter-in-law and grandchildren, they are all very important to me but if I don't have me I don't have them. The most important thing is my well-being.'

Apart from the overwhelming egotism of the remark the order of priority of his beloved relations is significant. Since Tom Jones put his wife Linda number three in that off-the-cuff answer, Linda has taken a large step away from the luxury of Bel-Air and made her most decisively independent move for thirty years, into Llwynddu House and out of Tom Jones' life for many months at a time.

INDEX

Note: Abbreviation TJ = Tom Jones

225

Lee-Potter, Lynda, 129
Lennon, John, 85
Lewis, Jerry Lee, 117
Locke, Albert, 70
Love, Darlene, 105, 108,
 109–10, 121, 161
Lulu, 49
Luna, Barbara, 174–5
Lynch, Kenny, 71

MacLaine, Shirley, 96
Manners, Dorothy, 85–6
Manson, Charles, 84–5
Maret, Michael, 112
Mather, Charles, 74
Meek, Joe, 23–4
Megarry, Mr. Justice, 87
Mills, Beverley, 151, 201,
 202, 207
Mills, Gordon: discovers
 TJ, 27–33, 35, 39; and
 TJ's success, 42–4, 45–6,
 47–8, 53, 75, 78, 114, 115;
 and TJ's group, 59–60,
 61–2, 90–2; and finan-
 cial arrangements, 87–8,
 132–7, 142; and TJ's
 entourage, 111, 113,
 148–151, 152–3, 154–7,
 206; affairs of, 120, 149,
 197, 200, 219–20; and
 TJ's film career, 143,
 164–6, 168–9, 170, 173;
 and TJ's fans, 184–5,
 186, 188; death of, 187,
 197–202

Mills, Jo: and TJ's career,
 28, 29–30, 42, 43, 45,
 48–9, 131–2, 134;
 relationship with
 husband, 142, 149, 150,
 197, 201, 219–20; other
 refs., 53, 54–5, 75, 144
Mills, Lorna, 197, 200
Mills, Tracey, 207
Montgomery, Chris, 86,
 194, 206
Montiel, Ruth, 186, 196
Moran, John, 156–7, 188,
 198, 199
Morley, Julia, 126, 127
Mostel, Zero, 100
Murphy, Eddie, 165

Naff, Nick, 73–7, 79–80,
 81, 83–4, 118, 119
Neill, Mr Brian, QC, 88
Nicholls, Roy, 16
Nicholson, Jack, 222
Nuizo, Jimmy, 204

Olalquiaga, Manuel, 111
O'Sullivan, Gilbert, 136–7,
 142, 145, 155

Paloma, Donna, *see*
 Woodward, Donna
Parker, Col. Tom, 79, 149,
 164
Parkinson, Michael, 200
Peers, Donald, 18